2017 U.S. Navy Illustrated Encyclopedia of Weapons, Ships, and Equipment: Updated Program Guide - Aircraft, Jets, Carriers, Submarines, Missiles, Electronics, Surface Combatants, Science, Technology

* * * * * * * * * * *

U.S. Government, U.S. Military, Department of Defense (DoD), U.S. Navy

* * * * * * * * * * *

Progressive Management

Questions? Suggestions? Comments? Concerns? Please contact the publisher directly at

bookcustomerservice@gmail.com

Remember, the book retailer can't answer your questions, but we can!

* * * * * * * * * * *

This is a privately authored news service and educational publication of Progressive Management. Our publications synthesize official government information with original material - they are not produced by the federal government. They are designed to provide a convenient user-friendly reference work to uniformly present authoritative knowledge that can be rapidly read, reviewed or searched. Vast archives of important data that might otherwise remain inaccessible are available for instant review no matter where you are. There is no other reference book that is as convenient, comprehensive, thoroughly researched, and portable - everything you need to know, from renowned experts you trust. For over a quarter of a century, our news, educational, technical, scientific, and medical publications have made unique and valuable references accessible to all people. Our books put knowledge at your fingertips, and an expert in your pocket!

Progressive Management Publications

experience

quarter of a century and counting

* * * * * * * * * * *

CONTENTS

* * * * * * * * * * * *

* * * * * * * * * * * *

Introduction

The U.S. Navy is ready to execute the Nation's tasks at sea, from prompt and sustained combat operations to everyday forward-presence, diplomacy and relief efforts. We operate worldwide, in space, cyberspace, and throughout the maritime domain. The United States is and will remain a maritime nation, and our security and prosperity are inextricably linked to our ability to operate naval forces on, under and above the seas and oceans of the world.

To that end, the Navy executes programs that enable our Sailors, Marines, civilians, and forces to meet existing and emerging challenges at sea with confidence. Six priorities guide today's planning, programming, and budgeting decisions: (1) maintain a credible, modern, and survivable sea based strategic deterrent; (2) sustain forward presence, distributed globally in places that matter; (3) develop the capability and capacity to win decisively; (4) focus on critical afloat and ashore readiness to ensure the Navy is adequately funded and ready; (5) enhance the Navy's asymmetric capabilities in the physical domains as well as in cyberspace and the electromagnetic spectrum; and (6) sustain a relevant industrial base, particularly in shipbuilding.

Our mission begins with these priorities in consonance with our overall charge "to conduct prompt and sustained combat incident to operations at sea." In today's security environment, we find ourselves looking ahead to a new reality of a more globalized world, with myriad state and non-state actors on the stage, and global forces that directly relate to our efforts at and from the sea. These forces include increased traffic in all aspects of the maritime world, including open oceans, constricted seas, and other waterways from the sea floor to space. The return to great power competition, accompanied by our competitors' increased capabilities and high-end warfighting systems, and the increasing capabilities of international terrorist groups threaten our forces ashore and in the littoral.

We will continue to faithfully serve our Nation along with our primary joint partner, the U.S. Marine Corps. Together we are America's "force in readiness," prepared to promptly respond to contingencies, crises, and conflicts anywhere America's people, interests, and partners are at risk.

Since 2014, we have continued our rebalance to the Pacific while maintaining our global commitments in every sea and ocean. Our partnerships in the Asia-Pacific region are crucial to safeguarding the free flow of goods, services, ideas, and access to the global maritime commons on which our Nation, allies, and partners rely. Throughout the Middle East, our forward-deployed naval forces assist our partners maintain peace, manage change, deter aggression, and address threats to stability in one of the world's key energy-producing regions. In Europe, our forward-deployed forces have supported partners throughout the region with afloat and ashore missile defense, and participate in exercises across the European region to ensure maritime security and stability.

Some of the program highlights since the last Program Guide was published in 2015 include the commissioning of the first DDG 1000, the USS Zumwalt; continued production of Virginia-class nuclear-powered fast-attack submarines; sea trials for the Gerald Ford, our next nuclear aircraft carrier class leader; and continuing progress in capabilities such as Aegis Ashore in Romania, NIFC-CA From-The-Sea, SM-6 missiles in multiple modes, F-35 Lightning II Joint Strike Fighter, P-8A Poseidon multi-mission maritime patrol aircraft, and many others.

We will balance future investments in these and emerging programs to ensure we are prepared to execute today's missions and unknown tasks in the future, all while maintaining the discipline of budgetary responsibility. We have aligned strategic and fiscal choices to achieve optimal warfighting capability without compromising the mission. The 2017 Navy Program Guide reflects those values. It is our duty to ensure that our Fleet will continue to meet the Nation's needs with people, platforms, and payloads ready for today and as far into the future we can see.

* * * * * * * * * * * *

SECTION I: NAVAL AVIATION

AIRCRAFT CARRIERS

CVN 68 Nimitz-Class and CVN 78 Ford-Class Aircraft Carrier Programs

AIRCRAFT

AH-1Z and UH-1Y Helicopter Upgrades

AV-8B Harrier 11+ Vertical/Short Take-Off and Landing (V/STOL) Aircraft

C-2A Greyhound Logistics Support Aircraft

C-40A Clipper Navy Unique Fleet Essential Airlift (NUFEA)

C-130T Hercules Intra-Theater Airlift Aircraft

CH-53E Super Stallion Helicopter

CH-53K King Stallion Heavy-Lift Replacement (HLR) Helicopter

CMV-22B Osprey Tilt-Rotor Aircraft

EA-6B Prowler Airborne Electronic Attack (AEA) Aircraft

EA-18G Growler Airborne Electronic Attack (AEA) Aircraft

F-35 Lightning II Joint Strike Fighter (JSF)

F/A-18A-D Hornet Strike-Fighter Aircraft

F/A-18E/F Super Hornet Strike-Fighter Aircraft

KC-130J Hercules Tactical Tanker and Transport

MH-60R/S Seahawk Multi-mission Combat Helicopter

MH-53E Sea Dragon Airborne Mine Countermeasures (AMCM) Helicopter

MQ-25 Carrier Based Aerial Refueling System

MV-22B Osprey Tilt-Rotor Aircraft

P-3C Orion Modification, Improvement, and Sustainment.

P-8A Poseidon Multi-mission Maritime Aircraft (MMA)

Naval Aviation Training Aircraft

Service Secretary Controlled Aircraft/Executive Airlift (SSCA/EA)

VH-92A Presidential Replacement Helicopter

AVIATION WEAPONS

AGM-88E Advanced Anti-Radiation Guided Missile (AARGM)

AGM-154 Joint Standoff Weapon (JSOW)

AIM-9X Sidewinder Short-Range Air-to-Air Missile (SRAAM)

AIM-120 Advanced Medium-Range Air-to-Air Missile (AMRAAM)

Joint Direct-Attack Munition (JDAM, GBU-31/32/38)

Laser JDAM (GBU-54)

Offensive Anti-Surface Warfare Increment 1 (OASuW Inc 1)

Long-Range Anti-Ship Missile (LRASM)

Paveway II Laser-Guided Bomb (LGB)

Dual-Mode LGB (GBU-10/12/16) and Paveway III (GBU-24) LGB

AVIATION SENSORS AND SYSTEMS

Airborne Electronic Attack (AEA) Next-Generation Jammer (NGJ)

ALQ-214 Integrated Defensive Electronic Countermeasures (IDECM)

ALR-67(V)3 Advanced Special Receiver (RWR)

APG-79 Active Electronically Scanned Array (AESA) Radar System

AAQ-24 Department of the Navy Large Aircraft

Infrared Countermeasures (DoN LAIRCM) System

ASQ-228 Advanced Targeting Forward-Looking Infra-Red (ATFLIR) Sensor

Joint Mission Planning Systems (JMPS)

SECTION 2: SURFACE WARFARE

SURFACE WARSHIPS

CG 47 Ticonderoga-Class Aegis Guided-Missile Cruiser Modernization

DDG 51 Arleigh Burke-Class Aegis Guided-Missile Destroyer

DDG 51 Arleigh Burke-Class Aegis Guided-Missile Destroyer Modernization

DDG 1000 Zumwalt-Class 21st-Century Destroyer Frigate (FF)

Littoral Combat Ship (LCS)

PC 1 Cyclone-Class Patrol Coastal Modernization Program

SURFACE WEAPONS

Mk 15 Phalanx Close-In Weapon System (CIWS)

Mk 38 Mod 2 Stabilized 25mm Chain Gun

Mk 45 Mod 4 5-Inch/62-Caliber Gun System Upgrade

Mk 46 Mod 2 Gun Weapon System (GWS)

Mk 51 Gun Weapon System (GWS)

Mk 54 Lightweight Torpedo (LWT)

Mk 60 Griffin Missile System (GMS)

RGM/UGM-109E Tomahawk Land-Attack Missile (TLAM)

RIM-7, Mk 57 NATO Seasparrow Surface Missile System (NSSMS) and RIM-162 Evolved Seasparrow Missile (ESSM)

RIM-66C Standard Missile-2 Blocks III/IIIA/IIIB

RIM-116A Rolling Airframe Missile (RAM)

SM-6 Standard Missile 6 Extended-Range Active Missile (ERAM) Block I/II

U.S. Coast Guard Navy-Type / Navy-Owned (NTNO) Program

SURFACE SENSORS AND COMBAT SYSTEMS

Aegis Ashore

Aegis Combat System (ACS)

Air and Missile Defense Radar (AMDR)

Enterprise Air Surveillance Radar (EASR)

Enterprise Air Warfare Ship Self-Defense Test and Evaluation

Littoral Combat Ship (LCS) Mission Packages (MPs)

Maritime Integrated Air and Missile Defense Planning System (MIPS)

Naval Integrated Fire Control-Counter Air (NIFC-CA) From the Sea (FTS)

Navigation Systems

Navy Aegis Ballistic Missile Defense (ABMD)

Ship Self-Defense System (SSDS)

SPQ-9B Radar Anti-Ship Cruise Missile (ASCM) Radar

SPY-1 (Series) Aegis Multi-Function Phased-Array Radar

SPY-3 Advanced Multi-Function Radar (MFR)

SPY-4 Volume Search Radar (VSR)

SQQ-89 Anti-Submarine Warfare (ASW) Combat System

Surface Ship Torpedo Defense (SSTD)

Tactical Tomahawk Weapon Control System (TTWCS)

Theater Mission Planning Center (TMPC)

SURFACE EQUIPMENT AND SYSTEMS

EXPEDITIONARY AND SPECIAL MISSION SHIPS AND CRAFT

Expeditionary Sea Base (ESB)

Expeditionary Transfer Dock (ESD)

Landing Craft Air Cushion (LCAC)

LCU 1610 Landing Craft Utility Vessels

LHA 6 America-Class Amphibious Assault Ship

134

LHD 1 Wasp-Class Amphibious Assault Ship

LPD 17 San Antonio-Class Amphibious Transport Dock Ship

LSD 41 / 49 Whidbey Island /Harpers Ferry-Class Dock Landing Ships   137

LX(R) Dock Landing Ship Replacement

MCM 1 Avenger-Class Mine Countermeasures Ship Modernization (MCM MOD)

Ship-to-Shore Connector (SSC) / LCAC 100 Surface Connector (X) Replacement (SC(X)R)

EXPEDITIONARY SYSTEMS

AES-1 Airborne Laser Mine Detection System (ALMDS)

Airborne Mine Neutralization System (AMNS)

AQS-20A Sonar Assault Breaching System (ABS)

Joint Counter Radio-Controlled Improvised Explosive Device (RCIED) Electronic Warfare (JCREW)

KSQ-1 Amphibious Assault Direction System (AADS)

Mk 62/63/65 Naval Quickstrike Mines

Submarine Launched Mobile Mine (SLMM)

WLD-1 Remote Minehunting System (RMS)

SECTION 5: INFORMATION WARFARE

Assured command and control

Afloat Electromagnetic Spectrum Operations Program (AESOP)

Automated Digital Network System (ADNS)

Automatic Identification System (AIS)

Base Communications Office (BCO)

Base Level Information Infrastructure (BLII)

Battle Force Tactical Network (BFTN)

Commercial Satellite Communications (COMSATCOM)

Consolidated Afloat Networks and Enterprise Services (CANES)

Defense Red Switch Network (DRSN)

Deployable Joint Command and Control Capability (DJC2)

Digital Modular Radio (DMR)

E-6B Mercury

Enterprise Services

Global Broadcast Service (GBS)

Global Command and Control System-Maritime (GCCS-M)

Information Systems Security Program (ISSP)

Integrated Broadcast Service / Joint Tactical Terminal (IBS/JTT)

Maritime Operations Center (MOC)

Maritime Tactical Command and Control (MTC2)

Mobile User Objective System (MUOS)

Navy Air Operations Command and Control (NAOC2)

Navy Multi-band Terminal (NMT)

Network Tactical Common Data Link (NTCDL)

Next-Generation Enterprise Network (NGEN)

OCONUS Navy Enterprise Network (ONE-NET)

Submarine Communications Equipment

Super-High-Frequency Satellite Communications (SHF SATCOMS)

Tactical Messaging

Tactical Mobile (TacMobile)

Telephony

BATTLESPACE AWARENESS

Airborne ASW Intelligence (AAI)

EP-3E ARIES II Spiral 3

Fixed Surveillance Systems (FSS)

Large Displacement Unmanned Undersea Vehicle (LDUUV)

MQ-4C Triton Unmanned Aircraft System (UAS)

MQ-8B/C Fire Scout Vertical Takeoff and Landing Tactical UAV (VTUAV)
System

RQ-7B Shadow Unmanned Air System (STUAS)

RQ-21 Blackjack Small Tactical Unmanned Air System (STUAS)

UQQ-2 Surveillance Towed Array Sensor System (SURTASS)

WQT-2 Surveillance Towed Array Sensor System (SURTASS) / Flow
Frequency Active (LFA)

INTEGRATED FIRES

Advanced Tactical Data Link Systems (ATDLS)

Cooperative Engagement Capability (CEC)

Distributed Common Ground System-Navy (DCGS-N)

E-2C/D Hawkeye Airborne Early Warning Aircraft

Joint Automated Deep Operations Coordination System (JADOCS)

Mk XIIA, Mode 5 Identification Friend or Foe (IFF) Combat ID

Nulka Radar Decoy System

SSQ-130 Ship Signal Exploitation Equipment (SSEE) Increment F

Surface Electronic Warfare Improvement Program (SEWIP)

UYQ-100 Undersea Warfare Decision Support System (USW-DSS)

OCEANOGRAPHY AND MARITIME DOMAIN AWARENESS

Hazardous Weather Detection and Display Capability (HWDDC)

Littoral Battlespace Sensing-Unmanned Undersea Vehicles (LBS-UUV)

Maritime Domain Awareness (MDA)

Meteorological Mobile Facility (Replacement) Next Generation [MetMF(R) NEXGEN]

Naval Integrated Tactical Environmental System-Next Generation (NITES-Next)

NAVSTAR Global Positioning System (GPS)

Precise Timing and Astrometry (PTA)

T-AGS Oceanographic Survey Ship

Task Force Climate Change (TFCC)

SECTION 6: SUPPLY AND LOGISTICS

Navy Electronic Procurement System (EPS)

Naval Operational Business Logistics Enterprise (NOBLE)

Naval Tactical Command Support System (NTCSS)

Navy Energy Program

Navy Enterprise Resource Planning (Navy ERP)

T-AH 19 Mercy-Class Hospital Ship

T-AKE 1 Lewis and Clark-Class Dry Cargo and Ammunition Ship

T-AO 187 Kaiser-Class and T-AO(X) Replenishment Oiler

T-AOE 6 Supply-Class Fast Combat Support Ship

T-ATS(X) Towing, Salvage and Rescue Ship

T-EPF 1 Spearhead-Class Expeditionary Fast Transport (formerly Joint High-Speed Vessel)

SECTION 7: SCIENCE AND TECHNOLOGY

Autonomous Aerial Cargo/Utility System (AACUS)

Autonomous Swarmboats

Discovery and Invention (D&I) Research

Electromagnetic Maneuver Warfare Command & Control (EMC2)

Electromagnetic Railgun (EMRG)

Energy System Technology Evaluation Program (ESTEP)

Forward-Deployed Energy and Communications Outpost (FDECO)

Future Naval Capabilities (FNC)

Lightweight and Modern Metals Manufacturing Innovation (LM3I) Institute / Lightweight Innovations for Tomorrow (LIFT)

Medium Displacement Unmanned Surface Vehicle "Sea Hunter"

Naval Research Laboratory (NRL)

Navy Manufacturing Technology Program (ManTech)

Netted Emulation of Multi-Element Signature against Integrated Sensors (NEMESIS)

ONR Global

Resilient Hull, Infrastructure, Mechanical, and Electrical Security (RHIMES)

Science, Technology, Engineering and Mathematics (STEM)

Solid State Laser

SwampWorks

TechSolutions

Total Platform Cyber Protection (TPCP)

* * * * * * * * * * * *

SECTION 1

Naval Aviation forces are the Nation's maritime "mailed fist" of credible combat power across the spectrum of crisis and conflict in the 21st-Century. From cyberspace to the ocean floor, from unmanned systems through the most complex crewed aircraft and aircraft carriers, Naval Aviation platforms, systems and, most importantly, Sailors provide the Navy and the Nation with an unmatched capability to fight and win—providing persistent forward presence and deterring adversaries wherever and whenever America's citizens, interests, and allies and partners might be at risk. In that regard we continue to field nuclear-powered aircraft carriers—including the next-generation Gerald Ford (CVN 78) class—with their multi-mission air wings, introduce the F-35C Lightning II Joint Strike Fighter, improve our land-based aviation capabilities with P-8A Poseidon Multi-mission Maritime Aircraft and Triton unmanned aircraft system, and delivering improvements in weapons and sensors across the board.

AIRCRAFT CARRIERS

CVN 68 Nimitz-Class and CVN 78 Ford-Class Aircraft Carrier Programs

Description

The U.S. Navy's nuclear-powered aircraft carriers (CVNs), in combination with their embarked air wings and strike group warships, provide the proper balance between forward presence and surge capability to conduct warfighting and peacetime operations around the globe in support of national priorities. Sailing the world's oceans, each carrier strike group is a versatile, lethal, and independent striking force capable of engaging targets at sea or hundreds of miles inland. The unique mobility and independence of aircraft carriers provide unmatched global access that requires no host-nation support. America's CVNs can remain on-station for months at a time, replenishing ordnance, spare parts, food, consumables, and aircraft fuel while simultaneously conducting air strikes and other critical missions. This capability demonstrates the carrier's remarkable operational flexibility and self-reliance so vital to conducting time-critical strike operations.

Aircraft carriers and their strike groups are always ready upon arrival and are either on-station ready to deliver or just a few days away from where they will be needed. To meet the demands of 21st-century warfare, U.S. aircraft carriers will deploy with air wings comprising the newest and most-capable aviation platforms, including the FA-18E/F Super Hornet, EA-18G Growler, F-35C Lightning II, E-2D Advanced Hawkeye, and, in the not-too-distant future, the MQ-25A Stingray. Joint concepts of operation, centered on the aircraft carrier, will additionally leverage the military strengths of all the services, bringing cooperative muscle to the fight and a potent synergy across the warfare continuum. Following the inactivation of the USS Enterprise (CVN 65) in December 2012, after more than 51 years of service, the Navy has been fulfilling its mission with a reduced force structure of ten aircraft carriers, as authorized by the National Defense Authorization Act for FY 2010. The force will increase to the statutory requirement of 11 aircraft carriers when Gerald R. Ford (CVN 78) is delivered to the Navy.

The lead ship of the first new class of aircraft carriers, CVN 78 has been under construction since 2008. The Ford-class is designed for increased efficiency throughout the ship—aimed at reducing the total operating cost by approximately $4 billion dollars per hull when compared to the Nimitz (CVN 68)-class carriers—while enhancing warfighting capabilities. In converting all auxiliary systems outside the main propulsion plant from steam to electric power, the requirement for costly steam, hydraulic, and pneumatic piping, as well as the maintenance and repair of those distributed systems, will be significantly reduced. The advanced and more efficient reactor plant provides an electrical generating capacity nearly three times that of a Nimitz-class carrier, enabling such new technologies such as the Electromagnetic Aircraft Launch System and advanced command-and-control systems. The new ship design, which is based on the Nimitz hull, also includes the Advanced Arresting Gear system and Dual-Band Radar. The redesigned flight deck, which incorporates a smaller island structure located further aft on the ship, allows greater flexibility during aircraft turnaround and launch-and-recovery cycles, leading to at least a 33 percent increase in daily sortie generation-rate capability. Combined, these new technologies and more efficient systems will enable the Ford-class ships to operate with about 900 fewer Sailors than the Nimitz class.

Status

Construction of Gerald R. Ford was 98 percent complete in August 2016 at Huntington Ingalls Industries, Newport News Shipbuilding. The keel for John F. Kennedy (CVN 79) was laid on August 22, 2015, and the ship was approximately 20 percent constructed as of August 2016.

Developers

Huntington Ingalls Industries Newport News, Virginia

* * * * * * * * * * *

AIRCRAFT

AH-1Z and UH-1Y Helicopter Upgrades

Description

The H-1 Upgrade Program upgrades legacy Huey/Venom UH-1N and Super Cobra AH-1W aircraft, ensuring that the Marine Air-Ground Task Forces possess credible rotary-wing attack and utility support platforms for the next 20 years. The H-1 program reduces life-cycle costs, significantly improves operational capabilities, and extends the service lives of both aircraft. There is 85 percent commonality between the two aircraft. This greatly enhances the maintainability and readiness of the systems by leveraging the ability to support and operate both aircraft within the same squadron structure.

The program includes a new, four-bladed, all-composite rotor system, coupled with a sophisticated, fully integrated glass cockpit. It also incorporates a performance-matched transmission, four-bladed tail rotor drive system, and upgraded landing gear. The integrated glass cockpit with modern avionics systems provides a more lethal platform as well as enhanced joint interoperability. Operational enhancements include a dramatic increase in range, speed, survivability, payload, and lethality of both aircraft, with a significant decrease in logistics footprint. Compared to legacy aircraft, the UH-1Y Huey/Venom helicopter operates at nearly twice the in-service range, with more than double the payload. The AH-1Z Super Cobra helicopter realizes similar performance increases, with the ability to carry twice the in-service load of precision-guided munitions.

Status

The H-1 Upgrades program of record is for 160 UH-1Ys and 189 AH-1Zs. Through the end of FY 2016, 266 H-1 aircraft were on contract (160 UH-1Y, 111 AH-1Z), with 139 UH-1Ys and 57 AH-1Zs delivered as of September 2016. The FY 2017 budget requests 24 H-1 Upgrade aircraft. AH-1Z full-rate production was achieved on November 28, 2010, and at the same time the H-1 Upgrades program was designated ACAT-1C. AH-1Z initial operational capability was reached on February 24, 2011 and the first successful deployment of the new attack helicopter occurred with the 11th Marine Expeditionary Unit (MEU) from November 2011 to June 2012. This MEU detachment was another program "first," as it was the first "all Upgrades" (UH-1Y/AH-1Z) deployment. All West Coast MEU deployments (11th, 13th, and 15th) comprise only UH-1Y and AH-1Z aircraft. The UH-1Y made its initial deployment with the 13th MEU from January to June 2009, and the UH-1Y has conducted sustained combat operations in Operation Enduring Freedom since November 2009. The Marine Corps' fleet of utility aircraft includes only UH-1Ys; the last UH-1N was retired in September 2014. The UH-1Y and AH-1Z have been aggressively deployed ahead of their respective material support dates, in an effort to support our deployed troops with the most capable aircraft available.

Developers

Bell Helicopter Textron Fort Worth, Texas

Amarillo, Texas

* * * * * * * * * * *

15

AV-8B Harrier II+ Vertical/Short Take-Off and Landing (V/STOL) Aircraft

Description

The AV-8B Harrier is a single-seat, light attack aircraft that supports the Marine Air-Ground Task Force (MAGTF) commander by engaging surface targets and escorting friendly aircraft, day or night, under all weather conditions during expeditionary, joint or combined operations. By virtue of its vertical/short takeoff and landing capability, the AV-8B can operate from a variety of amphibious ships, rapidly constructed expeditionary airfields, forward sites--e.g., roads and forward operating bases—and damaged conventional airfields. Two variants of the aircraft are in service, the AV-8B II Night-Attack Harrier and the AV-8B II+ Radar Harrier. The Night-Attack Harrier improved the original AV-8B design through incorporation of a navigation, forward-looking infrared sensor, a digital color moving map, night-vision goggle compatibility, and a higher-performance engine. The in-service Radar Harrier has all the improvements of the Night-Attack Harrier plus the APG-65 multi-mode radar. The fusion of night and radar capabilities allows the Harrier II+ to be responsive to the MAGTF's needs for expeditionary, night, and adverse-weather offensive air support.

Status

The Harrier Operational Flight Program H6.0 integrated the digital, improved triple-ejector racks for increased carriage capacity of the Joint Direct Attack Munition, fully integrated ALE-47 airborne warning hardware and software, adjustments for improving moving-target engagements, improved radar capability, safety improvements, and Advanced Medium-Range-Air-to-Air Missile AIM-120 A/B flight clearance. In 2015, the AV-8B received the H6.1 Operational Flight Program (OFP), enabling full integration of the Generation 4 LITENING targeting pod, as well as correcting software deficiencies to smart weapon employment and targeting.

It also brought a Common OFP for LITENING to the AV-8B, enabling the LITENING pod to be interchanged between F/A-18 Hornets and AV-8Bs without any software reloads. Airborne Variable Message Format terminals will be installed in the AV-8B, enabling joint standard digital-aided close-air support technology. Other near-term capability upgrades in FY 2016 included the digital video recorder, continued implementation of the BRU-70/A digital improved triple-ejector rack, and expanded carriage of the AIM-120 missile. The next major steps for the AV-8B II+ are Link-16 integration, continued development of digital interoperability in the future network infrastructure, and AIM-9X Short-Range-Air-to-Air Missile and AIM-120C integration.

Developers

The Boeing Company St. Louis, Missouri

* * * * * * * * * * * *

C-2A Greyhound Logistics Support Aircraft

Description

The C-2A Greyhound is the Navy's medium-lift/long-range logistics support aircraft. Capable of operational ranges up to 1,000 nautical miles, the C-2A can transport payloads up to 10,000 pounds between aircraft carrier strike groups and forward logistics sites. The Greyhound's cargo bay can be rapidly reconfigured to accommodate passengers, litter patients medical evacuation, and time-critical cargo. The large rear cargo ramp allows direct loading and unloading for fast turnaround and can be operated in light to airdrop supplies and personnel. Equipped with an auxiliary power unit for unassisted engine starts, the C-2A can operate independently from remote locations. The versatile Greyhound can also support special operations and distinguished visitor transport requirements.

Status

The aircraft has undergone several modifications and a service life extension program that extended the Greyhound fleet's service life until 2028.

Developers

Northrop Grumman Bethpage, New York

* * * * * * * * * * * *

C-40A Clipper Navy Unique Fleet Essential Airlift (NUFEA)

Description

The Naval Air Force Reserve provides 100 percent of the Navy's organic intra-theater logistics airlift capability via the Navy Unique Fleet Essential Airlift community. NUFEA provides Navy component commanders with short-notice, fast-response, intra-theater logistics support for naval power projection worldwide. The legacy C-9B and C-20G aircraft are being replaced by the C-40A Clipper, a modified Boeing 737-700/800 series aircraft. This state-of-the-art aircraft can transport 121 passengers (passenger configuration), 40,000 pounds of cargo (cargo configuration), or a combination of the two (combination configuration), at ranges greater than 3,000 nautical miles at Mach 0.8 cruise speed. Maximum gross takeoff weight is 171,000 pounds. The unique ability to carry cargo pallets and passengers simultaneously maximizes the operational capability, flexibility, safety, and capacity. The C-40A has an electronic light deck fully compliant with future communications, navigation, and air traffic control mandates; advanced technology Stage III noise-compliant, fuel-efficient engines; and an integral cargo door/ cargo handling system.

Status

Fifteen aircraft are in the C-40A inventory in late 2016. The Navy has purchased the aircraft via commercial-off-the shelf standards using standard best commercial practices. C-40A squadrons are located at Naval Air Station Oceana, Virginia; Naval Base Coronado/Naval Air Station North Island, California; Naval Air Station Jacksonville, Florida; Naval Air Station/Joint Reserve Base Fort Worth, Texas; and Naval Air Station Whidbey Island, Washington.

Developers

The Boeing Company Seattle, Washington

C-130T Hercules Intra-Theater Airlift Aircraft

Description

The Navy C-130T Hercules — a component of the Navy Unique Fleet Essential Airlift (NUFEA) community — provides heavy, over-, and outsized-organic airlift capability. These aircraft are deployed worldwide and provide rapid-response direct support to Navy component commanders' theater requirements. This aircraft can be reconfigured within minutes to transport up to 40,000 pounds of cargo or up to 75 passengers.

Status

The Navy has started a program to upgrade its C-130T aircraft to meet all current and future communications navigation surveillance/air traffic management requirements. These NUFEA, heavy-lift aircraft are stationed at Naval Air Station Jacksonville, Florida; Naval Air Station Joint Reserve Base New Orleans, Louisiana; Joint Base Andrews/Naval Air Facility Washington, DC; Naval Base Ventura County/Naval Air Station Point Mugu, California; and Joint Base McGuire/Dix/Lakehurst, New Jersey.

Developers

Lockheed Martin Bethesda, Maryland

Marietta, Georgia

* * * * * * * * * * * *

CH-53E Super Stallion Helicopter Description

The CH-53E entered service in 1981 and in late 2016 is the only heavy-lift helicopter in the Department of Defense (DoD) rotor-craft inventory. The 2017 force construct is eight active component HMH squadrons and one reserve component HMH. The Super Stallion fleet has enabled heavy-lift assault support operations in Afghanistan, Iraq, and the Horn of Africa and is forward deployed in support of Marine Expeditionary Units, Unit Deployment Program Okinawa, Marine Rotational Force-Darwin, and Special-Purpose Marine Air-Ground Task Forces. The past 15 years of combat operations and humanitarian crises have validated the relevance of vertical heavy lift by MAGTF and joint force commanders alike. The CH-53E inventory is 146 aircraft. Replacement production capacity does not exist, nor are there CH-53Es available in war storage. Flow aircraft inventory is aggravated by pipeline aircraft (aircraft receiving modifications, depot-level repairs, and standard depot-level maintenance), which creates a shortfall of physical assets available for tasking on the flight line. As a result of this shortfall, a squadron's primary aircraft inventory is 12 aircraft. Transition to the Heavy-Lift Replacement CH-53K will enable re-distribution of CH-53E aircraft, allowing squadrons to return to 16 aircraft.

Status

The CH-53E Readiness Recovery Effort (RRF) is addressing recommendations from the Super Stallion Independent Readiness Review conducted to assist the CH-53E community to achieve and maintain full readiness until CH-53K full operational capability in 2029. The recovery plan is a three-year process extending through FY 2019, and the "reset" of all 146 aircraft by 2020 is the main effort. Reset specification consists of all maintenance requirement cards including phase cycle and calendar/special inspections improving serviceability and material condition of the aircraft. Upon completion, the squadron will conduct a full functional check-light to ensure the aircraft is returned full mission capable with zero outstanding awaiting maintenance discrepancies.

Other RRF elements include procurement of the correct amount of individual material readiness list and support equipment, functional check-flight training for pilots and crew chiefs, procure five portable electronic maintenance aids per aircraft, ix all technical publication discrepancy reports, reconstitute MH-53Es stored at Aerospace Maintenance and Regeneration Group for stick and rudder aircraft at Marine Heavy Helicopter Training Squadron-302, Contract Maintenance Field Teams, and fully fund program related logistics.

It is imperative to sustain the CH-53E fleet, as the aircraft will continue to support the full spectrum of assigned combat operations and scheduled deployments during the transition to the CH-53K.

Developers

Sikorsky Aircraft Corporation Stratford, Connecticut

* * * * * * * * * * *

Image courtesy of Sikorsky Aircraft.

CH-53K King Stallion Heavy-Lift Replacement (HLR) Helicopter

Description

The CH-53K is the follow-on to the Marine Corps CH-53E Super Stallion heavy-lift helicopter. Major systems improvements of the newly manufactured helicopter include more powerful engines, expanded gross weight airframe, drive train, advanced composite rotor blades, glass cockpit, external and internal cargo handling systems, and enhanced survivability. The CH-53K will be capable of externally lifting 27,000 pounds on a standard sea level hot day (103° Fahrenheit) to a range of 110 nautical miles and delivering cargo in a landing zone at a pressure altitude of 3,000 feet and 91.5°F, a capability improvement nearly triple the in-service CH-53E. Additionally, the CH-53K will be capable of transporting 30 combat-loaded troops. The CH-53K's increased capabilities are essential to meeting the Marine Corps Expeditionary Force 21 Capstone Concept and ship-to-objective maneuver requirements. The CH-53K fully supports the joint operational concept of full-spectrum dominance by enabling rapid, decisive operations and the early termination of conflict by projecting and sustaining forces in denied environments. The expeditionary maneuver warfare concept establishes the basis for the organization, deployment, and employment of the Marine Corps to conduct maneuver warfare and provides the doctrine for effective joint and multinational operations.

Status

The Navy awarded Sikorsky Aircraft Corporation the post-Milestone B system development and demonstration contract on April 5, 2006. The program conducted preliminary design review during the fourth quarter FY 2008. The critical design review successfully completed ahead of schedule in the third quarter FY 2010, and the program has transitioned from the design to the manufacturing phase. The Navy awarded two contracts to Sikorsky to build a total of six System Demonstration Test Articles (SDTAs); the first was awarded in the third quarter FY 2013 for four SDTAs and the second in the fourth quarter FY 2016 for two SDTAs. The SDTAs will be the first fleet representative CH-53K helicopters delivered and will be used for operational test and evaluation. In early 2015, the ground test vehicle executed the ground test program; mounted to the test pedestal, the test vehicle completed bare head light off of all engines and initial shake down testing with all engines operating and rotor system turning. Four engineering demonstration models are conducting the light test phase that began on October 27, 2015 with first light. Major milestones planned for the CH-53K are to achieve Milestone C and receive a flow-rate initial production contract second quarter FY 2017 and reach initial operational capability in 2019 and full operational capability in 2009. The Marine Corps requirement is 200 aircraft.

Developers

Sikorsky Aircraft Corporation

Lockheed Martin Corporation Stratford, Connecticut

* * * * * * * * * * *

CMV-22B Osprey Tilt-Rotor Aircraft

Description

The CMV-22B Osprey will provide the Joint Force Maritime Component Commander time-critical logistics support, transporting personnel, mail, and priority cargo from advance bases to the sea base. As an aerial resupply/logistics for sea basing (AR/LSB) capability, the CMV-22B's primary mission is carrier onboard delivery, but it also fulfills secondary missions of vertical on-board delivery, vertical replenishment, medical evacuation, Naval Special Warfare support, missions of state (diplomatic presence and distinguished visitor movement), humanitarian assistance/disaster relief, and search and rescue. Two Fleet Logistics Support squadrons—located at Naval Air Station North Island, California, and Naval Station Norfolk, Virginia—and the Forward-Deployed Naval Forces detachment in Japan will operate CMV-22Bs. The Navy will leverage existing Marine Corps logistics, maintenance and training processes, including the V-22 Fleet Replacement Squadron at Marine Corps Air Station New River, North Carolina, for pilot and aircrew training. In a basic transport mission profile, the CMV-22B provides significant range/payload increase over the C-2 Greyhound.

Status

The Navy will procure 44 aircraft, achieving an initial operational capability in 2021 and full operational capability in 2023. The Navy issued a contract in the second quarter FY 2016 to develop the engineering change to meet the AR/LSB mission. This includes an extended-range fuel configuration, a public address system, and secure beyond-line-of-sight communications capability. Future developments include: production contract award in FY 2018; first aircraft delivery in FY 2020; complete CMV-22B AR/LSB developmental and operational testing in FY 2021; the first detachment of three aircraft able to deploy in FY 2021; and ability to support major combat operations in FY 2013.

Developers

Bell/Textron Fort Worth, Texas

The Boeing Company Philadelphia, Pennsylvania

Rolls Royce Indianapolis, Indiana

* * * * * * * * * * *

EA-6B Prowler

Airborne Electronic Attack (AEA) Aircraft Description

The EA-6B Prowler provides airborne electronic warfare (EW) attack capabilities against enemy systems operating within the radio frequency spectrum. EA-6B capabilities traditionally support the strike capabilities of joint force operations, aircraft carrier air wings, and Marine Air-Ground Task Forces (MAGTFs). The need for EW demonstrably increased during numerous joint and allied operations since 1991 against traditional and non-traditional target sets in support of ground forces. The enormous demand for AEA in support of worldwide airborne electronic attack requirements have driven EA-6B and AEA operational employment rates to record levels.

Status

The EA-6B Improved Capability (ICAP) III upgrade reached initial operational capability in September 2005. This generational leap in AEA capability deployed for the first time in 2006. ICAP III includes a completely redesigned receiver system (ALQ-218), new displays, and MIDS/Link-16, which dramatically improve joint interoperability. The Navy completed "sundown" of the Prowler and transitioned to an all EA-18G Growler force in April, 2016. The Marine Corps will fly the EA-6B ICAP III through 2019. The Joint Strike Fighter F-35B Lightning LL and a series of networked air and ground EW payloads on manned and unmanned platforms, forming a collaborative system of systems labeled "MAGTF EW," will replace and expand Prowler capabilities, providing increased EW capacity, flexibility, and scalability in direct support of the MAGTF commander and joint forces. The first implementation of MAGTF EW, the Intrepid Tiger II pod carried on the AV-8B Harrier LL+, made its initial deployment in May 2012 and on a Marine Corps F/A-18 Hornet in June 2014.

Developers

Naval Air Warfare Center,

Weapons Division Point Mugu, California

Northrop Grumman Bethpage, New York

* * * * * * * * * * * *

EA-18G Growler

Airborne Electronic Attack (AEA) Aircraft Description

The EA-18G Growler is replacing the Navy's EA-6B Prowler. The EA-18G provides full-spectrum airborne electronic attack (AEA) capabilities to counter enemy air defenses and communication networks, most notably anti-radiation missiles. These capabilities continue to be in high demand in overseas contingency operations, where Growler operations protect coalition forces and disrupt critical command and control links. The Growler maintains a high degree of commonality with the F/A-18F

Super Hornet, retaining a great deal of the latter's inherent strike-fighter and self-protection capabilities while providing air-to-air self-protection, thus freeing other assets for additional strike-fighter tasking.

Status

Growler reached initial operational capability in September 2009 and in late 2016 is in full-rate production. In December 2009, the Department of Defense decided to continue the Navy Expeditionary AEA mission and recapitalize the Navy EA-6B expeditionary force with the EA-18G. As a result, 26 additional aircraft were programmed for procurement for three active and one reserve expeditionary squadrons. All three active component expeditionary squadrons have transitioned to the EA-18G. The FY 2014 President's budget requested 21 additional EA-18Gs to stand-up two more expeditionary squadrons. The first EA-18G deployment occurred in November 2010 in an expeditionary role supporting Operation New Dawn and in March 2011 in support of Operations Odyssey Dawn and Unified Protector, during which the EA-18G conducted combat operations. The first carrier deployment occurred in May 2011 on board the USS George H. W. Bush (CVN 77). Final deliveries will complete in FY 2018. The inventory objective of 160 aircraft will support ten carrier-based squadrons, five active expeditionary squadrons, and one reserve squadron. Full operational capability is planned for FY 2017.

Developers

The Boeing Company St. Louis, Missouri

Northrop Grumman Bethpage, New York

* * * * * * * * * * * *

F-35 Lightning II Joint Strike Fighter (JSF) Description

The Joint Strike Fighter program is delivering a transformational family of next-generation strike aircraft, combining stealth and enhanced sensors to provide lethal, survivable, and supportable tactical jet aviation strike fighters. The F-35C carrier variant, the F-35B short takeoff and vertical landing, and F-35A conventional takeoff and landing "family of aircraft" designs share a high level of commonality and meet U.S. service and allied partner requirements. The keystone of this effort is a mission systems avionics suite that delivers unparalleled interoperability among U.S. armed services and coalition partners. Agreements for international participation in the program have been negotiated with Australia, Canada, Denmark, Italy, the Netherlands, Norway, Turkey, and the United Kingdom. Israel, Japan, and the Republic of Korea selected the F-35 through the U.S. Foreign Military Sales program. In U.S. service, the F-35C will replace F/A-18A-C aircraft and complement the F/A-18E/F Super Hornet. The F-35B will replace Marine F/A-18s, AV-8Bs and EA-6Bs.

Status

As of September 2016, the Department of the Navy had taken delivery of 52 F-35Bs and 24 F-35Cs. After successfully completing two amphibious ship developmental test (DT) periods, the F-35B variant successfully carried out its third and final DT trial in October 2016. The F-35C completed its third and final shipboard developmental test period in August 2016 on the USS George Washington (CVN 73). The Marine Corps declared F-35B initial operational capability in July 2015 and will permanently base its first operational squadron, VMFA-121, at Marine Corps Air Station Iwakuni, Japan, in January 2017. The first F-35B shipboard operational deployment is scheduled for spring 2018. The Navy's F-35C IOC is planned in 2018 and coincides with stand up of the first operational F-35C squadron at Naval Air Station Lemoore, California. The first F-35C shipboard operational deployment is scheduled for spring 2021.

Developers

Lockheed Martin Fort Worth, Texas

Pratt & Whitney Hartford, Connecticut

* * * * * * * * * * * *

F/A-18A-D Hornet Strike-Fighter Aircraft

Description

The F/A-18 Hornet is a multi-mission strike fighter that combines the capabilities of a fighter and an attack aircraft. The single-seat F/A-18A and two-seat F/A-18B became operational in 1983. Eventually, the Hornet replaced the Navy's A-6 Intruder, A-7 Corsair LL, and F-4 Phantom LL and the Marine Corps F-4 aircraft. Reliability and ease of maintenance were emphasized in the Hornet's design, and F/A-18s have consistently flown three times as many hours without failure as other Navy tactical aircraft while requiring half the maintenance time.

The F/A-18 is equipped with a digital fly-by-wire light control system that provides exceptional maneuverability and allows the pilot to concentrate on operating the aircraft's weapons system. A solid thrust-to-weight ratio and superior turn characteristics, combined with energy sustainability, enable the Hornet to defeat any adversary. The ability to sustain evasive action is what many pilots consider to be the Hornet's finest trait. The F/A-18 is the Navy's first tactical jet to incorporate digital-bus architecture for the entire avionics suite, making this component of the aircraft relatively easy to upgrade on a regular and affordable basis.

Following a production run of more than 400 F/A-18A/Bs, deliveries of the single-seat F/A-18C and two-seat F/A-18D began in September 1987. The F/A-18C/D models incorporated upgrades for employing updated missiles and jamming devices. These versions are armed with the AIM-120 Advanced Medium-Range Air-to-Air Missile and the infrared-imaging version of the AGM-65 Maverick. The Hornet is battle tested and a proven, highly reliable and versatile strike fighter. Navy and Marine Corps Hornets were in the forefront of strikes in Afghanistan in 2001 during Operation Enduring Freedom, where they continue to serve, and in Iraq in 2003 during Operations Iraqi Freedom/New Dawn. The latest lot of F/A-18C/D Hornets is far more capable than the first F/A-18A/Bs. Although the F/A-18C/D's growth is limited, the Hornet will continue to ill carrier air wings for years to come, before gradually giving way to the larger, longer-range and more capable F/A-18E/F Super Hornet and the F-35 Lightning LL Joint Strike Fighter. The last Hornet, an F/A-18D, rolled off the Boeing production line in August 2000.

Status

As of September 2016, the Navy and Marine Corps had 92 F/A-18A, 21 F/A-18B, 359 F/A-18C and 129 F/A-18D aircraft in service and test roles, and two NF/A-18C and two NF/A-18D versions in permanent test roles. Hornets equip 16 active Navy and Marine Corps and three Navy and Marine Corps Reserve strike fighter squadrons, two fleet replacement squadrons, three air-test and evaluation squadrons, the Navy's Flight Demonstration Squadron (Blue Angels), and the Naval Strike and Air Warfare Center.

Developers

The Boeing Company St. Louis, Missouri

General Electric Lynn, Massachusetts

F/A-18E/F Super Hornet Strike-Fighter Aircraft

Description

The multi-mission F/A-18E/F Super Hornet strike fighter is an evolutionary upgrade of the F/A-18C/D Hornet. The F/A-18E/F is able to conduct unescorted strikes against highly defended targets early in a conflict. The Super Hornet provides the carrier strike group with a strike fighter that has significant growth potential and more than adequate carrier-based landing weight, range, endurance, and ordnance-carrying capabilities comparable to those of the F-14 Tomcat and F/A-18A/C Hornet it replaces. The single-seat F/A-18E and the two-seat F/A-18F have a 25 percent larger wing area and a 33 percent higher internal fuel capacity that effectively increase endurance by 50 percent and mission range by 41 percent. It has five "wet" stations that give the Super Hornet in-light tanker capability.

The Super Hornet incorporates two additional wing stations that allow for increased payload flexibility in the mix of air-to-air and air-to-ground ordnance. The F/A-18E/F can carry a full array of the newest joint "smart" weapons, such as the Joint Direct-Attack Munition (JDAM) and the Joint Standoff Weapon (JSOW). The Super Hornet has the ability to recover aboard a carrier with optimum reserve fuel while carrying a load of precision-strike weapons; its carrier-recovery payload is more than 9,000 pounds.

The Super Hornet also has the space, power, and cooling capability needed to accommodate valuable but installation-sensitive avionics when they become available, including the Active Electronically Scanned-Array (AESA) radar that is installed on approximately 85 percent of delivered Super Hornets. Sophisticated systems such as the Integrated Defensive Electronic Countermeasures System, Advanced Targeting Forward Looking Infrared, Joint Helmet- Mounted Cueing System, JDAM and JSOW, AIM-9X Sidewinder Short-Range Air-to-Air Missile and AIM-120 Advanced Medium-Range Air-to-Air Missile, APG-79 AESA radar system, and advanced mission computers and displays make the F/A-18E/F an extremely capable and lethal strike platform. Future planned upgrades include the AIM-120D, the AGM-88E Advanced Anti-Radiation Guided Missile, and cockpit and display improvements. The first operational Super Hornet squadron (VFA-115) deployed on board the USS Abraham Lincoln (CVN 72) on July 24, 2002, for a ten-month deployment that included initial operations in support of Operation Iraqi Freedom. At the forefront of combat operations, Super Hornet squadrons are integrated into all ten Navy carrier air wings, and with future capability upgrades, are well suited to complement the F-35 Lightning LL Joint Strike Fighter.

Status

As of September 2016, there were 287 F/A-18E models and 259 F/A-18F models in U.S. Navy inventory. The FY 2016 program of record is 584 aircraft.

Developers

The Boeing Company St. Louis, Missouri

General Electric Lynn, Massachusetts

* * * * * * * * * * * *

KC-130J Hercules Tactical Tanker and Transport

Description

The KC-130J is a four-engine turbo-prop, multi-role, multi-mission tactical aerial refueler, and tactical transport aircraft that supports all six functions of Marine Aviation and is well suited to meet the mission needs of forward-deployed Marine Air-Ground Task Forces (MAGTFs). The Hercules provides the six functions:

(1) fixed-wing, rotary-wing, and tilt-rotor tactical air-to-air refueling; rapid ground refueling of aircraft and tactical vehicles;

(2) assault air transport of air-landed or air-delivered personnel, supplies, and equipment; (3) command-and-control augmentation; (4) battlefield illumination; (5) tactical aero medical evacuation; and (6) combat search and rescue. When equipped with the Harvest HAWK Intelligence Surveillance Reconnaissance Weapon Mission kit, the aircraft can perform multi-sensor image reconnaissance and provide close air support. With its increase in speed, altitude, range, performance, state-of-the-art light station that includes two heads-up displays, night vision lighting, an augmented crew station, fully integrated digital avionics, enhanced air-to-air refueling capability, and aircraft survivability enhancements, the KC-130J will provide the MAGTF commander with multi-mission capabilities well into the 21st Century.

Status

The Marine Corps requirement is 79 KC-130Js. As of September 2016, the KC-130J inventory totaled 50 aircraft. Fourteen KC-130T model aircraft operated by the Reserves are yet to be replaced.

Developers

Lockheed Martin Marietta, Georgia

* * * * * * * * * * *

MH-60R/S Seahawk Multi-mission Combat Helicopter

Description

The MH-60R and MH-60S Seahawk multi-mission combat helicopters are the two pillars of the Navy's 21st-Century air wing. MH-60R/S squadrons deploy on aircraft carriers, elements of the carrier air wing, and strike group surface warships. Expeditionary squadrons deploy as detachments embarked on amphibious assault ships, surface combatants, and logistics vessels. The MH-60R provides anti-submarine and surface warfare capability with a suite of sensors and weapons that includes airborne flow-frequency dipping sonar, surface search radar with automatic periscope detection and discrimination modes, electronic support measures, advanced forward-looking infrared (FLIR) sensors, precision air-to-surface missiles, and torpedoes. The MH-60R is the only airborne anti-submarine warfare asset in strike groups and on independently deploying warships. The MH-60S provides surface and mine countermeasure warfare capabilities, as well as robust Naval Special Warfare, search and rescue, combat search and rescue, and logistics capability, with air-to-ground weapons and the same FLIR and Link-16 capability as the MH-60R. Airborne mine countermeasure operations will use advanced sensor and weapons packages to provide detection, localization, and neutralization of adversary "weapons that wait." MH-60R/S platforms are produced with 85 percent common components (e.g., common cockpit and dynamic components) to simplify maintenance, logistics, and training.

Status

The MH-60R was authorized to enter full-rate production in March 2006 and the last aircraft are scheduled for delivery in FY 2018. The Navy plans to acquire 280 MH-60Rs. The MH-60S was approved for full-rate production in August 2002 and the 275th and final MH-60S rolled off the line in January 2016. At the end of FY 2016, there were 226 MH-60R and 275 MH-60S helicopters in the inventory.

Developers

Lockheed Martin Owego, New York

Sikorsky Aircraft Corporation Stratford, Connecticut

* * * * * * * * * * *

MH-53E Sea Dragon Airborne Mine Countermeasures (AMCM) Helicopter

Description

The MH-53E provides AMCM capability to naval forces through various mine-hunting and mine-sweeping systems. The MH-53E supports undersea warfare by defending the Fleet from surface and sub-surface mine threats and ensuring sea lines of communication remain passable for not only carrier and expeditionary strike groups, but also for vital commercial shipping. The MH-53E provides the Navy's only heavy-lift rotary-wing capability enabling over-the-horizon combat logistics support, pending delivery of the CH-53K King Stallion. Secondary missions include vertical onboard delivery, tactical aircraft recovery, humanitarian assistance and disaster relief, and Naval Special Warfare support.

The USS Ponce (AFSBI 15) has been designated an interim afloat forward-staging base and its replacement, the USNS Lewis B. Puller (T-ESB 3), has been designated an expeditionary sea base to provide staging for the MH-53E and associated airborne mine-hunting and mine-sweeping systems, enabling a more rapid and sustained deployment of AMCM forces.

Status

The MH-53E program is executing an in-service sustainment strategy to ensure continued AMCM and heavy-lift support to the sea base until the transition to the Littoral Combat Ship mine countermeasures mission package is complete. The sustainment strategy addresses fatigue, obsolescence, readiness, and safety issues. A fatigue life extension program has been completed, which extended the aircraft service life to 10,000 hours, enabling the Navy to maintain a dedicated AMCM capability through the 2025 timeframe.

Developers

General Electric Lynn, Massachusetts

Sikorsky Aircraft Corporation Stratford, Connecticut

* * * * * * * * * * *

MQ-25 Carrier Based Aerial Refueling System

Description

The Deputy Secretary of Defense Resource Management Decision for the FY 2017 budget request restructured the Unmanned Carrier Based Reconnaissance and Strike (UCLASS) program to the Carrier Based Aerial Refueling System. Officially designated MQ-25 on July 13, 2016, MQ-25 will enhance aircraft carrier (CVN) capability and versatility for the joint force through integration of a persistent, multi-mission aerial refueling and intelligence, surveillance, and reconnaissance (ISR) unmanned aircraft system (UAS) into the carrier air wing (CVW). The ability of the CVW to provide an organic refueling capability is essential for performing blue-water light operations and achieving meaningful, extended range combat strike capabilities. MQ-25 will significantly extend the range, reach, and mission effectiveness of the CVW. Prior to MQ-25, there was no program to replace the refueling capability provided by F/A-18E/F Super Hornet strike fighters. MQ-25 will free up these strike fighters to execute their primary missions and preserve fatigue-life expenditure. Additionally, MQ-25 will provide a long-endurance ISR capability to address the CVW organic ISR capability gap. MQ-25 will pioneer the integration of manned-unmanned operations, mature complex sea-based C4I (command, control, communication, computers, and intelligence) UAS technologies, and pave the way for future multi-mission UASs to pace emerging threats. MQ-25 will reach initial operational capability by the mid-2020s.

Status

The Navy awarded four sole-source concept-refinement contracts to Boeing, General Atomics, Lockheed Martin, and Northrop Grumman in the fourth quarter FY 2016. The concept refinement effort will include MQ-25 technical and task analyses and, when applicable, also include prototyping and non-lying demonstration events. These activities will identify key system technologies, attributes, and approaches to optimize cost, schedule, and technical risk during engineering and manufacturing development (EMD) phase of the program. The program is on-track to release a final air system EMD request for proposal in the third quarter FY 2017 for a third quarter FY 2018 air system EMD contract award.

Developers

To be determined.

* * * * * * * * * * * *

MV-22B Osprey Tilt-Rotor Aircraft

Description

The MV-22 Osprey is the world's first production tilt-rotor aircraft and blends the vertical light capabilities of helicopters with the speed, range, altitude, and endurance of fixed-wing transport aircraft. This combat multiplier represents a quantum improvement in strategic mobility and tactical flexibility for the Marine Corps, Navy, and Air Force. The Osprey has a 370-nautical mile combat radius, can cruise at 260 knots, and can carry 24 combat-equipped Marines or a 12,500-pound external load. With a 2,200 nautical-mile single-aerial refueling range, the aircraft also has a strategic self-deployment capability. Specific missions for the MV-22 include medium-lift expeditionary assault support, aerial delivery, tactical recovery of aircraft and personnel, casualty and humanitarian evacuation, rapid insertion and extraction, and airborne resupply/logistics support to the sea base. The MV-22 is the cornerstone of Marine Corps assault support capability, with the speed, endurance, and survivability needed to fight and win on tomorrow's battlefields.

Status

The Marine Corps transition to the MV-22 was 75 percent complete at the end of 2016; more than 280 of 360 aircraft have been delivered to 14 of 16 operational squadrons. In the years ahead, the MV-22 will remain the Nation's crisis-response platform of choice, and future MV-22s will provide aerial refueling of F/A-18, AV-8, and F-35 aircraft. Additionally, through Link-16 and software reprogrammable radios, the Osprey is digitally linked to the Marine Air-Ground Task Force, enhancing interoperability of ground and air forces during long-range operations. The Osprey will field an ability to provide all-aspect reactive fires and effective ballistic protection in hostile environments. Finally, the program is pursuing a common configuration, readiness, and modernization, ensuring operational relevance at a lower cost for decades to come.

Developers

Bell Helicopter Textron Fort Worth, Texas

Boeing Defense and Space Group, Helicopter Division Philadelphia, Pennsylvania

Rolls Royce Indianapolis, Indiana

* * * * * * * * * * *

P-3C Orion Modification, Improvement, and Sustainment

Description

The legacy P-3C Orion maritime patrol aircraft provides antisubmarine warfare (ASW), anti-surface warfare (ASUW), and intelligence, surveillance, and reconnaissance (ISR) capabilities to naval and joint task force commanders and contributes directly to maritime domain awareness across the globe. Squadrons are based in Jacksonville, Florida; Whidbey Island, Washington; and Kaneohe Bay, Hawaii. Because of the P-3's range, endurance, and multi-mission capabilities, the aircraft has been in high demand for the past five decades and is nearing its end of service life.

The Navy's P-3 roadmap focuses on three areas: (1) airframe sustainment; (2) mission systems obsolescence; and (3) recapitalization to the P-8A Poseidon Multi-mission Maritime Aircraft. Regarding airframe sustainment, 39 aircraft were grounded on 27 December 2007, a result of on-going Fatigue Life Management Program analysis that revealed the aft lower surface of the outer-wing (Zone 5) experienced fatigue at higher levels than previously estimated. The Chief of Naval Operations approved a P-3 Recovery Plan that included a dual-path approach encompassing Zone 5 modifications to replace outer-wing components and manufacture new outer-wing assemblies where needed. The mission system sustainment program improves aircraft availability through replacement and upgrades to obsolete systems with modern hardware systems and software. These programs ensure the P-3C continues to meet Navy's ASW, ASUW, and ISR requirements through completion of the transition to the P-8A Poseidon in FY 2019.

34

Status

The Navy has successfully implemented its P-3C Fatigue Life Management Program. Through FY 2016, 60 of the 61 Special Structural Inspection-Kits and 89 of 90 Zone 5 modifications have been completed. Procurement of outer wing assemblies began in 2008, and installs commenced in 2011. By the end of FY 2016, 26 outer wing assemblies have been completed, with the last three aircraft in work.

Developers

Lockheed Martin Marietta, Georgia

Eagan, Minnesota Greenville, South Carolina Manassas, Virginia

* * * * * * * * * * * *

P-8A Poseidon Multi-mission Maritime Aircraft (MMA) Description

The P-8A Poseidon recapitalizes and improves the broad-area anti-submarine warfare (ASW), anti-surface warfare (ASUW), and intelligence, surveillance, and reconnaissance (ISR) capability resident in the legacy P-3C Orion. The P-8A combines the proven reliability of the commercial Boeing 737 airframe, powerplants, and avionics with an open architecture that enables the affordable integration of modern sensors and communications networks. The P-8A leverages global logistics support infrastructure and commercial training applications to provide both higher operational availability and improved warfighting readiness. The P-8A program invested in high-fidelity simulation to attain a 70/30-percent simulator/aircraft training ratio, significantly reducing life cycle costs for the life of the platform. The P-8A will be built with three incremental upgrades that include improved ASW sensors, network-enabled ASW and ASUW weapons, sensor and targeting enhancements, and improved communications capability.

Status

The P-8A Poseidon is meeting all cost, schedule, and performance parameters in accordance with the acquisition program baseline. In August 2010, the program successfully passed Milestone C and the first flow-rate initial-production (LRIP) aircraft delivered to Patrol Squadron Thirty (VP-30) at Naval Air Station Jacksonville, Florida in March 2012. The first operational VP squadron commenced transition from P-3C to P-8A in July 2012. The program achieved initial operational capability in December 2013, when the first P-8A squadron (VP-16) deployed to Kadena, Japan. The program was approved for full-rate production (FRP) in January 2014, and the Navy awarded the FRP Lot I contract for 16 aircraft in

February 2014. By the end of FY 2016, seven lots of LRIP/ FRP aircraft, including 80 aircraft and associated trainers, spares and support equipment, were on contract with Boeing Defense Space and Security. Six fleet squadrons have completed transition to P-8A, with 45 aircraft delivered on or ahead of schedule. The seventh fleet squadron began transition in October 2016. The P-8A program continues to execute its evolutionary acquisition strategy. Increment 2 will deliver improved ASW capabilities as a series of three engineering change proposals (ECPs): multi-static active coherent high-altitude anti-submarine warfare sensors; high-altitude ASW weapon capability; and targeting enhancements. These ECPs will be incorporated in-line with production or via retrofit. Increment 3 will continue advanced development as a series of four ECPs, with initial operational capability in FY 2023. Increment 3 improves the warfighting capability of baseline P-8A to pace future threats and integrates a network-enabled ASUW weapon, advanced ASW and ISR sensors, precision targeting, and architecture upgrades to satisfy the Net-Ready Key Performance Parameter. The P-8A warfighting requirement is 117 aircraft.

Developers

The Boeing Company Renton, Washington

* * * * * * * * * * *

36

Naval Aviation Training Aircraft

Description

The Commander, Naval Air Training Command's (CNATRA) mission is to train and safely produce the world's finest combat aviation professionals—Naval Aviators and Naval Flight Officers—and deliver them at the right time, in the right numbers, and at the right cost to the Fleet for follow-on tasking. This mission is essential to generate the readiness the Fleet requires. CNATRA's training aircraft inventory includes the T-6A/B Texan LL, T-45 Goshawk, TH-57 Sea Ranger, T-44 Pegasus, and the TC-12 Huron.

All undergraduate military light officers (UMFOs) begin primary light training in the T-6B Texan LL. Built by Beechcraft Defense Corporation, the T-6B features a Pratt & Whitney PT-6A-68 engine with increased horsepower, ejection seats for increased safety, cockpit pressurization, onboard oxygen-generating systems, and a completely digital "glass" cockpit.

The T-45C Goshawk, a carrier-capable derivative of the British Aerospace Hawk, is used for intermediate and advanced training in the strike syllabus for jet pilots. Future upgrades include resolution of an engine-surge issue to enhance fuel efficiency and safety, and preservation of current aircraft through service life assessment and service life extension programs.

The TH-57 Sea Ranger, the Navy version of the commercial Bell Jet Ranger, is used for advanced training in the rotary-wing (helicopter) pilot syllabus.

The T-44 Pegasus and the TC-12 Huron are twin turboprop, pressurized, fixed-wing aircraft that are used for intermediate and advanced training for multi-engine and tilt-rotor pilots. Continued improvements to the T-44 include the replacement of wing wiring, simulator upgrades, and the conversion from analog to digital cockpits. The T-44 training system has received new simulators to replace the obsolete legacy instrument light trainers.

VFA (attack) and VAQ (electronic warfare) advanced UMFO training is in the T-45C. The T-45, integrated with the Virtual Mission Training System (VMTS), an embedded synthetic radar system, is used for the tactical maneuvering and advanced phase radar training portion of the VFA and VAQ UMFO syllabus. CNATRA has charted a course to revolutionize UMFO training by employing the T-6A, the T-45C with VMTS, and high-fidelity simulators to train future VFA and VAQ UMFOs. VP, VQ and VAW advanced UMFO training will be conducted in the multi-crew simulator (MCS). The MCS will focus on crew resource management, communications, and sensor integration and will provide intermediate and advanced training for all NFOs.

Status

The T-6 has completed production with an inventory of 295 aircraft, with the final lot aircraft delivered in June 2016. The TH-57B (visual light) and the TH-57C (instrument light) will be receiving minor avionics upgrades that will allow continued operation past 2020. The TC-12 will be phased out of advanced training by 2017.

Developers

The Boeing Company (T-45) St. Louis, Missouri

Hawker Beechcraft (T-6) Wichita, Kansas

* * * * * * * * * * *

Service Secretary Controlled Aircraft/ Executive Airlift (SSCA/EA)

Description

The Department of the Navy maintains Service Secretary Controlled Aircraft/Executive Airlift in accordance with the Department of Defense Directive 4500.56. The SSCA aircraft are designated by the secretaries of the military departments for transportation of their senior Service officials. The offices of the Secretary of the Navy, Chief of Naval Operations, and Commandant of the Marine Corps coordinate with Fleet Logistics Support Squadron One (VR-1) for scheduling Navy and Marine Corps senior leader travel. At the discretion of the Secretary of the Navy, other SSCA/ EA aircraft are stationed outside of the continental United States to support senior leader travel. Three C-37Bs (Gulfstream-550), one C-37A (Gulfstream-V), and one C-20 (Gulfstream-LV) provide executive transport services. The C-37A/B meets all international-imposed air traffic management communications, navigation, and surveillance requirements.

Status

The first C-37 aircraft was delivered in 2002, a second aircraft in 2005, and two more in 2006. The Navy's first and only C-37A is based at Hickam Air Force Base, Hawaii. The C-37Bs and C-20Ds are based at Joint Base Andrews/Naval Air Facility Washington, D.C., and are assigned to Fleet Logistics Support Squadron One. Additionally, the Navy bases a C-20 at Naval Air Station Sigonella, Italy.

Developers

Gulfstream (General Dynamics) Savannah, Georgia

* * * * * * * * * * * *

Image courtesy of Sikorsky Aircraft.

VH-92A Presidential Replacement Helicopter

Description

A replacement is required for the 41-year-old VH-3D Sea King and 25-year old VH-60N WhiteHawk helicopters that provide transportation for the President of the United States, foreign heads of state, and other dignitaries as directed by the White House Military Office. The Replacement Presidential Helicopter will provide a survivable, mobile command-and-control "VIP" transportation capability and a system-of-integrated-systems necessary to meet presidential transport mission requirements, including the ability to be globally transportable via Air Force Strategic Lift.

Status

The Presidential Helicopter Fleet Replacement Program became a formal ACAT-1D acquisition program in March 2014 when it successfully completed a Milestone B and the Defense Acquisition Board approved the program to enter the engineering manufacturing and development (EMD) phase. In May 2014, the Navy awarded an EMD contract with production options to Sikorsky Aircraft Corporation. Under the contract, Sikorsky will use its in-production S-92A medium-lift helicopter to integrate government-defined mission systems and install an executive interior. The program successfully completed critical design review in July 2016. First light and the beginning of contractor test are planned for April 2017, with the initial operational capability planned for 2020.

Developers

General Electric Lynn, Massachusetts Lockheed Martin Mission Systems and Training Owego, New York Sikorsky Aircraft Corporation, Lockheed Martin Stratford, Connecticut

* * * * * * * * * * * *

AVIATION WEAPONS

AGM-88E Advanced Anti-Radiation Guided Missile (AARGM)

Description

The U.S. Navy's AGM-88E AARGM is the latest evolution of the High-Speed Anti-Radiation Mission (HARM) weapon system. Prior to AARGM, HARM was the Navy's only anti-radiation, defense-suppression, air-to-surface missile. Employed successfully in naval operations for decades, HARM can destroy or suppress broadcasting enemy electronic emitters, especially those associated with radar sites used to direct anti-aircraft guns and surface-to-air missiles. Fielded configurations of HARM include AGM-88B (Block IIIA), AGM-88C (Block V), and AGM-88C (Block VA). The HARM program is a Navy-led joint-service (Navy, Air Force, and Marine Corps) program.

The AGM-88E program upgrades some of the existing HARM missile inventory with a new guidance section and a modified control section to incorporate multi-sensor, multi-spectral, digital anti-radiation homing detection capability, global positioning system/inertial navigation system guidance, and a millimeter-wave terminal seeker. AARGM also includes a netted situation awareness/targeting capability and weapon impact assessment reporting via direct connectivity with national technical means. The Department of Defense and the Ministry of Defense of the Republic of Italy have signed an international memorandum of agreement for cooperative development of AGM-88E. The AARGM system is a transformational and affordable upgrade to the legacy HARM.

Status

The AGM-88E program completed initial operational testing and evaluation and reached initial operational capability during the third quarter FY 2012. The full-rate production (FRP) decision was approved and first FRP contract was awarded in the fourth quarter FY 2012. AARGM is integrated on F/A-18C/D/E/F Hornet/ Super Hornet and EA-18G Growler aircraft. The Italian air force will integrate AARGM on the Tornado ECR aircraft in accordance with the international cooperative development program agreements. AARGM Block I software will be delivered to the Fleet in FY 2017, addressing discrepancies identified during operational test, which will increase lethality of the weapon. AARGM Extended Range began as a program of record in 2016 and will significantly increase the range of the AARGM weapons system and will allow for internal carriage in the F-35C Joint Strike Fighter. Initial operational capability is planned for 2023.

Developers

ATK Woodland Hills, California

AGM-154 Joint Standoff Weapon (JSOW)

Description

The JSOW is a family of weapons that enables naval aircraft to attack targets at standoff distances using global positioning system/ inertial navigation system for guidance. All JSOW variants share a common body, but can be configured for use against area targets, bunker penetration, and ship attack. Defeating emergent, time-critical threats, whether in close-in proximity or over the horizon, requires an all-weather weapon capable of penetrating defended sanctuaries and destroying hostile targets while minimizing the danger of collateral damage to friendly and neutral shipping as well as friendly/neutral assets and personnel ashore. The JSOW Unitary (JSOW-C) variant adds an imaging infrared seeker and autonomous target acquisition to attack point targets with precision accuracy. The JSOW-C-1 incorporates new target-tracking algorithms into the seeker for moving targets, giving the joint force commanders an affordable, air-delivered, standoff weapon that is effective against fixed and re-locatable land and maritime targets. Used in conjunction with accurate targeting information and anti-radiation weapons, JSOW-C-1 will provide the capability to defeat enemy air defenses while creating sanctuaries that permit the rapid transition to flow-cost, direct-attack ordnance.

Status

AGM-154A reached initial operational capability (IOC) in 1999, and the AGM-154C variant achieved IOC in FY 2005. JSOW C-1 began procurement in FY 2011 and achieved IOC in June 2016. JSOW C-1 was procured through FY 2016.

Developers

Raytheon Tucson, Arizona

* * * * * * * * * * * *

AIM-9X Sidewinder Short-Range Air-to-Air Missile (SRAAM)

Description

The AIM-9X Sidewinder is a fifth-generation all-aspect infrared (IR) day and night, beyond-visual-range, lock-on-after-launch missile with superior detection and tracking capability, high off-bore sight capability, robust IR counter-countermeasures, enhanced maneuverability, and growth potential via software improvements. The AIM-9X development leveraged existing AIM-9M components to minimize development risk and cost. Obsolescence and pre-planned product improvements efforts have been ongoing since initial operational capability in 2003. A series of independent engineering change proposals provided improved performance in the way of faster processors in the guidance control unit and an improved fuze/target detector (DSU-41) and data link component. These improvements led to the AIM-9X Block II missile program in FY 2011.

Status

The AIM-9X Block II procurement began in FY 2011. The AIM-9X Block II completed operational testing in FY 2015 and achieved initial operational capability in March 2015. AIM-9X Block II+ is being procured in 2017 for a 2019 delivery, which will provide F-35B/C Lightning LL additional survivability improvements compared to when carrying an AIM-9X Block II. Under the System Improvement Program III effort, the Navy is also addressing obsolescence concerns and cost avoidance measures and will ultimately field 9.4/10.4 software in 2020, improving the lethality of the weapons system.

Developers

Raytheon Tucson, Arizona

* * * * * * * * * * *

AIM-120 Advanced Medium-Range Air-to-Air Missile (AMRAAM)

Description

The AIM-120 AMRAAM is an all-weather, all-environment, radar-guided missile developed by the Air Force and Navy. The missile is deployed on the AV-8B Harrier, FA-18A-D Hornet, FA-18E/F Super Hornet, EA-18G Growler, and F-35B Lightning LL. AMRAAM will be deployed on F-35C Lightning LL when it achieves initial operational capability (IOC). Entering service in September 1993, AMRAAM has evolved to maintain air superiority through pre-planned product improvement programs. This modernization plan includes clipped wings for internal carriage, a propulsion-enhancement program, increased warhead lethality, and enhanced electronic counter-countermeasures capabilities through hardware and software upgrades. Additionally, the missile has improved capabilities against flow- and high-altitude targets in an advancing threat environment. AIM-120C7 completed production and AIM-120D production began in FY 2008. With the "sundown" of the AIM-7 Sparrow missile in 2018, AMRAAM will be the Services' sole medium/beyond-visual-range missile.

Status

The AIM-120C7 missile variant reached IOC in FY 2008. The AIM-120D completed operational test in fourth quarter FY 2014. The Navy achieved IOC of the latest hardware variant AIM-120D in January 2015. To pace the threat, the Navy has fielded the Electronic Protection Improvement Program (EPIP) Basic for AIM-120C3-C7 missiles and the System Improvement Program (SIP) 1 for AIM-120D in 2016. Advanced EPIP for AIM-120C7 is planned for 2017, and SIP 2 for AIM-120D will follow in 2018 to improve lethality further against the advancing threat.

Developers

Raytheon Tucson, Arizona

* * * * * * * * * * * *

Joint Direct-Attack Munition (JDAM, GBU-31/32/38) / Laser JDAM (GBU-54)

Description

The JDAM is an Air Force-led joint program for a global positioning system (GPS)-aided, inertial navigation system (INS) guidance kit to improve the precision of existing 500-pound, 1,000-pound, and 2,000-pound general-purpose and penetrator bombs in all weather conditions. JDAM addresses a broad spectrum of fixed and re-locatable targets at medium-range and releasing aircraft at high altitudes. The weapon is autonomous, all weather, and able to be employed against pre-planned targets or targets of opportunity. This weapon system has proven to be a true force multiplier, allowing a single aircraft to attack multiple targets from a single release point, and has proven its value during operations in Kosovo, Iraq, and Afghanistan.

In September 2006, the Departments of the Navy and Air Force put in place a flow-cost, non-developmental enhancement to the GBU-38 (500-pound) JDAM to address moving targets. Open competition and source selection completed in February 2010, and the Air Force awarded a contract to Boeing for a version of Laser JDAM (LJDAM) that provides a direct-attack moving-target capability. LJDAM (GBU-54) is a 500-pound dual-mode weapon that couples the GPS/INS precision of the JDAM and laser-designated accuracy of the laser-guided bomb into a single weapon. LJDAM also provides added capability and flexibility to the Fleet's existing inventory of precision-guided munitions to satisfy the ground moving-target capability gap.

Status

LRIP for the 2,000-pound kits began in FY 1997, and Milestone III was reached in FY 2001. The 1,000-pound JDAM kit reached initial operational capability (IOC) in FY 2002, and IOC for the 500-pound weapon occurred during the second quarter of FY 2005. LJDAM reached IOC in FY 2012. The Navy is developing the GBU-58 Laser JDAM for the BLU-109 penetrator to field in 2018 to replace the legacy GBU-24 Paveway III weapons systems.

Developers

The Boeing Company St. Louis, Missouri

Lockheed Martin Bethesda, Maryland

* * * * * * * * * * * *

Offensive Anti-Surface Warfare Increment 1 (OASuW Inc 1) Long-Range Anti-Ship Missile (LRASM)

Description

The Long-Range Anti-Ship Missile program will provide the first increment of next-generation anti-ship capabilities for the Navy and Air Force. The combatant commanders have an unmet urgent operational need to field improved anti-surface warfare capability. LRASM/ OASuW Increment 1 ills the most urgent air-launched requirement, significantly reduces joint force warfighting risks, and positions the Department of Defense (DoD) to address evolving surface warfare threats. In 2016, the Navy requested funds to begin the OASuW Increment 2 program to be a full and

45

open competition to address the "sundown" of Harpoon 1C and SLAM-ER ASUW weapons in the mid 2020s.

Status

The OASuW Inc 1 program is a joint (DoN lead/USAF) accelerated acquisition program scheduled for early operational capability on the B-1 Lancer in the fourth quarter FY 2018 and on the FA-18E/F Super Hornet in the fourth quarter FY 2019. The OASuW Inc 1 capability development document (CDD) has been approved by the Joint Requirements Oversight Council (JROC), and the program passed its Knowledge Point 3 (Milestone B equivalent) in March 2016. The Navy has staffed the CDD for OASuW Increment 2 requirements for JROC validation in FY 2017.

Developers

Raytheon Tucson, Arizona

* * * * * * * * * * *

Paveway II Laser-Guided Bomb (LGB) / Dual-Mode LGB (GBU-10/12/16) and Paveway III (GBU-24) LGB

Description

The Paveway II/III laser-guided bomb program is an Air Force-led joint effort with the Navy. LGBs include GBU-10, -12, and -16, using Mk 80/Bomb-Live Unit (BLU) series general-purpose bomb bodies, and GBU-24, using the BLU-109 bomb body with updated guidance and control features. GBU-12 is a 500-pound class weapon; GBU-16 is a 1,000-pound class weapon; and GBU-10 is a 2,000-pound class weapon. An LGB has a Mk 80/BLU-series warhead fitted with a laser-guidance kit and computer control group mounted on the bomb nose. Legacy LGBs will remain in the Navy inventory through FY 2020. The Dual-Mode LGB (DMLGB) retrofits legacy LGBs to a dual-mode configuration using common components. This provides increased flexibility to the warfighter by combining proven laser terminal guidance technology with the all-weather, fire-and-forget capability of inertial navigation system/global positioning system. The DMLGB reached initial operational capability in September 2007 on the AV-8B Harrier LL+ and FA-18 Hornet/Super Hornet aircraft.

Status

Approximately 7,000 DMLGB kits have been procured. No future funding for DMLGB is planned, given the development of the dual-mode Laser Joint Direct Attack Munition.

Developers

Lockheed Martin Bethesda, Maryland

Raytheon Tucson, Arizona

* * * * * * * * * * *

AVIATION SENSORS AND SYSTEMS

Airborne Electronic Attack (AEA) Next-Generation Jammer (NGJ)

Description

The Next-Generation Jammer is the replacement for the ALQ-99 Tactical Jamming System (TJS). Fielded in 1971, ALQ-99 is the only airborne tactical jamming system in the Department of Defense inventory. ALQ-99 is facing material and technological obsolescence and cannot counter all current, much less future, threats. The NGJ will provide significantly improved jamming capabilities with an open-system architecture that will support software and hardware updates to rapidly counter a wide variety of technically complex systems. It will be a full-spectrum jammer, developed in increments, and will initially be fielded on the EA-18G Growler. NGJ will be the prime contributor for the airborne electronic attack mission.

Status

NGJ Increment 1 achieved Milestone B in March 2016 and in late 2016 is executing the engineering, manufacturing and development (EMD) phase. The EMD contract was awarded to Raytheon in April 2016. Increment 2 is a FY 2016 new-start program. In FY 2017 Increment 2 is conducting technology studies, validating technology readiness levels, building and testing pod prototypes, and performing system-engineering tests.

Developers

The Boeing Company (Platform Prime) St. Louis, Missouri Raytheon (Pod Prime) El Segundo, California

* * * * * * * * * * *

ALQ-214 Integrated Defensive Electronic Countermeasures (IDECM)

Description

The IDECM system is employed on the F/A-18 series Hornet/ Super Hornets to defend against radar-guided surface-to-air and air-to-air missile systems. Through either a towed decoy or onboard transmitters, the ALQ-214 produces complex waveform radar jamming that defeats advanced threat systems.

Status

IDECM has been developed in three phases: (1) ALQ-165 On Board Jammer and ALE-50 towed decoy (initial operational capability, IOC, in FY 2002); (2) ALQ-214 On-Board Jammer and ALE-50 towed decoy (IOC FY 2004); and (3) ALQ-214 On Board Jammer and ALE-55 Fiber-Optic Towed Decoy (IOC FY 2011). The ALE-55 Fiber-Optic Towed Decoy replaces the ALE-50 towed decoy. IDECM is entering a fourth phase with development of the production Block 4 ALQ-214 On-Board Jammer for the F/A-18C/D/E/F Hornet/Super Hornet aircraft and is in full-rate production. The software improvement program will achieve IOC in FY 2017.

Developers

BAE Systems Nashua, New Hampshire

Excelis, Inc. Clifton, New Jersey

* * * * * * * * * * *

ALR-67(V)3 Advanced Special Receiver (RWR)

Description

The ALR-67(V)3 will meet Navy requirements through the year 2020. It enables the Navy Hornet/Super Hornet family of aircraft to detect threat radar emissions, enhancing aircrew situational awareness and aircraft survivability.

Status

The ALR-67(V)3 program successfully completed the engineering and manufacturing development phase and operational testing in 1999 and entered full-rate production in FY 2013. Production quantities will eventually outfit all F/A-18 Hornet/Super Hornet aircraft.

Developers

Arete Associates Tucson, Arizona

Raytheon Goleta, California

* * * * * * * * * * * *

APG-79 Active Electronically Scanned Array (AESA) Radar System

Description

The APG-79 AESA Phase I upgrade provides multi-mode function flexibility while enhancing performance in the air-to-air arena (including cruise missile defense) as well as the air-to-ground arena. The Phase II upgrade provides enhanced performance in hostile electronic countermeasure environments and provides significant electronic warfare improvements. Growth provisions will allow for future reconnaissance capability through the use of synthetic aperture radar technology and improved hardware and software. The APG-79 AESA radar is installed on Block II F/A-18E/F Super Hornet and all EA-18G Growler aircraft.

Status

The APG-79 completed subcontractor competition in November 1999; the Navy awarded the engineering and manufacturing development contract in February 2001; and the radar achieved initial operational capability in 2007. AESA Milestone C and flow-rate initial production approvals were received in January 2004 for initial delivery with Lot 27 Super Hornets in FY 2005. Full-rate production was achieved in June 2007 following completion of the initial operational test and evaluation in December 2006. The first deployment of the AESA system was with the VFA-22 "Fighting Redcocks" in 2008. Retrofit installations into Block II Lot 26-29 F/A-18E/Fs began in 2013. All Block II F/A-18E/F and EA-18G aircraft will be equipped with the APG-79 AESA radar by 2019.

Developers

The Boeing Company St. Louis, Missouri

Raytheon El Segundo, California

* * * * * * * * * * * *

AAQ-24 Department of the Navy Large Aircraft Infrared Countermeasures (DoN LAIRCM) System

Description

The AAQ-24(V)25, DoN LAIRCM System is an ACAT II Special Interest program. The system consists of advanced, two-color infrared (IR) missile warning that cues an inexhaustible laser countermeasure and ALE-47 expendables to defeat shoulder-launched missiles. The current IR missile warning sensors are being retrofitted to provide advanced threat warner (ATW) capability. ATW sensors will improve missile-warning performance and will provide laser warning (LW), and hostile fire indication (HFI), as well as threat point of origin for better situational awareness. ATW will improve countermeasures accuracy and enable tactical responses to surface to air threats including small arms, anti-aircraft artillery, rocket propelled grenades and laser-guided weaponry. The DoN LAIRCM and ATW configuration includes four major components: (1) IR MWS sensors; (2) a dedicated processor; (3) a control indicator unit for cockpit display; and (4) Guardian laser turret assembly that consists of a four-axis stabilized gimbaled system, a fine-track sensor, and a Viper TM laser.

The system is deployed on Marine Corps CH-53E Super Stallion helicopters. The CH-53E systems are being upgraded to the ATW configuration, and ATW is also being installed on the MV-22 and KC-130J aircraft, and will be installed on the CH-53K in the future. The Naval Air Systems Command (NAVAIR) began DoN LAIRCM integration on CH-53Es in 2009 and Navy C-40 Clipper and Marine Corps KC-130J Hercules aircraft in FY 2012.

A Marine Corps urgent universal need statement signed in April 2014 directed NAVAIR to install DoN LAIRCM/ATW on 24 Special-Purpose Marine Air-Ground Task Force MV-22 Ospreys. The ATW follow-on test and evaluation (FOT&E) was called out of test in July 2015, and ATW retrofit and initial installation kits were fielded based on the operational test (OT) report. ATW sensor retrofit will initially be fielded on MV-22 in the second quarter FY 2017 based on a Quick Reaction Assessment. During this same period KC-130J completed Non-Recurring Engineering to integrate DoN LAIRCM. KC-130J testing and fielding was planned for the first quarter FY 2017. The CH-53K baseline DECM configuration includes DoN LAIRCM with OT planned in the first quarter FY 2019. Upon completion of OT testing, the CH-53K will be upgraded to the ATW configuration to meet emergent threats.

The DoN LAIRCM program Office provided government-furnished equipment to the P-8A Poseidon program to support a 2015 urgent operational need.

Status

DoN LAIRCM initial operational capability was achieved in May 2009, and a full-rate production decision was approved in January 2010. Advanced threat warning operational test and evaluation began in FY 2013, and finished FOT&E in FY 2015. Delivery began in FY 2016. The DoN LAIRCM Program Office works closely with its counterpart the Air Force LAIRCM program to leverage contracts, test and evaluation, and sustainment efforts, and is working closely with the Army to provide support during the transition to a new missile warning system.

Developers

Northrop Grumman Rolling Meadows, Illinois

* * * * * * * * * * * *

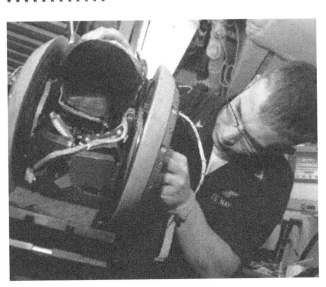

ASQ-228 Advanced Targeting Forward-Looking Infra-Red (ATFLIR) Sensor

Description

The ATFLIR provides the F/A-18A+/C/E/F Hornet and Super Hornet aircraft with a significantly enhanced capability to detect, track, and attack air and ground targets, compared to the legacy AAS-38/46 NITEHAWK Targeting Forward-Looking Infrared (FLIR) system. Laser-guided and global positioning system standoff weapons systems and higher-altitude attack profiles require improved performance. The ATFLIR provides a significant improvement in operational effectiveness to support precision-strike mission requirements. Improved reliability and maintainability increase operational availability while reducing total ownership costs. The ATFLIR consists of a mid-wave FLIR and electro-optical sensor, laser spot tracker, and a tactical laser for designation and ranging. Improvements to the ATFLIR include the addition of an infrared marker, ROVER data link, and moving-target track improvements.

Status

ATFLIR completed Phase I operational test and evaluation in September 2003 and was determined to be operationally suitable and effective; it was recommended for further fleet introduction and achieved initial operational capability in September 2003. It has demonstrated its combat capability during Operations Iraqi Freedom and Enduring Freedom. The ATFLIR production contract is complete with a total procurement of 410 pods.

Developers

The Boeing Company St. Louis, Missouri

Raytheon El Segundo, California

* * * * * * * * * * * *

Joint Mission Planning Systems (JMPS)

Description

The Joint Mission Planning System is the core of the Naval Mission Planning Systems (NavMPS) portfolio. JMPS enables weapon system employment by providing the information, automated tools, and decision aids needed to plan missions; to load mission data into aircraft, weapons, sensors, and avionics systems; and to conduct post-mission analysis. Navy and Marine Corps aircrews use JMPS for mission planning at different classification levels for a variety of Navy/Marine Corps aviation platforms and air-launched weapons. JMPS software is fielded to the Fleet as a platform-tailored mission planning environment (MPE) that combines a common JMPS framework with NavMPS applications (e.g., WASP and TOPSCENE) and components that support platform-specific capabilities and tactical missions. JMPS replaced and improved upon legacy MPS capabilities, increasing commonality among platforms, and integrating new technologies to support evolving platform capabilities and interoperability requirements.

Status

JMPS is fielded directly to squadrons and supports approximately 40 aircraft type/model series. These include: (1) all F/A-18 Hornet/Super Hornet variants, EA-18G Growler, EA-6B Prowler, AV-8B Harrier LL, MV-22B Osprey, C-2A Greyhound, E-2C/D Hawkeye, P-3C Orion, and EP-3E ARLES LL: (2) Navy and Marine Corps helicopters—MH-53E Sea Dragon and MH-60R/S Seahawk, AH-1W/Z Super Cobra, UH-1Y Venom, CH-53E Super Stallion, VH-3D Sea King and VH-60N WhiteHawk presidential helicopters; and (3) Naval Aviation training aircraft. Future JMPS platforms include the CH-53K King Stallion helicopter and MQ-4C Triton unmanned aerial system.

In 2006 JMPS was designated the single MPS for Naval Aviation, replacing legacy, platform-unique MPS. In 2014 JMPS began fielding platform-tailored MPEs upgraded with a new JMPS framework and Windows 7 operating system (OS).

JMPS will transition MPEs to Windows 10 OS in compliance with Department of Defense cybersecurity mandates. JMPS is also transitioning from a 32-bit to a 64-bit architecture that increases memory and processing capabilities to meet fleet requirements. The JMPS program is fielding mobile "electronic kneeboard" devices to support aircrew planning and execution of flight requirements in support of "paperless cockpit" initiatives.

Developers

DCS Corporation Lexington Park, Maryland

Lockheed Martin Marlton, New Jersey

Northrop Grumman San Pedro, California

* * * * * * * * * * *

SECTION 2

"Distributed Lethality" means that the Navy's Surface Forces are the world's premier multi-domain naval warfighting force. Multi-mission guided-missile cruisers and destroyers, coupled with our smaller littoral combat ships and next-generation frigates, are crucial to deterring and defeating threats through all-domain access, power projection, air and missile defense, precision strike, and maritime security and sea control. Through forward-deployed operations augmented by surface warship homeports in Japan and Spain, the Surface Force maximizes its access to vital world regions in support of the Nation's interests as well as protecting the global maritime commons to safeguard world commerce.

SURFACE WARSHIPS

CG 47 Ticonderoga-Class Aegis Guided-Missile Cruiser Modernization

Description

Ticonderoga-class guided-missile cruisers (CGs) provide multi-mission offensive and defensive capabilities and can operate independently or as part of aircraft carrier strike groups and surface action groups in global operations. Ticonderoga-class cruisers have a combat system centered on the Aegis Weapon System and the SPY-1B/(B)V multi-function, phased-array radar. The combat system includes the Mk 41 vertical launching system that employs Standard Missile surface-to-air missiles, Tomahawk land-attack cruise missiles, advanced undersea and surface warfare systems, embarked sea-control helicopters, and robust command, control, and communications systems in a potent, multi-mission warship.

The oldest 11 cruisers have been extensively modernized, including hull, mechanical, and electrical (HM&E) upgrades as well as improved quality of life, mission-life extension, integrated ship's control, all-electric auxiliaries, and weight and moment modifications. Combat systems upgrades include an open-architecture computing environment. Specific improvements to Cooperative Engagement Capability and SPY radar, maritime force-protection with the Mk 15 Close-In Weapon System Block 1B, Evolved Seasparrow Missile, Nulka decoy, and SPQ-9B radar, and the SQQ-89A(V)15 anti-submarine warfare suite address capability upgrades. Open architecture cruiser modernization warfighting improvements will extend the Aegis Weapon System's capabilities against projected threats well into the 21st Century.

The Navy has commenced a modernization plan of the Fleet's 11 newest cruisers, which will update the ships' combat systems and HM&E systems. This updated modernization plan provides the added benefit of extending the service lives of these ships from 35 to 40 years, ensuring a minimum of 11 relevant and capable purpose-built air defense-commander platforms for carrier strike groups into the mid-2030s.

Status

Combat systems modernization commenced in FY 2008 with the USS Bunker Hill (CG 52). Seven ships have completed Advanced Capability Build (ACB) 08 combat systems modernization, and three have completed ACB-12 combat systems modernization. Aegis CGs 52-62 have completed extensive HM&E upgrades, and in 2015 the USS Gettysburg (CG 64) and USS Cowpens (CG 63) were inducted into phased modernization. The USS Chosin (CG 65) and USS Vicksburg (CG 69) were inducted into phased modernization in 2016.

Developers

Huntington Ingalls Industries,

Ingalls Shipbuilding Pascagoula, Mississippi

Lockheed Martin Moorestown, New Jersey

* * * * * * * * * * *

DDG 51 Arleigh Burke-Class Aegis Guided-Missile Destroyer

Description

Arleigh Burke-class guided-missile destroyer combat system is centered on the Aegis Weapon System and the SPY-1D(V) multifunction, phased-array radar. The combat system includes the Mk 41 vertical launching system, an advanced anti-submarine warfare system, advanced anti-air warfare missiles, and Tomahawk land-attack cruise missiles. Incorporating all-steel construction and gas-turbine propulsion, DDG 51 destroyers provide multi-mission offensive and defensive capability, operating independently or as part of an aircraft carrier strike group or surface action group. Flight IIA variants incorporate facilities to support two embarked helicopters, significantly enhancing the ship's sea-control capability. A Flight III variant, which will incorporate the advanced Air and Missile Defense Radar (AMDR) SPY-6(V), is in development. Studies are ongoing to identify additional technology insertions to improve capability in other warfare area missions for Flight III.

Status

Following completion of the original DDG 51 acquisition program, the line was restarted in FY 2010 to continue production of this highly capable platform. Contracts for four Flight IIA ships were awarded from FY 2010 through FY 2012. The first of the "restart" Flight IIA ships, John Finn (DDG 113), successfully completed builder's trials in August 2016. DDG 113 is fitted with the Aegis Weapon System Baseline 9, which enables the ship to simultaneously track and target ballistic missiles and traditional air warfare threats. In June 2013, the Navy awarded a multi-year contract for Flight IIA DDG 51s in FY 2013 through FY 2017. In June 2014, the Navy modified these contracts reflecting engineering change proposals to the Flight III configuration starting with the second ship procured in FY 2016. The Flight III configuration will include the SPY-6(V) next-generation integrated air and missile defense radar, power and cooling enhancements to support SPY-6(V), and additional technology insertions to improve capability and life cycle costs in other warfare area missions. Initial operational capability is scheduled for FY 2023 after delivery of the first ship in FY 2021.

Developers

General Dynamics Bath Iron Works Bath, Maine

Huntington Ingalls Industries, Ingalls Shipbuilding Pascagoula, Mississippi

Lockheed Martin Moorestown, New Jersey

* * * * * * * * * * * *

DDG 51 Arleigh Burke-Class Aegis Guided-Missile Destroyer Modernization

Description

Arleigh Burke-class guided-missile destroyers commenced mid-life modernization in FY 2010 with DDGs 51 and 53. The program was originally accomplished in two phases. The first phase concentrated on hull, mechanical, and electrical (HM&E) systems and included new gigabit ethernet connectivity in the engineering plant, a digital video surveillance system, an integrated bridge system, an advanced galley, and other habitability and manpower-reduction modifications. A complete open-architecture computing environment is the foundation for warfighting improvements in the second phase of the modernization for each ship. The upgrade plan consists of an improved multi-mission signal processor, which integrates air and ballistic missile defense capabilities, and enhancements improving radar performance in the littoral regions. Upon the completion of the modernization program, the ships will have the following weapons and sensors: Cooperative Engagement Capability; Evolved Seasparrow Missile; Mk 15 Close-In Weapon System Block 1B; Surface Electronic Warfare Improvement Program; and Nulka decoys. The Mk 41 vertical launching system is upgraded to support SM-3 and newer variants of the Standard Missile family. These two phases are accomplished on each ship approximately two years apart. Modernized DDG 51-class guided-missile destroyers will continue to provide multi-mission offensive and defensive capabilities with the added benefit of sea-based ballistic missile defense (BMD).

Status

The HM&E modernization modifications have been designed into the most recent new-construction Arleigh Burke-class destroyers. Incorporating modernization design in new construction optimizes risk reduction and proof of alteration in the builder's yard, reducing overall risk in the modernization program. Six Flight I DDGs have completed the Advanced Capability Build (ACB-12/ BMD 5.0) process of providing software upgrades for combat systems modernization. DDG modernization initially concentrates on the Flight I and II ships (DDGs 51-78), but is intended as a modernization program for the entire class. The Flight IIA modernization as a single combined HM&E and combat system modernization is scheduled to begin in FY 2017.

Developers

General Dynamics Bath Iron Works Bath, Maine

Lockheed Martin Moorestown, New Jersey

* * * * * * * * * * * *

DDG 1000 Zumwalt-Class 21st Century Destroyer

Description

The Zumwalt-class guided-missile destroyer is an optimally crewed, multi-mission surface combatant tailored for land attack and littoral control. This advanced warship will provide offensive, distributed, and precision fires in support of forces ashore and a credible forward naval presence while operating independently or as an integral part of naval, joint or combined strike forces. To ensure effective operations in the littoral, it will incorporate signature reduction, active and passive self-defense systems, and enhanced survivability features. It will field an undersea warfare suite capable of in-stride mine avoidance, as well as robust self-defense systems to defeat littoral submarine threats, anti-ship cruise missiles, and small boats. Additionally, it will provide valuable lessons in advanced technology, such as the integrated power system and advanced survivability features, which can be incorporated into other ship classes.

Status

Zumwalt (DDG 1000) fabrication commenced in February 2009, and the ship delivered in May 2016. Expected to reach initial operational capability in FY 2020, Zumwalt was christened in FY 2014 and commissioned in Baltimore, Maryland, on October 15, 2016. Michael Monsoor (DDG 1001) fabrication commenced in February 2010, and the ship is scheduled to deliver in FY 2017. Fabrication of Lyndon B. Johnson (DDG 1002) commenced in April 2012, and the ship is scheduled to deliver in FY 2019. General Dynamics Bath Iron Works is building the three-ship Zumwalt class, with Huntington Ingalls Industries manufacturing the composite superstructure for DDG 1000 and 1001.

Developers

BAE Systems Minneapolis, Minnesota

General Dynamics Bath Iron Works Bath, Maine Huntington Ingalls Industries,

Ingalls Shipbuilding Pascagoula, Mississippi

Raytheon Systems, Inc. Sudbury, Massachusetts

* * * * * * * * * * * *

Frigate (FF) Description

The next-generation frigate (FF) will be a modified littoral combat ship (LCS) with enhanced lethality and survivability. It will be a multi-mission reconfigurable ship with the simultaneous ability to support surface warfare (SUW) and anti-submarine warfare (ASW) missions. The addition of over-the-horizon missiles will add significant combat capability to support the Navy's distributed lethality concept and blue water operations with larger task forces and high-value units. The FF will provide excellent escort and screening capabilities, with an improved 3-D radar and upgraded electronic warfare suite, providing flexibility in the employment of larger surface combatants while lowering the overall warfighting risk. Its ability to operate in the littorals and "blue water" addresses warfighting capability gaps against asymmetric anti-access threats and thus play a vital role in American maritime security.

The contract award and down-select to either the Freedom or Independence variant FF is planned for FY 2019, but may be as early as FY 2018, with initial operational capability scheduled for 2023. Regardless of the variant chosen, COMBATSS-21 (an Aegis Weapon System derivative) will be the combat management system. This will leverage synergies with other surface warships that use the Aegis combat system and ensure the FF can support the range of naval operations with larger combatants through all phases of conflict. Due to similar maintenance, training requirements, and rotational crewing processes as LCS, FF will fold into the preexisting logistical infrastructure, training support programs, and facilities. Taking advantage of the previous institution of processes and systems for the LCS will enable the FF to quickly contribute to the small surface combatant operational demand, meeting the validated fleet requirements for small surface combatants.

Status

In February of 2014, the Secretary of Defense Chuck Hagel directed Navy to submit proposals for a more lethal and capable small surface combatant to follow LCS 1 through 32. A Small Surface Combatant Task Force (SSCTF) subsequently analyzed and evaluated potential alternatives to LCS. In December 2014, the SSCTF presented its findings to the Defense Secretary, who concurred with the Navy's recommendation to pursue a small surface combatant design based on a modified LCS. The following January, Secretary of the Navy Ray Mabus announced the modified LCS would be called Frigate to emphasize the enhanced lethality, survivability, and multi-mission capability FF would offer to the warfighter. In December 2015, Secretary of Defense Ash Carter directed the Navy to reduce the small surface combatant program of record from 52 to 40 ships for budgetary reasons. In accordance with this direction, Navy has truncated the LCS/FF program to 28 LCS and 12 FF. The last LCS keel will begin construction in 2017, with FF construction beginning as early as 2018 but not later than 2019.

Developers

To be determined.

* * * * * * * * * * * *

Littoral Combat Ship (LCS)

Description

The Littoral Combat Ship is a modular, reconfigurable ship designed to meet validated fleet requirements in the littoral region. The LCS addresses warfighting capability gaps against asymmetric anti-access threats and is already playing an important role in American maritime security; it will eventually compose a significant portion of the Navy's future surface combatant fleet. Through its innovative modular design, each LCS can be configured for surface warfare (SUW), anti-submarine warfare (ASW), or mine countermeasures (MCM) missions. This versatility enables the Navy to provide warfighters with the most capable, cost-effective solution to counter threats from the littoral regions to the open ocean.

There are two variants of LCS, the Freedom variant (all odd-numbered ships) and Independence variant (all even-numbered ships). The Freedom variant is a steel semi-planing monohull with an aluminum superstructure, constructed by Lockheed Martin in Fincantieri Marinette Marine's shipyard in Marinette, Wisconsin. The Independence variant is an all-aluminum, stabilized mono-hull (trimaran) constructed by Austal USA (formerly teamed with General Dynamics) in Mobile, Alabama. Both ship variants have an open-architecture design and embark one of three interchangeable mission packages to execute SUW, ASW, or MCM missions, as well as having the organic capability to conduct numerous secondary missions. The LCS modular architecture will also enable the rapid upgrade of weapon systems and sensors without requiring expensive and time-consuming shipyard periods. The ships operate on a rotational crewing concept which will provide more than twice the on-station time compared to other, single-crewed ships, resulting in a significant cost savings to the Navy and continuous presence in important world regions. By 2030, six out of every ten U.S. Navy warships deployed worldwide will be LCS ships due to this unique crewing concept. The Navy is also aggressively pursuing forward-/back-it LCS lethality and survivability upgrades to support LCS ability to fold seamlessly into the surface Navy's distributed lethality concept.

Status

The LCS program began in February 2002, and in May 2004 the Navy awarded two contract options to Lockheed Martin and General Dynamics/Austal USA to build the first research-and-development variants. Through highly effective competition between industry bidders in 2010, the LCS program achieved significant cost savings with a fixed-price dual-block buy of 20 LCS (ten of each variant) through FY 2015. By the spring 2017, the Navy had 26 LCS (13 of each variant) at sea, under construction, or under contract. As of early 2017, LCSs 1-8 have been commissioned. LCSs 9-26 will be delivered to the Navy by the end of 2020. In November 2014, the USS Fort Worth (LCS 3) commenced a 16-month deployment to Singapore, beginning continuous LCS presence in the Western Pacific and the implementation of the rotational crewing concept. During the first 14 months of her deployment, she participated in a search and rescue effort for Air Asia flight QZ8501, made 12 port visits, and participated in ten bilateral and multi-lateral exercises across the Indo-Asia-Pacific region. Prior to her scheduled maiden deployment, the Navy upgraded the USS Coronado with a Harpoon SUW missile system and conducted a successful structural test firing during the "Rim of the Pacific" 2016 multilateral naval exercise. She is now equipped with a fully functional and certified missile system for the 2016-2017 Southeast Asia deployment. The USS Jackson (LCS 6) completed shock trials for the Independence variant during the summer 2016, validating and frequently exceeding survivability expectations; the USS Milwaukee (LCS 5) completed shock trials for the Freedom variant in the fall 2016. The long-term testing and deployment schedule is under review by the Fleet following improvements to the rotational construct to improve deployed presence, maintenance execution, and crew ownership.

Developers

Austal USA Mobile, Alabama

Lockheed Martin and Marinette Marine Marinette, Wisconsin

* * * * * * * * * * *

PC 1 Cyclone-Class Patrol Coastal Modernization Program

Description

The Cyclone-class Patrol Coastal ships are essential for conducting theater security cooperation tasks, maritime security operations, and intelligence, surveillance, and reconnaissance missions. The PCs are uniquely suited to operating with maritime partner navies and coastguards, particularly in the green-water/brown-water "seam." Fourteen Cyclone-class ships were built, 13 are operating in the Navy in late 2016, and one was transferred to the Philippine navy in 2004. The PC Modernization improvements correct the most significant maintenance and obsolescence issues and will extend the life of the class by 15 years, to a 30-year expected service life. The program supports significant alterations, such as a main propulsion diesel engine pool and upgrading diesel generators and reverse-osmosis units. Additional hull, mechanical, and electrical modifications and updates to the weapons systems and C4ISR (command, control, communications, computers, intelligence, surveillance, and reconnaissance) suite are also included. As part of the Navy's counter-swarm strategy, for example, a 7.62mm coaxial mount Gatling gun is integrated into the forward and aft Mk 38 Mod 2 25mm electro-optical/infrared machine gun system to augment the PC's surface warfare capabilities for layered self-defense. In addition to the Mk 38 Mod 2 upgrade, the Mk 60 Griffin missile system installation is planned for all ten PCs deployed to Bahrain.

Status

The 13-ship Cyclone-class modernization program commenced in FY 2008 and is scheduled for completion by FY 2017. Ten PCs are forward deployed to Bahrain; the remaining three PCs are home-ported in Mayport, Florida. The forward and aft Mk 38 Mod 2 upgrade and Mk 60 Griffin missile system installation have been completed on all ten Bahrain-homeported PCs.

Developers

Bollinger Shipyards Lockport, Louisiana

* * * * * * * * * * *

SURFACE WEAPONS

Mk 15 Phalanx Close-In Weapon System (CIWS)

Description

The Mk 15 Mod 21-28 Phalanx Close-In Weapon System is an autonomous combat system that searches, detects, tracks (radar and electro-optic), and engages threats with a 20mm Gatling gun capable of firing 4,500 tungsten penetrator rounds per minute. Integral to ship self-defense and the anti-air warfare defense-in-depth concept, CIWS provides terminal defense against anti-ship missiles and high-speed aircraft penetrating other fleet defenses. Phalanx CIWS can operate autonomously or be integrated with a ship's combat system. The Block 1B configuration provides expanded defense against asymmetric threats such as small, fast surface craft, slow-lying aircraft, and unmanned aerial vehicles through the addition of an integrated forward-looking infrared system. Block 1B also incorporates an optimized gun barrel (OGB) for tighter ordnance dispersion. Enhanced-lethality cartridges can be used with the OGB for improved target penetration. Mk 15 Mod 31 is the

SeaRAM system. SeaRAM is based on the Block 1B Phalanx configuration, with the gun subsystem replaced by an 11-round Rolling Airframe Missile (RAM) launcher, capable of firing RAM Block 1 or Block 2 missiles. SeaRAM can be integrated with a ships' combat system or operate autonomously.

Status

More than 250 Mk 15 Phalanx CIWS systems are deployed in the Navy. CIWS Block 1B is installed on all CVNs (three mounts), LHDs (three mounts), LHAs (three mounts), LSDs (two mounts), DDGs (one or two mounts), and CGs (two mounts). By the end of 2019, a fleet-wide upgrade of Phalanx radar systems to Baseline 2 configuration will be complete. SeaRAM systems are employed on the four forward-deployed guided-missile destroyers homeported in Rota, Spain, and also on the Independence (LCS 2) variant littoral combat ship. It is scheduled for the new-construction Freedom-variant LCSs.

The Army procured 45 Land-based Phalanx Weapon System (LPWS) units, with one system since retired from service. Approximately half of the LPWS units are deployed at forward operating bases in theater and the other half are continental U.S.-based, primarily for use in training. LPWS has executed more than 275 successful defensive combat engagements in Iraq and Afghanistan operations.

Developers

Raytheon (Engineering) Tucson, Arizona

Raytheon (Production/Depot) Louisville, Kentucky

* * * * * * * * * * * *

Mk 38 Mod 2 Stabilized 25mm Chain Gun

Description

The Mod 2 program upgrades the Mk 38 Mod 1 25mm chain gun by adding stabilization, remote operation, fire control, and an electro-optical sensor. These additions significantly expand the effective range, lethality, and nighttime capability of the weapon. The program reduces risk for surface ship self-defense by engaging

64

asymmetric threats to ships at close range. It provides the capability to bridge current and future targeting and weapons technology in a close-range force-protection environment, including protection in port, at anchor, transiting choke points, or while operating in restricted waters.

Status

The Navy initiated the Mk 38 Mod 2 program in 2003 to improve ship self-defense against small-boat threats by developing and fielding a mid-term capability for surface ships that is simple, stabilized, and affordable. The Mk 38 Mod 2 program received an approval for initial operational capability in FY 2006. At the end of FY 2016, the program has fielded 257 systems, 64 percent of the planned total. The Mk 38 Mod 2 machine gun system is being installed on aircraft carriers, guided-missile cruisers and destroyers, amphibious warfare ships, patrol coastal ships, command ships, and riverine squadron patrol boats.

An ordnance alteration (ORDALT) has been developed to implement a 7.62mm coaxially mounted automatic gun. This ORDALT completed live-fire testing in late FY 2016 and will complete safety qualification in FY 2017. In addition, improvements to the Mk 38 Mod 2 have been implemented, including an enhanced electro-optical/infrared sensor with increased range and resolution for tracking and Identification to counter swarm fast-attack craft/fast in-shore-attack craft. Mk 38 Mod 3 is assigned for this improved configuration. The Mk 38 Mod 3 has completed environmental qualification and live-fire testing in late FY 2016 and will complete safety qualification in FY 2017.

Developers

BAE Louisville, Kentucky

Rafael USA, Inc. Haifa, Israel

* * * * * * * * * * *

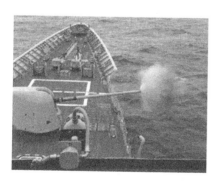

Mk 45 Mod 4 5-Inch/62-Caliber Gun System Upgrade

Description

The Mk 45 Mod 4 5-inch/62-caliber gun is a modification of the 5-inch/54-caliber gun with higher firing energies to support long-range munitions. The gun retains the functionality of the 5-inch guns, including ability to fire all existing 5-inch rounds. The modified design also improves maintenance procedures and provides enhanced anti-surface and anti-air warfare performance. Modifications include a longer (62-caliber) barrel, an ammunition recognition system, and a digital control system.

Status

The Mk 45 Mod 4 gun was added to the new-construction Arleigh Burke (DDG 51)-class destroyers, starting with the USS Winston S. Churchill (DDG 81).

Developers

BAE Systems Minneapolis, Minnesota

* * * * * * * * * * * *

Mk 46 Mod 2 Gun Weapon System (GWS)

Description

The Mk 46 Mod 2 is a 30mm GWS with a two-axis stabilized gun that can fire up to 200 rounds per minute. The system uses a forward-looking infrared sensor, a flow-light television camera, and laser range finder with a closed-loop tracking system to optimize accuracy against small, high-speed surface targets. Adapted from the Marine Corps expeditionary fighting vehicle gun, the Mk 46 Mod 2 GWS is an upgrade to the Mk 46 Mod 1 GWS. Both systems build upon commercial off-the-shelf /non-development items (COTS/NDI) technology using open-system architecture to allow for rapid and cost-effective use of COTS/NDI components and software.

Status

The Mk 46 Mod 2 GWS is being installed on the San Antonio (LPD 17)-class amphibious transport dock ships and the Zumwalt (DDG 1000)-class destroyers as well as the littoral combat ship surface warfare mission package.

Developers

General Dynamics Land Systems Sterling Heights, Michigan

* * * * * * * * * * * *

Mk 51 Gun Weapon System (GWS)

Description

The Mk 51 GWS is a 155mm (6-inch) advanced gun system (AGS) being installed in the three Zumwalt (DDG 1000)-class destroyers to provide precision, volume, and sustained fires in support of distributed joint and coalition forces ashore. The Mk 51 GWS is a fully integrated, automatic gun and magazine weapon system that will support the Zumwalt-class naval surface fire support mission. Each system will be capable of independently firing up to ten rounds per minute. The Mk 51 GWS was designed to meet DDG 1000 optimal manning and radar-signature requirements.

Status

Mk 51 manufacturing is underway at two facilities—Cordova, Alabama, and Louisville, Kentucky—and is meeting ship-production schedules. Mk 51 magazines and guns have been installed on DDG 1000, with follow-on mount/magazine fabrication and installation in progress or completed in DDG 1001 and 1002.

Developers

BAE Systems Minneapolis, Minnesota

* * * * * * * * * * * *

Mk 54 Lightweight Torpedo (LWT)

Description

The Mk 54 Lightweight Torpedo is a modular upgrade to the lightweight torpedo inventory and adds the capability to counter quiet diesel-electric submarines operating in the littoral. Mk 54 LWT combines existing torpedo hardware and software from Mk 46, Mk 50, and Mk 48 advanced capability programs, with advanced digital commercial off-the-shelf electronics. The resulting Mk 54 LWT offers significantly improved shallow-water capability at reduced life-cycle costs. The Mk 54 LWT modernization plan will introduce new hardware and software updates providing stepped increases in probability of kill, while reducing life-cycle cost and allowing the torpedo to remain ahead of the evolving littoral submarine threat. Mk 54 is also replacing the Mk 46 as the payload in the vertical-launch anti-submarine rocket.

Status

Mk 54 torpedoes are being delivered for fleet use to meet the total munitions requirement. FY 2020 will be the final year of Mk 54 Mod 0 production. Mk 54 Mod 1 has begun developmental testing, and operational testing begins in FY 2018. Initial operational capability for Mk 54 Mod 1 is planned for FY 2023.

Developers

Raytheon Mukilteo, Washington

Mk 60 Griffin Missile System (GMS)

Description

The Griffin Missile System combines a lightweight laser and global positioning system/inertial navigation system in an integrated guided-missile system that has been adapted for use on forward-deployed Cyclone (PC 1)-class Patrol Coastal ships. The GMS was originally designed as an air-to-ground precision-engagement missile for U.S. Air Force MC-130 gunships. The Navy modified the GMS as a rapid deployment capability in support of fleet operational needs to improve small-vessel engagement capacity. The Griffin Block II is a 5.5-inch missile with a 13-pound blast-fragmentation warhead and semi-active laser seeker. The GMS uses the Brite Star II electro-optic infrared laser designator sensor ball mounted on the PC's mast to provide target Identification and illumination.

Status

At-sea testing completed in July 2013, and GMS proved capable against small-vessel threats. The first operational system was installed on the USS Monsoon (PC 4) in 2012, and the remaining nine installs were completed by the end of FY 2016.

Developers

Naval Surface Warfare Center Dahlgren, Virginia

Raytheon Tucson, Arizona

RGM/UGM-109E Tomahawk Land-Attack Missile (TLAM)

Description

Deployed on surface warships and attack- and guided-missile submarines, the Tomahawk land-attack missile is the Department of Defense's premier, all-weather, long-range, subsonic land-attack cruise missile. The Block IV Tactical Tomahawk (TACTOM, RGM-109E/UGM-109E) preserves Tomahawk's long-range precision-strike capability while significantly increasing responsiveness and flexibility. TACTOM improvements include in-light retargeting, the ability to loiter over the battlefield, and in-light missile health and status monitoring via a satellite data link. TACTOM also facilitates rapid mission planning and execution via global positioning system (GPS) onboard the launch platform and features an improved anti-jam GPS. A seeker variant is under development to add anti-surface warfare capability. Future payloads could include smart sub-munitions, a penetrator warhead, and a multiple-response warhead. Plans call for the Navy to procure more than 4,000 TACTOM weapons prior to program termination. TLAM Block III missiles will be retired from service by 2020.

Status

A full-rate production contract was signed in August 2004. It was Navy's first multi-year contract for TACTOM procurement of more than 1,500 missiles. This contract ended in FY 2008, and all missiles have been delivered. Tomahawk Block IV procurement in FY 2009 to FY 2016 was executed via firm, fixed-price contracts. The Navy will continue to procure TACTOM through FY 2017. A recertification and modernization program has been funded to start in FY 2019 to add an additional 15 years' service life to each missile in the TACTOM Block IV inventory.

Developers

Raytheon Missile Systems Tucson, Arizona

* * * * * * * * * * * *

RIM-7, Mk 57 NATO Seasparrow Surface Missile System (NSSMS) and RIM-162 Evolved Seasparrow Missile (ESSM)

Description

The Mk 57 NATO Seasparrow Surface Missile System (NSSMS) and its associated RIM-7P Seasparrow Missile and the RIM-162 Evolved Seasparrow Missile (ESSM) serve as the Navy's primary surface-to-air ship self-defense missile system. NSSMS is deployed on aircraft carriers, surface warships, and landing helicopter dock amphibious assault ships, and is being installed on the newest class of landing helicopter assault ships. The Mk 57 Target Acquisition System (TAS) is a combined volume-search radar and control element that determines threat evaluation and weapon assignment.

A kinematic upgrade to the RIM-7P missile, the ESSM Block 1 is the next-generation Seasparrow Missile that serves as a primary self-defense weapon on aircraft carriers and large-deck amphibious warships and provides layered-defense for Aegis cruisers and destroyers. ESSM Block 1 upgrades include a more powerful rocket motor, tail control section for quick response on vertical-launch system ships, upgraded warhead, and a quick-reaction electronic upgrade. Enhanced ESSM kinematics and warhead lethality leverage the robust RIM-7P guidance capability to provide increased operational effectiveness against high-speed, maneuvering, hardened anti-ship cruise missiles at greater intercept ranges than the

RIM-7P. Operational in FY 2004, ESSM Block 1 continues to be procured as part of the NATO Seasparrow Consortium involving ten NATO countries. To pace evolving threats, the next-generation ESSM Block 2 is being developed cooperatively by the consortium, replacing the missile guidance section with an active/semi-active dual-mode seeker.

Status

ESSM Block 1 is fielded on Ticonderoga (CG 47)-class guided-missile cruisers, Arleigh Burke (DDG 51)-class destroyers with Aegis Baselines 6.3 and higher, aircraft carriers (CVNs) and select amphibious ships (LHD 7-8, LHA 6). It will be deployed on the three Zumwalt (DDG 1000)-class destroyers, Wasp-class amphibious assault ships (LHDs 1-6), America class (LHA 7-8), and in-service Aegis cruisers and destroyers as well as new-construction destroyers. ESSM (Block 1 and Block 2) joint universal weapon link (JUWL) development is on schedule, and interrupted continuous wave illumination (ICWI) capability has already been incorporated. DDG 1000 and CVN 78 will require a unique variant of ESSM Block 1, incorporating both ICWI and JUWL. ESSM Block 2 development is in the engineering and manufacturing development phase. ESSM Block 2 achieved Milestone B in FY 2015 and will achieve initial operational capability in 2020 on Aegis ships and FY 2022 for non-Aegis ships.

Developers

Raytheon Tucson, Arizona

* * * * * * * * * * * *

RIM-66C Standard Missile-2 Blocks III/IIIA/IIIB

Description

The RIM-66C Standard Missile 2 (SM-2) is the Navy's primary air-defense weapon. SM-2 Block III/IIIA/IIIB configurations are all-weather, ship-launched, medium-range, surface-to-air missiles in service with the Navy and 15 allied navies. SM-2 enables forward naval presence, littoral operations, and projecting and sustaining U.S. forces in anti-access and area-denied environments. SM-2 Block III/IIIA/IIIB missiles are launched from the Mk 41 vertical launching system installed in Aegis cruisers and destroyers. Block III features improved performance against flow-altitude threats and optimizes the trajectory-shaping within the Aegis command guidance system by implementing shaping and fuse altimeter improvements. Block IIIA features a new directional warhead and a moving-target-indicator fuse design for improved performance and lethality against sea-skimming threats. Block IIIB adds an infrared-guidance mode capability developed in the missile homing-improvement program to improve performance in a stressing electronic countermeasure environment. Blocks IIIA/IIIB will be the heart of the SM-2 inventory for the next 20 years. The latest generation of Block IIIB missiles includes a maneuverability upgrade (SM-2 Block IIIB w/MU2) to enhance weapon performance against flow-altitude, supersonic maneuvering threats.

Status

The Navy established a depot (FY 2013) and rocket motor regrain program (FY 2014) to maintain the inventory out to the 2030+ timeframe. This will allow the SM-2 inventory to keep pace with Navy's 30-year shipbuilding plan, keep infrastructure in place to convert SM-2 Block IIIA missiles to the unique interrupted continuous wave illumination/joint universal weapon link variant for the three Zumwalt (DDG 1000)-class warships, and support projected increases in fleet proficiency firings. In addition, to avoid significant hardware obsolescence impacts, a modification to SM-2 to incorporate SM-6 technology will result in a supportable missile with commonality benefits to the Standard Missile family. This effort will begin in FY 2017 and will result in increased SM-2 capability from the incorporation of this latest technology.

Developers

Raytheon Tucson, Arizona

* * * * * * * * * * *

RIM-116A Rolling Airframe Missile (RAM)

Description

The Rolling Airframe Missile is a high rate-of-fire, flow-cost system, with the Block 0 configuration based on the AIM-9 Sidewinder, designed to engage anti-ship cruise missiles (ASCMs). RAM is a surface-to-air missile with passive dual-mode radio frequency/ infrared (RF/IR) guidance and an active-optical proximity and contact fuse. RAM has minimal shipboard control systems and is autonomous after launch. While effective against a wide spectrum of existing threats, RAM enhancements have been developed to improve and keep pace with emerging threats. RAM Block 1 IR upgrade incorporates IR all-the-way-homing to improve performance against evolving passive and active ASCMs. RAM Block 2, in flow-rate initial production (LRIP), provides increased kinematic capability against highly maneuvering threats and improved RF detection against flow probability of intercept threats. The RAM program is a cooperative development, production, and in-service program with Germany.

Status

RAM is installed in the Tarawa (LHA 1)- and Wasp (LHD 1)-class amphibious assault ships, Whidbey Island (LSD 41)- and Harpers Ferry (LSD 49)-class dock landing ships, aircraft carriers, and San Antonio (LPD 17)-class landing platform dock ships. RAM is also installed on the USS Freedom (LCS 1), the Lockheed

Martin variant of the littoral combat ship. The Block 0 and Block 1 configurations have completed production with the Block 2 missile in the fifth year of flow-rate initial production. Block 2 achieved initial operational capability in May 2015 with a full-rate production decision planned for FY 2018. A RAM Block 2 capability enhancement commenced development in FY 2016 to improve system performance against a stream raid threat scenario with plans to deliver the new capability in two incremental phases (FY 2019 and FY 2021).

Developers

RAMSYS GmbH Ottobrunn, Germany

Raytheon Tucson, Arizona

* * * * * * * * * * *

SM-6 Standard Missile 6 Extended-Range Active Missile (ERAM) Block I/II

Description

The Standard Missile 6 Extended-Range Active Missile is the Navy's next-generation extended-range anti-air warfare interceptor. The introduction of active-seeker technology to air defense in the Surface Force reduces the Aegis Weapon System's reliance on illuminators. It also provides improved performance against stream raids and targets employing advanced characteristics such as enhanced maneuverability, flow-radar cross-section, improved kinematics, and advanced electronic countermeasures. The SM-6 acquisition strategy is characterized as a

74

flow-risk development approach that leverages SM-2 Block IV/IVA program non-developmental items and Raytheon's Advanced Medium-Range Air-to-Air Missile Phase 3 active seeker program from Naval Air Systems Command. The SM-6 missile will be fielded on Arleigh Burke (DDG 51)-class destroyers and Ticonderoga (CG 47)-class cruisers.

Status

The Navy established the SM-6 extended-range air defense program in FY 2004. In March 2013, the Resources and Requirements Review Board directed a program of record increase from 1,200 missiles to 1,800. The SM-6 program inventory objective increase results from fleet threat analysis and evolving mission sets, as well as anticipated new threats. The program improves fleet defense and ensures sufficient missile inventory is available. SM-6 Block I was authorized to enter into full rate production in July 2013 and achieved initial operational capability in November 2013. The SM-6 Block IA variant was incorporated into production in FY 2015, and Block IA initial operational test and evaluation is planned for FY 2017.

Developers

Raytheon Tucson, Arizona

* * * * * * * * * * * *

U.S. Coast Guard Navy-Type / Navy-Owned (NTNO) Program

Description

The Navy-Type/Navy-Owned Program provides legacy and new-construction Coast Guard cutters with sensors, weapons, and communications capabilities. A few examples of the more than 20 systems that make up the NTNO program are the: Mk 110 57mm naval gun system; Mk 38 25mm machine gun system; Mk 15 Phalanx Close-In Weapon System; and SLQ-32 electronic warfare system. The NTNO program ensures commonality and interoperability between Navy and Coast Guard fleets. Coast Guard cutters serve as force multipliers across all combatant commanders' areas of responsibility, conducting naval warfare tasks, sea control, maritime domain awareness, vessel boarding search and seizure, high-value unit protection, and international engagement in support of DoD and Navy missions.

Status

In addition to supporting the Coast Guard's legacy fleet of more than 80 in-service platforms ranging from high- and medium-endurance cutters to its patrol boat fleet, the NTNO program is an integral part of the Coast Guard's ongoing cutter modernization efforts. The Coast Guard continues to field the Legend (WMSL 750)-class national security cutters and Sentinel-class fast response cutters, and is preparing to begin construction on the offshore patrol cutters.

Developers

Multiple sources.

* * * * * * * * * * *

SURFACE SENSORS AND COMBAT SYSTEMS

Aegis Ashore

Description

On September 17, 2009, the President announced the plan to provide regional missile defense to U.S. deployed forces and allies called a European Phased Adaptive Approach (EPAA). The EPAA tailors U.S. ballistic missile defense (BMD) capabilities to specific theater needs, to enhance integrated regional missile defenses against short-, medium-, and intermediate-range ballistic missiles. Aegis Ashore is an adaptation of Navy's proven Aegis BMD capability and uses components of the Aegis Weapon System that are installed in modular containers and deployed to prepared sites of host nations to provide a shore-based BMD capability. The Department of Defense Missile Defense Agency (MDA) is the Aegis Ashore material developer and funds development, procurement, and installation of BMD systems, peripherals, and Standard Missile (SM-3) missiles. The Director, MDA is designated the Acquisition Executive for the U.S. Ballistic Missile Defense System, and in this capacity MDA exercises all source-selection and milestone decision authorities for all elements of the BMDS up to, but not including, production issues.

Status

The first Aegis Ashore site, Aegis Ashore Missile Defense Test Complex at Pacific Missile Range Facility, Kauai, Hawaii, was completed in FY 2014. The first forward operating site in Romania was declared technically capable in December 2015. In July 2016, NATO declared initial operational capability of the Aegis Ashore Missile Defense Site Romania and was transferred to NATO control the next month. The second AAMDS in Poland will be operational by late 2018. The Naval Sea Systems Command and

MDA established an Aegis Ashore Hybrid Program Office within the Aegis BMD Directorate that is closely coordinating the efforts with Program Executive Office for Integrated Warfare Systems, which oversees Aegis Ashore development and deployment.

Developers

Black & Veatch Corporation Overland Park, Kansas

Carlson Technology Inc. Livonia, Michigan

Gibbs & Cox Inc. Arlington, Virginia

Lockheed Martin Moorestown, New Jersey

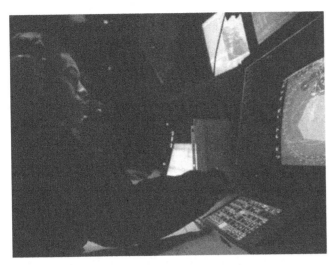

Aegis Combat System (ACS) Description

The Aegis Combat System is a centralized, automated, command-and-control, and weapons control system. ACS integrates combat capabilities, developed in other Navy programs, into the Ticonderoga (CG 47)-class and Arleigh Burke (DDG 51)-class warships, providing effective capability to counter current and future air, surface, and sub-surface threats. ACS is an element of the Aegis Shipbuilding Acquisition Category (ACAT) I program of record.

Status

ACS was introduced to the Fleet in 1983 and continues to serve as the foundation platform for new capabilities, weapons, and sensor systems. The Aegis Modernization (AMOD) program is producing system upgrades via the advanced capability build (ACB) process being implemented as part of the cruiser and destroyer modernization, DDG 51 restart, and DDG 51 Flight III programs to keep pace with evolving threats and challenging littoral environments.

The first iteration of this process, ACB-08/Technology Insertion (TI) 08, brought CGs 52 through 58 increased warfighting capabilities during modernizations that began in 2009. ACB-08 separated hardware from software, allowing for commercial-off-the-shelf computer processors, while integrating improved system capabilities.

The ongoing ACB-12 has transitioned to Aegis Baseline 9 and brings increased warfighting capability with regard to Integrated Air and Missile Defense (IAMD), Naval Integrated Fire Control-Counter Air (NIFC-CA), the SM-6 Extended-Range Active Missile, the Evolved Seasparrow Missile (ESSM), Close-In Weapon System (CIWS) Block 1B, and Multi-Mission Signal Processor.

ACB 16 builds upon ACB 12 and integrates the following additional capabilities: Improved IAMD capability with new Standard Missiles; SPQ-9B radar; MH-60R helicopter; Surface Electronic Warfare Improvement Program (SEWIP) Block II with radar-designated decoy launch; and updates to Total Ship Training Capability

(TSTC) training, interoperability, and C4I (command, control, communications, computers, and intelligence) capabilities.

Baseline 9 initiated a Common Source Library (CSL) program for Aegis and brought in the first third-party developed software element, the track manager/track server, as well as the competitively awarded common display system and common processor system. The CSL enables software reuse and commonality across all modernized and new-construction Aegis Combat System configurations. Specifically, the Aegis CSL allows for the use of common tactical software across four different Aegis configurations: (1) air-defense cruisers; (2) IAMD destroyers with integrated air and ballistic missile defense (BMD) capabilities; (3) new-construction IAMD destroyers; and (4) Aegis Ashore with integrated BMD capability.

The next effort to modernize the ACS is through the development of ACB 20. ACB 20 will reside in Flight III destroyers, the first of which is scheduled to arrive in FY 2023. ACB 20 will introduce the new AN/SPY-6 Air and Missile Defense Radar (AMDR), which brings a functional replacement to the legacy AN/SPY-1 radar, enhancing AAW and BMD capabilities. ACB 20 will integrate BMD 6.0, CIWS sensor data, an upgraded Link-16 J3.4 message, Mk 160 gun computer system upgrades, ESSM Block 2, and SEWIP Block 3.

ACBs are bringing new capabilities to existing ships in single packages vice the legacy method of installing capability improvements through individual deliveries. The Navy awarded a contract in March 2013 for an Aegis Combat System Engineering Agent, which will fully integrate these capabilities into the Aegis Combat System for maximum effectiveness. In addition, there will be greater commonality across ACBs, which will ultimately result in improved capability deliveries at a reduced cost.

Developers

Lockheed Martin Moorestown, New Jersey

Naval Surface Warfare Center Dahlgren, Virginia

Port Hueneme, California

* * * * * * * * * * *

Image courtesy of Raytheon.

Air and Missile Defense Radar (AMDR)

Description

The Air and Missile Defense Radar system, also known as SPY-6, is being developed to ill capability gaps identified by the Maritime Air and Missile Defense of Joint Forces Initial Capabilities Document. AMDR is a multi-function, active-phased array radar capable of simultaneous search, detection, and tracking of airborne missile targets and ballistic missile targets for engagement support. The AMDR suite consists of an S-band radar (AMDR-S), an X-band radar (SPQ-9B for the first 12 shipsets), and a radar suite controller (RSC). The radar will be developed to support multiple ship classes, the first being the Arleigh Burke (DDG 51) Flight III warships. The multi-mission capability will be effective in air dominance of the battle space (area air defense) and defense against ballistic missiles. In addition to its integrated air and missile defense capability, AMDR will support requirements for surface warfare, anti-submarine warfare, and electronic warfare.

Status

AMDR is an ACAT 1D program with Milestone B approval and in FY 2016 is in the engineering and manufacturing development (EMD) phase. The Navy awarded the AMDR contract to Raytheon on October 10, 2013 and after a protest and withdrawal, the EMD phase began on January 9, 2014. AMDR successfully completed the systems Critical Design Review on April 29, 2015. Following the array build-up and line replaceable unit testing in December 2015, the SPY-6 array successfully underwent near-field range testing in Sudbury, Massachusetts, to verify subsystem technical performance measures, transmit/receive patterns, and calibration testing. The array was then packed and shipped to the Navy's Pacific Missile Range Facility in Hawaii in June 2016 and conducted a successful light-off in July 2016. With integration complete, live (formal) testing began in October 2016 and will continue system testing through June 2017, including integrated air and ballistic missile defense against live targets. The program remains on track to receive Milestone C approval in late FY 2017 and achieve initial operational capability on the first DDG 51

Flight III warship in FY 2023.

Developers

Raytheon Waltham, Massachusetts

* * * * * * * * * * * *

Enterprise Air Surveillance Radar (EASR)

Description

The Enterprise Air Surveillance Radar (EASR) is a modern 3-D air search radar that addresses aircraft carrier and amphibious warfare ship requirements and closely conforms to existing combat system interfaces. It is designed to be installed within existing shipboard space, weight, and power limits. The architecture is intended to lower cost by using core technologies for fixed-face and rotating array systems. EASR will replace the SPY-4 volume search radar in future CVN 78 class carriers and the SPS-48/49 radar systems in new construction LHA and L(X)R classes.

Status

In 2016, Raytheon was awarded a cost-plus-incentive-fee contract for EASR engineering and manufacturing development of an engineering development model. EASR will consist of two configuration variants: Variant 1, a rotating phased array; and Variant 2, a three-face fixed-phased array. Follow-on procurements of production radars will be timed to meet the required in yard delivery dates for Variant 1: LHA 8, and L(X)R; and Variant 2: John F. Kennedy (CVN 79) and Enterprise (CVN 80).

Developers

Raytheon Electronic Systems Sudbury, Massachusetts

* * * * * * * * * * * *

Enterprise Air Warfare Ship Self-Defense Test and Evaluation

Description

The Air Warfare (AW) Ship Self-Defense (SSD) Enterprise Test and Evaluation (T&E) strategy is a cost-effective way of assessing combat systems effectiveness by providing "end-to-end" mission operational testing in a realistic operational environment through the use of the Self Defense Test Ship, lead ship testing, and

81

modeling and simulation data. The T&E Enterprise consolidates all AW SSD at-sea testing across multiple programs to provide the probability of raid annihilation (PRA) metric for LHA 6, LCS, LSD 41/49, DDG 1000, and CVN 78 ship classes.

Status

In FY 2015-2016, Enterprise T&E completed testing in support of Rolling Airframe Missile Block 2 initial operational capability and SSDS Mk 2 Mod 4B for LHA 6. In FY 2017, a PRA assessment will be conducted to evaluate the operational effectiveness and suitability of the LHA 6 ship class. In addition, AW operational testing will begin for CVN 78 and DDG 1000 ship classes.

Developers

Multiple sources.

* * * * * * * * * * * *

Littoral Combat Ship (LCS) Mission Packages (MPs)

Description

The littoral combat ships have innovative designs featuring interchangeable mission systems for rapid mission reconfiguration and modernization. The LCS design is configured to ill three warfare capability gaps: surface warfare (SUW); mine countermeasures (MCM); and anti-submarine warfare (ASW). This versatility gives the Navy the operational flexibility to meet changing warfighting requirements, as well as rapidly field upgrades or incorporate new technology to meet emerging threats. A mission package (MP) consists of mission modules (MM), which include: unmanned vehicles, sensors, communication systems, and weapons; a Mission Package Detachment, which consists of 15-19 Sailors specializing in the specific MP; and an Aviation Detachment, which includes pilots, aircrew, maintainers, helicopters, and unmanned aerial vehicles.

The SUW MP provides the ability to perform maritime security operations while delivering effective firepower, including offensive and defensive capabilities against multiple groups of fast-attack-craft and fast-inshore-attack craft. The SUW MP consists of the Maritime Security Module (two 11m rigid-hull inflatable boats for visit, board, search, and seizure operations), the Gun Mission Module (two Mk 46 30mm gun systems), an MH-60R Seahawk helicopter armed with Hellfire missiles, and a vertical-takeoff and landing tactical unmanned aerial vehicle (VTUAV). In 2018, the Surface-to-Surface Missile Module (Longbow Hellfire missiles) will be added to the SUW MP.

The MCM MP provides the capability to detect and neutralize mines throughout the water column using off-board manned and unmanned vehicles. The MCM MP consists of an unmanned towing platform equipped with the AQS-20A mine hunting sonar, an MH-60S helicopter equipped with ASQ-235 Airborne Mine Neutralization System or the Airborne Laser Mine Detection System, and a VTUAV with the Coastal Battlefield Reconnaissance and Analysis mine-detection system. In the future, the MCM MP will include an Unmanned Influence Sweep System and Knifefish unmanned underwater vehicle for buried/high clutter minehunting. By using multiple off-board assets, the MCM MP dramatically improves the speed an area can be searched and cleared of mines while keeping the ship and crew out of the mine danger area—a major improvement over existing fleet capabilities.

The ASW MP enables the LCS to detect, classify and engage diesel, air-independent propulsion, and nuclear submarines. The ASW MP includes active and passive detection systems to conduct area search and high-value unit escort missions; a torpedo counter-measure system to enhance survivability in an ASW environment; MH-60R helicopter with airborne flow-frequency sonar, sonobuoys, Mk 54 lightweight torpedoes; SQR-20 multi-function towed array; and variable-depth sonar.

Status

As of late FY 2016, seven SUW MPs, three MCM MPs, and the advanced development model ASW MP have been delivered. The ASW mission package completed its initial integration test on board the USS Freedom (LCS 1) in FY 2014. The Navy will select the variable-depth sonar and multi-function towed array to be used for the ASW MP in FY 2017. ASW MP shipboard testing will be conducted in FY 2018, and the Navy's first deployment of the ASW mission package is scheduled for FY 2019. Three phases of MCM MP developmental testing have been completed. The MCM MP program is undergoing an assessment of potential bottom and volume minehunting solutions to inform an FY 2019 decision. The Phase II SUW MP (Maritime Security Module, Gun Mission Module) has completed initial operational test and evaluation on both variants of the LCS. In 2015, the Navy completed successful launch demonstrations of the Hellfire Longbow missile as part of the Surface-to-Surface Missile Module and will be added as Phase III of the package in 2018.

Developers

Northrop Grumman Integrated Systems, Mission Package Development and Integration Falls Church, Virginia

* * * * * * * * * * *

Image courtesy of Thales.

Maritime Integrated Air and Missile Defense Planning System (MIPS)

Description

MIPS is a software and hardware display tool that supports operational level integrated air and missile defense (IAMD) planning and asset allocation, assessments of alternative courses of action and near real-time monitoring during IAMD mission execution. In a complex joint warfighting environment, MIPS provides the joint force maritime component commander staff with a planning tool for allocating resources and assessing operational risks in a rapidly developing deployment of Navy air and missile defense assets. The MIPS output is an operational-level plan detailing optimized use of forces developed with the warfighter's knowledge and judgment. MIPS is deployed across the numbered fleet maritime operations centers and on command ships.

Status

The MIPS program was designated a Navy ACAT III acquisition program on February 11, 2011. MIPS has completed its technical refresh to replace legacy and obsolete hardware and has delivered the first increment of a software update, with Increment 2 expected to deliver in third quarter FY 2018. Both increments include enhanced planning capabilities and capacity for IAMD as well as an improved interface between the Aegis Ballistic Missile Defense Mission Planner and the Command, Control, Battle Management, and Communications System. PEO IWS 6 has completed the school house classroom refurbishment and received funding for instructors to begin the first classroom training in the fourth quarter FY 2016.

Developers

General Dynamics Advanced information Systems Fairfax, Virginia

* * * * * * * * * * * *

85

Naval Integrated Fire Control-Counter Air (NIFC-CA) From the Sea (FTS)

Description

The Naval Integrated Fire Control-Counter Air From the Sea kill chain provides both an engage on remote (EOR) and over the horizon (OTH) air defense capability, taking advantage of the full kinematic range of the Navy's missiles, manned aircraft and cruise missiles. NIFC-CA is a non-ACAT project established to ensure the alignment of the SM-6 missile, Cooperative Engagement Capability, E-2D Advanced Hawkeye, and Aegis Weapon System. The NIFC-CA "System of 51 Systems" project overcomes traditional radar horizon limitations and expands on CEC sensor netting capability to provide an EOR capability to kill targets OTH at greater ranges than conventional organic fire-control systems.

Status

The NIFC-CA project has conducted more than 200 live-tracking events. All seven live-fire tests have successfully verified NIFC-CA capability. One of these tests, conducted in June 2014, was the longest Standard Missile engagement in history. The first deployment of initial capability deployed in FY 2015. Three live-fire events were conducted in the fall of 2016: an integration demonstration with F-35 Joint Strike Fighter; an at-sea test event; and stream raid presentation.

Developers

Multiple sources.

* * * * * * * * * * * *

Navigation Systems

Description

Navigation systems provide position, altitude, and timing information for all surface ships, aircraft carriers, and amphibious ships. The program consists of inertial navigators, gyrocompasses, speed logs, fathometers and Electronic Chart Display and Information System-Navy (ECDIS-N). In addition to supporting safety of navigation, shipboard navigation systems provide altitude information to Tomahawk land-attack missiles and ballistic missile defense systems.

Status

Modernization efforts are ongoing across the portfolio of navigation equipment. Legacy inertial navigators are being upgraded to the WSN-12 fiber optic gyroscopes, while the next generation Navy ECDIS system is being developed for fielding across the Fleet. The legacy navigation sensor system interface system (NAVSSI) is being upgraded and will be replaced with the military (M-code) compliant global positioning, navigation and timing system (GPNTS) in development. GPNTS will be paired with the advanced digital antenna production (ADAP) and future multi-platform anti-jam antennas to improve operations in stressing environments.

Developers

Northrop Grumman Sperry Marine Charlottesville, Virginia Raytheon Systems Harlow, United Kingdom

* * * * * * * * * * *

Navy Aegis Ballistic Missile Defense (ABMD)

Description

Aegis ballistic missile defense includes modifications to the Aegis Weapons System and integration of the Standard Missile (SM-3) with its hit-to-kill kinetic warhead. This combination gives select Aegis cruisers and destroyers the capability to intercept short-, medium-, and some intermediate-range ballistic missiles in the midcourse phase of exo-atmospheric trajectories. Additionally, Aegis BMD provides surveillance and tracking capability against longer-range intermediate- and intercontinental-range ballistic missile threats. Together, these capabilities contribute to robust defense-in-depth for U.S. and allied forces, critical political and military assets, population centers, and large geographic regions against the threat of ballistic missile attack. The Missile Defense Agency (MDA) and the Navy initially deployed the Aegis BMD long-range surveillance and tracking capability as an element of the U.S. Ballistic Missile Defense System in October 2004. The Aegis BMD engagement capability was certified for operational use in August 2006.

Status

At the end of FY 2016, 33 cruisers and destroyers had been modified to conduct BMD, with additional warships to be modified in the future. The Aegis BMD 3.6 program capability has been installed on 19 Aegis warships, and BMD 4.0 has been installed on ten others. The first true integrated air and missile defense Aegis Baseline, Baseline 9C, includes Aegis BMD 5.0. Baseline 9C has been installed on four DDGs and is deployed operationally in the Fleet. This most advanced baseline is scheduled for seven Flight I and II destroyers and all Flight IIA destroyers as part of the Aegis Modernization program. BMD ships also have long-range surveillance and tracking capability to provide cueing in defense of the homeland, and a BMD engagement capability using the SM-3 missile to conduct active defense against short-to-intermediate-range ballistic missiles. The SM-2 Block IV inventory has been modified for the terminal ballistic-missile defense mission. This capability provides an endo-atmospheric, lower-tier capability, resulting in a layered defense against enemy ballistic missiles. The Navy and MDA have collaborated to provide a more advanced sea-based terminal-defense capability using the advanced Standard Missile 6 interceptor.

Developers

Lockheed Martin Moorestown, New Jersey

Raytheon Tucson, Arizona

Ship Self-Defense System (SSDS)

Description

The Ship Self-Defense System is a centralized, automated, command-and-control system for non-Aegis warships. An upgrade of the Advanced Combat Direction System (ACDS), SSDS provides an integrated combat direction system for aircraft carriers and all amphibious ships, enabling them to keep pace with evolving anti-ship cruise missile (ASCM) threats. The SSDS open architecture system integrates detection and engagement elements of the combat system with automated weapons control doctrine, Cooperative Engagement Capability (CEC), and tactical data links for enhanced battle space awareness. SSDS provides a robust self-defense capability for six ship classes.

Status

SSDS Mk 1 began full-rate production following operational testing in 1997 and is fielded in all 12 Whidbey Island- and Harpers Ferry (LSD 41/49)-class ships.

SSDS Mk 2, which provides strike group interoperability via CEC and Tactical Data Information Link-Joint (TADIL-J), achieved initial operational capability in 2005 and continues fleet installation. The Navy plans to upgrade periodically the SSDS federated and technically decoupled architecture via commercial-off-the-shelf technology insertion and preplanned product improvement. SSDS Mk 2 is programmed for all aircraft carriers and amphibious ships. SSDS Mk 2 began replacing ACDS on LHD 1-class ships in FY 2013 and SSDS Mk 1 on LSD 41/49-class ships in FY 2014. SSDS Mk 2 is scheduled to complete in-service ship fielding by 2023 and in-line for new-construction ships in the future.

Advanced Capability Build (ACB) 12 is in development, with Gerald R. Ford (CVN 78) as the lead ship, and will incorporate the integration of dual band radar, Surface Electronic Warfare Improvement Program (SEWIP) Block 2, MH-60R Seahawk helicopters, and Identification Friend or Foe Mode 5 with SSDS.

The Fire Control Loop Improvement Project (FCLIP) will add significant improvements to the SSDS Integrated Combat System, increasing system-of-systems performance. Integration of Mk 15 Close-In Weapon System, Evolved Seasparrow Missile (ESSM) communications link, and CEC engage on remote are just a few of the improvements projected to field as part of FCLIP starting in FY 2020.

Follow-on ACB development and continuous fire control loop modernization will integrate into SSDS the Enterprise Air Surveillance Radar suite, SEWIP Block 3 with Advanced Offboard Electronic Warfare/Softkill Coordinator, and ESSM Block 2.

Developers

Raytheon San Diego, California

* * * * * * * * * * * *

SPQ-9B Radar Anti-Ship Cruise Missile (ASCM) Radar

Description

The SPQ-9B Anti-Ship Cruise Missile Radar is a phased-array, rotating radar that significantly improves a ship's ability to detect and track flow-altitude anti-ship cruise missiles in a heavy-clutter environment. This capability is in addition to and improves upon the surface search and gunfire control capability retained from previous versions of the SPQ-9 radar. It is a high-resolution track-while-scan, X-band, pulse-doppler radar that enables track detection at ranges that allow combat systems to engage subsonic or supersonic sea-skimming missiles at the outer edge of a ship's engagement envelope. A modification adding a periscope-detection and discrimination capability is incorporated in production systems and is being fielded to in-service systems via back-it kits.

Status

The SPQ-9B is an integral part of the Cruiser Modernization Program, providing an ASCM cue to the Aegis Combat System. The SPQ-9B integrates with Ship Self Defense Surface Mk 2 on aircraft carriers and amphibious assault ships, enabling those ships' ASCM defense capabilities to pace the evolving worldwide threat. The radar is Navy Type/Navy Owned equipment on the U.S. Coast Guard's new-construction Legend (WMSL 750)-class national security cutters. The SPQ-9B is planned for deployment in conjunction with future guided-missile destroyer modernizations and the initial DDG 51 Flight III destroyers.

Developers

Northrop Grumman Baltimore, Maryland

* * * * * * * * * * * *

SPY-1 (Series) Aegis Multi-Function Phased-Array Radar

Description

The SPY-1 S-band radar system is the primary air and surface radar for the Aegis Combat System installed in the Ticonderoga (CG 47)- and Arleigh Burke (DDG 51)-class warships. The SPY-1 is a multi-function, passive phased-array radar capable of search, automatic detection, tracking of air and surface targets, and missile-guidance support. The SPY-1A, SPY-1B, and SPY-1B(V) variants are fielded in cruisers, and the SPY-1D and SPY-1D(V) variants are fielded in destroyers. The latest variant of this radar, SPY-1D(V), improves the radar's capability against flow-altitude and reduced radar cross-section targets in littoral clutter environments and in the presence of intense electronic counter-measures. Radars in selected Aegis cruisers and destroyers can also detect, track, discriminate, and support engagement of ballistic missile threats.

Status

The SPY-1D(V) littoral radar upgrade superseded the SPY-1D in new-construction Flight IIA destroyers. Initial operational testing and evaluation were completed in the fall 2005. Full rate production decision occurred in 2012. SPY-1D (V) is, or will be, installed in DDGs 91 through 122. A new multi-mission signal processor (MMSP) was developed to deliver SPY-1D(V) equivalent capability to SPY-1D radars in support of integrated air and missile defense tasks, including ballistic-missile defense requirements. The MMSP upgrades are installed during Destroyer Modernization program combat system upgrade availabilities. The MMSP upgrade is likewise integrated with the SPY-1D(V) radar in new-construction destroyers, starting with DDG 113, and in Aegis Ashore ballistic-missile defense systems. Outfitted with the MMSP upgrade to the AN/SPY-1D Radar in 2013, the USS John Paul Jones (DDG 53) was the first destroyer to complete the combat system radar modernization upgrade. DDG 53 completed testing and certification in 2015.

Developers

Lockheed Martin Mission

Systems and Training Moorestown, New Jersey

Raytheon Electronic Systems Sudbury, Massachusetts

* * * * * * * * * * *

SPY-3 Advanced Multi-Function Radar (MFR)

Description

The SPY-3 Advanced Multi-Function Radar is an X-band active phased-array radar designed to meet all horizon-search and fire-control requirements for the 21st-Century Surface Fleet. The SPY-3 is designed to detect the most advanced anti-ship cruise missile threats and support fire-control illumination requirements for the Evolved Seasparrow Missile (ESSM), the Standard Missile (SM-2), and future missiles. SPY-3 also supports the new ship-design requirement for reduced radar cross-section, significantly reduced manning (no operators), and total ownership cost reduction. SPY-3 is on board the Zumwalt (DDG 1000)-class destroyers and as a component of the dual-band radar on the USS Gerald R. Ford (CVN 78). For DDG 1000-class, SPY-3 will be modified to provide above-horizon and volume-search capability.

Status

In 2006, SPY-3 engineering development model radar arrays were installed and tested at the Wallops Island Engineering Test Center, Wallops Island, Virginia, and on board the Navy's Self-Defense Test Ship. The SPY-4 volume search radar was also installed at the Wallops Island facility for radar test and SPY-3 integration events that completed at the end of FY 2010. SPY-3 development, testing, and production schedules are planned to support equipment delivery schedules for DDG 1000-class ships and CVN 78.

Developers

Raytheon Electronic Systems Sudbury, Massachusetts

* * * * * * * * * * *

*Image courtesy of Huntington Ingalls Industries,
Newport News Shipbuilding.*

SPY-4 Volume Search Radar (VSR)

Description

The SPY-4 volume search radar is an S-band active phased-array radar that meets all above-horizon detection and tracking requirements for 21st-Century ships without area air-defense missions, specifically the Gerald R. Ford (CVN 78)-class aircraft carriers. SPY-4 VSR will provide long-range situational awareness with above-horizon detection and air control functionality, replacing in-service SPS-48E and SPS-49 radars. With three fixed phased-array radar faces, SPY-4 VSR provides the requisite track revisit times to address fast, flow/small, and high-diving missile threats, and provides cueing for the SPY-3 Multi-Function Radar (MFR) to execute tracking and fire control functions above the horizon.

Status

Along with the SPY-3 MFR, SPY-4 VSR underwent radar test and integration events that completed at the end of FY 2010. VSR production arrays are in construction and testing at Lockheed Martin facilities in Moorestown, New Jersey. VSR will be deployed with SPY-3 MFR as an integrated radar suite, referred to as the dual-band radar, on CVN 78. SPY-4 development, testing, and production schedules are planned to support the in-progress light-off and testing of the radar installed in CVN 78.

Developers

Lockheed Martin Mission Systems and Training Moorestown, New Jersey

Raytheon Electronic Systems Sudbury, Massachusetts

* * * * * * * * * * *

SQQ-89 Anti-Submarine Warfare (ASW) Combat System

Description

The SQQ-89 Anti-Submarine Warfare Combat System suite provides cruisers and destroyers with an integrated undersea warfare detection, classification, display, and targeting capability. SQQ-89 is the surface ASW system-of-systems that integrates sensors, weapons, and underwater self-defense capabilities. The latest variant, the A(V)15, is replacing legacy SQQ-89 systems on Arleigh Burke-class guided-missile destroyers (DDGs) and guided-missile cruisers via the DDG and CG modernization programs. A(V)15 is also being installed in new-construction Flight IIA and Flight III DDGs. The A(V)15 includes a multi-function towed array (MFTA) for improved detection capabilities. The SQQ-89 A(V)15 is a modularized, open-architecture system using commercial off-the shelf (COTS) technology processing to provide revolutionary ASW warfighting improvements, and continuous upgrades to the following subsystems of the ASW detect-to-engage sequence: MFTA; Mk 54 lightweight torpedo; Mk 54 vertical launch antisubmarine rocket; and fire-control algorithms. These include the echo tracker classifier and active classification algorithms, sonar performance and prediction algorithms, environmental models, computer-aided dead-reckoning table interfaces, and torpedo detection, classification, and localization. The integrated high-fidelity surface ASW synthetic trainer (SAST) provides revolutionary ASW warfighting improvements for deep-water as well as shallow-water littoral environments.

Status

The first A(V)15 installation was completed on the USS Mason (DDG 87) in September 2009. It included the MFTA and marked the first towed-array installation in a DDG Flight IIA warship. By the end of FY 2016, the Navy had installed 35 production A(V)15 systems. The advanced capability build (ACB) process of providing software upgrades every two years and technology inserts on a four-year cycle mitigates commercial-off-the-shelf obsolescence and facilitates future capability upgrades. The first ASW ACB 11 was installed on the USS Bulkeley

(DDG 84) in FY 2012. It included SAST and major upgrades that improve torpedo threat detection. SAST is also installed as part of the ACB 11 trainers at the Fleet ASW Training Center in San Diego, California, and is planned for incorporation into the future design of the shore-based ASW trainers. The first installations of ACB 13 began in September 2016.

Developers

Adaptive Methods Centerville, Virginia

Advanced Acoustic Concepts Hauppauge, New York

Alion Sciences Fairfax, Virginia

Lockheed Martin Syracuse, New York

* * * * * * * * * * * *

Surface Ship Torpedo Defense (SSTD)

Description

The Surface Ship Torpedo Defense system comprises a layered approach and a family-of-systems acquisition strategy to provide anti-torpedo soft-kill and hard-kill capability. Soft-kill capability resides in the SLQ-25 Nixie towed system and acoustic device countermeasure (ADC) Mk 2 Mod 4/6 that are deployed on board aircraft carriers, cruisers, destroyers, amphibious ships, and combat logistics force (CLF) ships. The Nixie system is a towed acoustic and non-acoustic persistent countermeasure system. ADC Mk 2 Mod 4/6 is a hand-deployed acoustic countermeasure system. Hard-kill capability is achieved with the torpedo warning system (TWS) that provides torpedo detection, classification, and localization (TDCL) capability on aircraft carriers. The TWS prepares launch solutions, presets, and operator interfaces to launch anti-torpedo torpedoes (ATTs) for a hard-kill capability. The countermeasure anti-torpedo (CAT) integrates the ATT with self-contained launch energetics in all-up-round equipment to defeat torpedo threats. Together, the TWS and CAT systems form the anti-torpedo torpedo defense system (ATTDS).

Status

SLQ-25C Nixie system is installed on all in-service aircraft carriers, cruisers, destroyers, amphibious ships, CLF ships and will be installed on Zumwalt (DDG 1000)-class ships. The SLQ-25C installations will continue to improve reliability and acoustic countermeasure capability, provide a littoral-optimized tow cable, and add enhanced non-acoustic improvements to counter threat torpedoes. SLQ-25C EC-2 will provide a technology refresh of the in-service SLQ-25 architecture; fielding begins in FY 2020. As of late 2016, four ATTDS systems have been fielded on CVN 77, CVN 69, CVN 71, and CVN 75. A fifth installation is in progress on CVN 68 in late 2016. These five systems will be maintained, and a quick reaction assessment in FY 2017 will demonstrate a potential upgrade to the CAT/TWS software package.

Developers

Penn State Applied

Research Laboratory State College, Pennsylvania

Science Applications

International Corporation Arlington, Virginia

Ultra Electronics / 3 Phoenix Chantilly, Virginia

* * * * * * * * * * * *

Tactical Tomahawk Weapon Control System (TTWCS)

Description

The Tactical Tomahawk Weapon Control System initializes, prepares, and launches Block III and Block IV Tomahawk land-attack missiles. TTWCS also provides capability for firing units to plan Block III and Block IV global positioning system-only missions, retarget Block IV missiles to alternate targets, and monitor missiles in flight. The initial release of TTWCS reduced equipment racks required on board surface ships, introduced common software for the various TLAM-capable platforms (U.S. Navy guided-missile cruisers and destroyers, attack submarines, and guided-missile submarines, and Royal Navy attack submarines), and reduced overall reaction and engagement planning timelines. The TTWCS Viability Build, Version 5.4.0.2, improves the TTWCS system architecture to maintain existing Tomahawk Weapons System functionality, provides for future growth, and enhances command-and-control interoperability. Version 5.4.0.2 maintains interoperability with evolving systems and modernizes interfaces in accordance with joint mandates (e.g., Internet Protocol Version 6). Version 5.4.0.2 also improves operator interaction with the system, reduces system complexity, and provides an integrated training capability at all levels.

Status

TTWCS V5 incorporates Tomahawk integrated training architecture, changes for Aegis cruiser modernization, and the addition of Ohio (SSGN 726)-, Seawolf (SSN 21)-, and Virginia (SSN 774)-class guided-missile/attack submarines to the common weapon control system build. The initial operational capability of v5.4.0 was the first step toward TTWCS viability, refreshing hardware and porting resource-intensive

98

software executing on x86 processors with a Linux operating system. The next software version of the weapons control system, v5.4.0.2, will improve C4I (command, control, communications, computer, and intelligence) interoperability, refresh the hardware and software to improve performance, introduce a new human-computer interface, and align TTWCS with Department of Defense mandates.

Developers

Lockheed Martin Valley Forge, Pennsylvania

Naval Surface Warfare Center Dahlgren, Virginia

Naval Undersea Warfare Center, Keyport Newport, Rhode Island Southeastern Computers Consultants Inc. Austin, Texas

* * * * * * * * * * *

Theater Mission Planning Center (TMPC) Description

The Theater Mission Planning Center provides subsystems for precision targeting, route planning, mission distribution, and strike management for Tomahawk land-attack missile (TLAM) missions. The TMPC is the mission-planning and execution segment of the Tomahawk Weapon System (TWS) and optimizes all aspects of the TLAM mission to engage a target. TMPC develops and distributes missions for the Tomahawk missile; provides command information services for TWS; provides strike planning, execution, coordination, control, and reporting; and provides maritime component commanders the capability to plan or modify TLAM missions. TMPC has evolved into scalable configurations deployed in five configurations at 180 sites: three cruise missile support activities (CMSAs); three Tomahawk strike mission planning cells with Fifth, Sixth and Seventh Fleets; 133 carrier strike groups and firing units; 11 command and control nodes; five laboratories; and six training classrooms. TMPC or its components are employed by the United Kingdom under two separate Foreign Military Sales cases (TLAM and Storm Shadow). TMPC allows planners to exploit the full capabilities of the Tomahawk in either deliberate planning conditions or for battlefield time-sensitive planning operations, including executing all post-launch missile-control operations.

Status

TMPC version 4.3, which achieved initial operational capability (IOC) on May 26, 2012, featured improved system usability and completes the migration of the precision targeting workstation (PTW) functionality to the service-oriented architecture-based targeting and navigation toolset, permitting PTW retirement. In addition, TMPC 4.3 includes more than 1,000 modifications proposed by users. In October 2011, the last TMPC 4.2.2 was installed in Seventh Fleet. The next version of TMPC 5.0.1 reached IOC in FY 2014, with primary focus on human-computer interface updates for improved usability and has been installed at CMSAs in the United States and United Kingdom and the Fleet Tomahawk Strike and Mission Planning cells. All Tomahawk missiles fired operationally from Operation Desert Storm through Operation Odyssey Dawn have been planned and executed with TMPC components.

Developers

BAE Systems San Diego, California

SAIC McLean, Virginia

Tapestry St. Louis, Missouri

VENCORE San Jose, California

* * * * * * * * * * * *

SURFACE EQUIPMENT AND SYSTEMS

Authorized Equipage Lists (AEL) and Naval Security Forces Vest (NSFV)

Description

The visit, board, search, and seizure (VBSS) authorized equipage list provides equipment to perform compliant and non-compliant vessel VBSS missions integral to expanded maritime interception operations, maritime counter-proliferation interdiction, and maritime domain awareness. The anti-terrorism/force protection (AT/FP) physical security equipment AEL provides individual personal protection, training and entry control point equipment for use by the ships' self-defense forces while in port, transiting the littoral, and operating in restricted maneuverability environments. The AEL includes the enhanced body armor naval security forces vest (NSFV) providing improved protection against ballistic and fragmentation hazards. The NSFV also uses the enhanced small-arms protective inserts for increased protection.

Status

NSFV has been fielded as a replacement for both the concealable tactical response carrier and legacy Navy flak vest for consolidation and uniformity among fleet AELs. Designs for the next-generation body armor system (Maritime Armor System (MAS)) are underway in late 2016. This new system (certified to National Institute of Justice (NIJ) standards) will combine the inherent advantages of the Navy's legacy tactical flotation vest (TFV) with the NSFV to form a single standardized body armor system for all AT/ FP and VBSS missions. Another significant AEL upgrade includes the integration of the SRX-2200 combat radio as a replacement device for the legacy XTS-5000 AT/FP and XTS-2500 VBSS radio systems. Designed with battle-ready features such as embedded Individual Location Information (ILI), tactical over-the-air rekey (OTAR), and radio-to-radio text messaging, the system will allow for ease of use under often less-than-ideal conditions (whether voice or data), to include seamless operations and integration with land mobile radio (LMR) systems. Procurement and fielding of the SRX-2200 system to aircraft carriers, cruisers, destroyers, and patrol craft began in September 2014 and is expected to be completed by December 2020. Amphibious transport (LPD) and dock landing (LSD) ships will receive radios for VBSS teams during the same time period, but with a later date for initial procurement.

Developers

Naval Surface Warfare Center Crane, Indiana

* * * * * * * * * * * *

Biometrics / Identity Dominance System (IDS)

Description

The Personnel Identification Version One (Plv1), also known as the PX-1 Identity Dominance System (IDS), provides enhanced biometric and limited forensic collection capabilities for Navy visit, board, search, and seizure (VBSS) teams conducting maritime interception operations. The program provides VBSS teams with the means to rapidly capture, store, and share trusted information related to the identity of unknown individuals between the enterprise, inter-agencies, and international partners. Plv1 collects facial images ("mugshots"), iris images, fingerprints, contextual data, and cell phone media for exploitation, and conducts match/ no-match searches against an onboard biometrics-enabled watchlist of known or suspected terrorists or persons of interest.

Status

Fleet VBSS teams use commercial-off-the-shelf biometric collection devices to collect and transmit biometric information to the DoD's authoritative biometric database for intelligence analysis, and "match/no-match" analysis. Advanced research and development efforts continue to deliver next-generation capabilities, including robust multi-modal biometric, and enhanced document and media exploitation functionality through the Personnel Identification Version One (Plv1) program of record. Initial operational capability was achieved in FY 2013, with full operational capability planned for FY 2017. More than 270 tactical kits have been fielded as of late 2016. A technology refresh is planned for FY 2019 to maintain this capability.

Developers

Aware Inc. Bedford, Massachusetts

Naval Surface Warfare Center Dahlgren, Virginia

* * * * * * * * * * *

Chemical, Biological, Radiological and Nuclear Defense Dismounted Reconnaissance, Sets, Kits and Outfits (CBRN DR SKO)

Description

Chemical, biological, radiological, and nuclear dismounted reconnaissance sets, kits, and outfits compose an organic suite of specialized CBRN detection and protection equipment. The equipment provides Navy boarding teams with additional CBRN capability to conduct efficient and thorough CBRN reconnaissance survey and monitoring missions on vessels of interest. It provides visit, board, search, and seizure (VBSS) teams with the capability to detect the presence of weapons of mass destruction (WMD) in support of WMD interdiction missions. In addition to enhanced detection and Identification capability for radiological and nuclear material, chemical and biological warfare agents, toxic industrial chemicals/toxic industrial materials (TIC/TIM), the DR SKO provides detection capabilities for deficient oxygen levels and combustible gases, and some explosives and drugs.

Status

The Navy's participation in this program responds to Commander, U.S. Naval Forces Central Command's urgent operational need to provide VBSS teams with enhanced capabilities to identify and detect CBRN/WMD material. A "stop-gap" capability was initially deployed in response to this request. Approximately 163 radiation detection/hazardous atmospheric kits were procured in FY 20072008, with each kit consisting of six UDR-15 personal radiation detectors, six handheld radiation monitors, one Thermo IdentiFinder Ultra NGM (used to identify isotopes), one Chameleon TIC vapor and gas detector, one GAMIC 4 gas analyzer, and one NIK drug testing kit. Recognizing the enduring nature of the request, Navy in FY 2015 took measure to transition the full-spectrum CBRN/ WMD detection requirement into the DR SKO as a joint program of record for proper resourcing and long-term sustainment. Initial operational capability for the DR SKO end items (11 kits) was achieved in September 2014; full operational capability is expected in FY 2020.

Developers

FLIR/ICx Elkridge, Maryland

JPM-NBC CA Aberdeen PG, Maryland

* * * * * * * * * * * *

Chemical, Biological, Radiological and Nuclear Defense-Individual Protection Equipment-Readiness Improvement Program (CBRND-IPE-RIP)

Description

The Individual Protective Equipment-Readiness Improvement Program for forces afloat manages millions of individual pieces of equipment for Sailors deploying into potential chemical, biological, radiological, and nuclear (CBRN) threat environments. Through centralized management, this program ensures that afloat and deployed expeditionary Sailors are provided with correctly maintained and properly fitted individual protection ensembles and a chemical protective mask, ready for immediate retrieval in response to the mission-oriented protective-posture condition. Historically, maintenance and logistics functions required to maintain the material readiness of this equipment required an extraordinary number of organizational man-hours that could be better used supporting operations and training. Ninety-day pre-deployment readiness visits by the Naval Sea Systems Command RIP Team relieve the ships of this burden. The cornerstone of the RIP is the NAVSEA Consolidated Storage Facility located at Ft. Worth, Texas.

Status

This program continues to improve fleet CBR readiness. In addition to IPE and gas masks, the RIP manages interceptor body armor, dorsal auxiliary protective systems, and lightweight helmets for expeditionary forces; provides protective CBRN equipment to Navy individual augmentees as they process through designated Army training centers; and manages CBR and nuclear-defense IPE for the Military Sealift Command as well as medical counter-measures for BUMED. In addition, the Navy has shifted from its traditional lifecycle replacement program and has implemented a condition-based obsolescence program to better sustain fleet CBRN-defense equipment. The Joint Program Executive Office for Chemical and Biological Defense Programs (JPEO CBDP) has adopted this efficiency plan for implementation across the entire CBDP enterprise.

Developers

Battelle Memorial Institute Columbus, Ohio

General Dynamics Information Technology Fairfax, Virginia Gryphon Technologies Washington, D.C.

Naval Surface Warfare Center Panama City, Florida

* * * * * * * * * * * *

Improved (Chemical Agent) Point Detection System (IPDS)-Lifecycle Replacement

Description

The Improved (Chemical Agent) Point Detection System-Life-cycle Replacement is a it, form, and function life-cycle replacement for legacy IPDS systems providing naval ships an automated chemical (vapor) point-detection capability afloat with enhanced detection and reliability. The system is designed to automatically detect and identify chemical vapors by agent class (nerve, blister, and blood) and type agent within a specified concentration level and time period. Successful detection of a chemical vapor at the required threshold concentration warns a ship of an imminent chemical attack to provide sufficient time for the crew to seek shelter inside a collective protected zone or don personal protective equipment, including a filtered mask, before the concentration reaches a critical level.

Status

IPDS-LR achieved initial operational capability in March 2013 with more than 30 systems fielded for ships, training facilities, and spares. IPDS-LR achieved 17 installs in FY 2016, and 18 installs are scheduled for FY 2017.

Developers

Bruker Billerica, Massachusetts

* * * * * * * * * * * *

Joint Biological Tactical Detection System (JBTDS)

Description

The Joint Biological Tactical Detection System Acquisition Category III program will be a lightweight biological agent system that will detect, warn, and provide presumptive Identification and samples for follow on confirmatory analysis. JBTDS will provide a local alarm and when networked a cooperative capability with reduced probability of false alarms. JBTDS will provide a biological detection capability to detect, collect, and identify biological aerosol hazards to support mission-oriented protective-posture decisions and downwind hazard warning at the tactical and operational levels. JBTDS will be operable across the full spectrum of operations in multiple environments. The system will support naval forces during periods of increased biological threat, as well as during routine biological surveillance operations, by providing near real-time detection of biological attacks and notification to personnel in the potential hazard area. JBTDS will ultimately support force protection and survivability and maximize combat effectiveness by enhancing medical response decision making.

Status

JBTDS Milestone B was achieved May 2014 and will reach Milestone C in FY 2018 with fielding planned for numerous ship classes (e.g., aircraft carriers, cruisers, destroyers, small combatants, amphibious ships, mine countermeasures ships, command ships, and combat logistics force vessels), and initial operational capability in FY 2020.

Developers - Multiple sources.

Next-Generation Chemical Detection (NGCD)

Description

The Next-Generation Chemical Detector comprises several detection systems for multi-phase matter sampling, locating of liquid and solids on surfaces, and vapor and aerosol monitoring. NGCD will detect and identify nontraditional agents (NTAs), chemical warfare agents (CWAs), and toxic industrial chemicals (TICs) in the air and on surfaces. NGCD will provide improved CWA/ TIC selectivity and sensitivity on multiple platforms as well as multiple environments. These sensors will improve detection, consequence management and reconnaissance, and weapons of mass destruction interdiction capabilities. The three detectors are as follows: (1) Detector Alarm provides NTA aerosol detection, (e.g., chemical event warning) and improved CWA and TIC vapor detection (e.g., naval ship contamination survey); (2) Survey Detector provides rapid interrogation of NTA and CWA liquid and solid detection on surfaces, (e.g. dismounted reconnaissance/ VBSS operations); and (3) Sample Analysis provides analytical identifier of solids, liquids, aerosols and vapors, (e.g., to support characterization of the residual hazard after a chemical event to inform protection decisions).

Status

The acquisition strategy for this program is technology driven. The Joint Project Manager for Nuclear, Biological and Chemical Contamination Avoidance (JPM NBC CA) is procuring prototypes for the program's technology maturation risk reduction phase with final prototype testing and early operational assessment scheduled for FY 2017. The Joint Project Manager NBC CA will use the final prototype test results to inform the Milestone B decision, engineering manufacturing development, and request for proposal release anticipated in mid-late 2017.

Developers

Multiple sources.

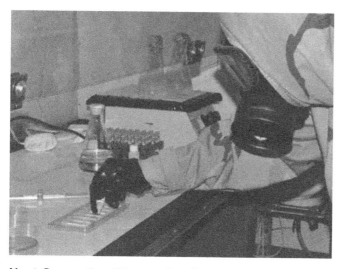

Next-Generation Diagnostics System (NGDS)

Description

The Next-Generation Diagnostics System family-of-systems will provide incremental chemical biological radiological and nuclear (CBRN) diagnostic capabilities across echelons of naval health care and provide common biological Identification materiel solutions across DoD. The NGDS Increment 1 (Inc. 1) Deployable Component is a U.S. Food and Drug Administration cleared reusable, portable biological pathogen diagnostic and identification system capable of rapidly analyzing clinical and environmental samples. NGDS diagnostic capabilities will be employed in Navy (Role 2 and 3) Fleet Deployable Combat Health Support units for the Identification and diagnosis of biological warfare agents and other pathogens of operational concern in support of individual patient treatment decision making, force health protection decision making, and CBRN situational awareness. NGDS Inc. 1 will be capable of connecting to CBRN defense, medical, and bio-surveillance network applications (e.g., Joint Warning and Reporting Network, and Composite Health Care System), if required. The NGDS Inc. 1 technology will be adapted for environmental sample analysis applications through collaboration with the Common Analytical Laboratory System (CALS) and the Joint Biological Tactical Detection System program offices. In collaboration with the CALS program for environmental capability requirements, NGDS Inc. 1 will replace the Joint Biological Agent Identification and Diagnostic System. NGDS Inc 2 will expand the program's CBRN assay capabilities and push some of the capabilities far-forward for enhanced diagnostics at the "point of injury/care" as part of the NGDS family-of-systems strategy.

Status

NGDS Inc. 1 is in its technology development phase with an initial operational capability (IOC) planned for FY 2018. NGDS Inc. 2 is scheduled to achieve IOC in FY 2021.

Developers

BioFire Diagnostics, Inc. (BFDx) Salt Lake City, Utah

* * * * * * * * * * *

Total Ship Training Capability (TSTC)

Description

Total Ship Training Capability consists of the Advanced Training Domain, Battle Force Tactical Trainer, Aegis Combat Training System, Battle Force Electronic Warfare Trainer scenario generators, and numerous Aegis and Ship Self-Defense System (SSDS) interfaces and display systems. Together, the capability provides realistic combat systems tactical scenario training supporting both unit level and strike group integrated training and certification.

Status

Training systems are installed on 128 in-service systems on Aegis and SSDS warships. Established in 2012, the TSTC program of record was created to address reliability, simplicity, functionality, and fidelity shortfalls within these systems and the supporting ships' weapon systems. TSTC has demonstrated through pier-side integrated training events an achieved savings compared to at-sea live exercises. A continual TSTC investment is required to maintain constant alignment between tactical modernization, warfare training capabilities, and operator and crew weapon system proficiency.

Developers

Lockheed Martin Chesapeake, Virginia

Naval Surface Warfare Center Dam Neck, Virginia

NOVONICS Arlington, Virginia

SYS Technologies San Diego, California

* * * * * * * * * * *

The Submarine Force supports all priorities identified in the Chief of Naval Operations' 2016 Navigation Plan: sustaining superior warfighting capability with ready and trained crews and superior submarines, weapons, and sensors. The start of the Ohio Replacement Program, coupled with the superior readiness of the 14 in-service Ohio-class nuclear-powered ballistic missile submarines, will ensure the Nation's sea-based strategic deterrent remains invulnerable and completely credible in the eyes of our allies and friends as well as potential adversaries and aggressors. At the same time, the highly successful Virginia-class fast-attack submarines generate a stealthy global presence and conduct warfighting operations in an increasingly "high end" competition at sea. In short, our submarine force continues to be the superior force that it has been since the dawn of the nuclear age.

SUBMARINES AND UNDERSEA VEHICLES

SSBN 726 Ohio-Class Replacement (OR) Fleet Ballistic-Missile Submarine (SSBN)

Description

The Navy's nuclear-powered fleet ballistic-missile submarines support the Nation's strategic nuclear triad—long-range strategic bombers, land-based intercontinental ballistic missiles, and SSBNs armed with long-range submarine-launched ballistic missiles (SLBMs)—by providing a flexible and survivable deterrent with an assured-response capability. The sea-based strategic deterrent mission remains the Navy's top priority, and maintaining and modernizing the undersea "leg" of the strategic deterrent triad is the Navy's number-one acquisition priority. The 2017 force of 14 Ohio-class SSBNs begins to retire at a rate of one hull per year starting in 2027. Prudent engineering practices prevent further extending their operational lives without incurring unacceptable risk.

The Navy is focused on ensuring a seamless and successful transition to the Columbia-class OR SSBN to meet U.S. Strategic Command requirements in the 2030s and beyond. The 12 OR SSBNs will provide a survivable strategic deterrent capability well into the 2080s at a responsible cost. The Navy is designing the Columbia class to ensure survivability against threats into the late 21st Century. Concurrent with the U.S. OR program, the United Kingdom (U.K.) will recapitalize its sea-based strategic-deterrent platforms, the Vanguard-class SSBNs, which also employ the Trident II/D5 SLBM. The OR SSBN incorporates the Common Missile Compartment (CMC), which is under joint development with the United Kingdom to reduce design and construction costs, thus continuing the long-standing SSBN partnership between the U.S. and Royal navies. Additional ownership and production cost-reduction initiatives include a life-of-ship reactor core, modular construction techniques, and the re-use of selected Virginia (SSN 774)- and Ohio-class submarine systems.

Status

The OR program achieved Milestone A in 2011 and in 2017 is in the technology development phase. The Joint Requirements Oversight Council validated the OR SSBN Capability Development Document in August 2015, which documents the platform's requirements and guides the technology development effort. The Navy Gate 4 Review in November 2015 locked the technical baseline of the OR design, allowing for proper design maturity prior to construction start in FY 2021. Early research and design efforts include prototyping and demonstrating construction techniques for the first new-design SLBM tubes since the delivery of the USS Louisiana (SSBN 743) in 1997. Specifications for the U.S. and U.K. CMC quad pack were approved in August 2012, and quad pack construction commenced in August 2016. U.S. and U.K. CMC design and construction efforts remain synchronized. The OR lead ship is on track for a FY 2021 construction start to support its first strategic deterrent patrol in October 2030.

Developers

General Dynamics Electric

Boat Corporation Groton, Connecticut

Huntington Ingalls Industries-Newport News Newport News, Virginia

* * * * * * * * * * * *

SSN 774 Virginia-Class Nuclear-Powered Attack Submarine (SSN)

Description

The Virginia-class submarine is specifically built for multi-mission operations in the littoral while retaining the Submarine Force's strength in traditional open-ocean anti-submarine and anti-surface missions. These submarines have advanced acoustic stealth technology that allows unimpeded operation within an adversary's defensive perimeter, defeating his warfighting strategies and operations. Using these asymmetric advantages, Virginia-class submarines are configured to conduct sea control, land attack, mine reconnaissance, Special Operations Forces (SOF) insertion/extraction, intelligence collection, and surveillance missions that enable successful access and follow-on operations by larger general-purpose forces. The Virginia class can serve as host for various SOF delivery methods, including mini-submersibles and raiding craft via an embarked dry-deck shelter, or directly to sea via integral lockout chambers.

Virginia-class submarines are built under an innovative teaming arrangement between General Dynamics Electric Boat and Huntington Ingalls Industries-Newport News using a modular construction process in which each shipyard builds portions of each ship, with integration and delivery of completed submarines alternating between the shipyards. Modular construction also allows for assembly and testing of systems prior to installation in the hull, thereby reducing costs, minimizing rework, and simplifying system integration. The modular design and extensive use of open-architecture electronics systems facilitate technology insertion in future submarines during new construction and those already in the Fleet, enabling each Virginia-class submarine to keep pace with emerging threat capabilities throughout its 33-year service life.

Status

In 2008, the Navy negotiated a multi-year procurement contract for a total of eight submarines between 2009 and 2013. In 2010, the Virginia-class program completed Milestone C review, receiving full-rate production authority and achieving full operational capability. In 2011, the Navy increased the procurement rate to two submarines per year, the first time the Navy has procured two submarines in the same year since 1991. The USS Mississippi (SSN 782), the ninth Virginia-class submarine, delivered one year early in May 2012, and the USS Minnesota (SSN 783), the tenth ship of the class, also delivered ahead of schedule in June 2013, continuing the positive trend of constructing submarines ahead of schedule and within budget. SSN 784 through SSN 791 comprise the third block of Virginia-class submarines that began construction in 2009. Virginia Block III captures learning-curve efficiency initiatives that will help lower production costs even more. The first Block III ship, the USS North Dakota (SSN 784), delivered early on August 29, 2014. On April 28, 2014, the Navy awarded the contract for ten Virginia Block IV submarines (SSN 792 through SSN 801) that will include improvements to reduce total ownership costs. The Navy also received funds from Office of the Secretary of

Defense for research, development, and design efforts for Virginia Block V, which will incorporate the Virginia Payload Module (VPM). VPM will increase Tactical Tomahawk land-attack cruise missile strike capacity and provide improved capability to support follow-on payloads. The Virginia-class submarine inventory objective is 48 SSNs.

Developers

General Dynamics Electric

Boat Corporation Groton, Connecticut

Huntington Ingalls Industries-

Newport News Newport News, Virginia

* * * * * * * * * * *

Submarine Rescue Systems

Description

The Navy's submarine rescue capability is provided by two systems: the venerable Submarine Rescue Chambers Fly-away System (SRCFS) and the more capable Submarine Rescue Diving and Recompression System (SRDRS). Both are ground-, sea-, and air-transportable for rapid worldwide deployment on vessels of opportunity in the event of a submarine accident. The SRCFS provides non-pressurized shallow-water rescue to a depth of 850 feet. The SRDRS comprises three distinct systems: (1) Assessment Underwater Work System (AUWS); (2) Pressurized Rescue Module System (PRMS); and (3) Surface Decompression System (SDS). AUWS includes the Atmospheric Diving System (ADS2000), a one-atmosphere, no-decompression manned diving system capable of depths to 2,000 feet, and a remotely operated vehicle (ROV) for clearing and preparing a submarine hatch for seating a rescue platform. The PRMS is a manned, tethered, and remotely piloted vehicle capable of rescuing personnel from a stricken submarine to depths of 2,000 feet. The SRDRS will enable transfer under pressure (TUP) for surface decompression of personnel rescued from a pressurized submarine environment. The SRDRS is a government-owned, contractor-operated system maintained at the Navy's Undersea Rescue Command (URC).

Status

The manned AUWS was introduced to the Fleet in 2007, and URC continues to maintain four ADS2000 suites in support of submarine rescue system requirements. The Navy has approved replacement of ADS2000 with ROVs beginning in FY 2016. The PRMS element of the SRDRS became operational in 2008, replacing the Navy's aging and cost-prohibitive Deep Submergence Rescue Vehicle capability. The PRMS underwent repair from a February 2013 accident until July 2015. The

113

program was then re-baselined in November 2015. The complete SRDRS, including the TUP capability, is expected to reach initial operational capability in FY 2018 and is scheduled for delivery to the Fleet and full operational capability in FY 2019. Meanwhile, the Navy has programmed the legacy SRCFS for continued service.

Developers

Environmental Tectonics

Corporation Southampton, Pennsylvania

Oceaneering International Upper Marlboro, Maryland

OceanWorks International Vancouver, California

Southwest Research Institute San Antonio, Texas

* * * * * * * * * * *

SUBMARINE WEAPONS

Mk 48 Advanced Capability (ADCAP) Common Broadband Advanced Sonar System (CBASS) Torpedo

Description

The Mk 48 Advanced Capability heavyweight torpedo is the Navy's sole submarine-launched weapon for anti-submarine and anti-surface warfare. The ADCAP torpedo program was authorized for full-rate production of the Mk 48 Mod 5 ADCAP in 1990,

and the final production all-up-round torpedo was delivered to the Navy in 1996. Since then, the Navy has employed an open-architecture model to provide hardware and software improvements to the ADCAP torpedo inventory, converting the Mod 5 to Mod 6 and Mod 7. The ADCAP torpedo features sophisticated sonar, all-digital guidance and control systems, digital fuzing systems, and improved torpedo acoustic stealth compared to the legacy Mk 48 Mod 4 torpedo. The Mod 7 CBASS torpedo with Advanced Processor Build (APB) Spiral 4 software is the latest

114

and most capable configuration of the Mk 48 torpedo. Phase I of the CBASS program introduced the new broadband sonar analog receiver to the Fleet in 2006, and beginning in May 2013 Phase II provided APB Spiral 4 software improvements and common sonar upgrades leveraged from the Mk 54 Lightweight Torpedo program. The CBASS upgrade to the ADCAP torpedo is part of an ongoing Armaments Cooperative Program with the Royal Australian Navy (RAN). In addition to the RAN, the Brazilian, Canadian, and Netherlands navies also acquired versions of the Mk 48 torpedo through the Navy's Foreign Military Sales program.

Status

In FY 2016, the Navy restarted production of the Mk 48 Mod 7 CBASS torpedo to address a warshot inventory shortfall as a result of a FY 2012 warfighting inventory requirement increase. Separately, the Navy continues to procure Mod 7 CBASS upgrade kits for eventual conversion of all Mod 6 torpedoes. In parallel, the APB program continues to improve torpedo performance through software upgrades and hardware technology insertions (TIs) in challenging areas, such as the shallow-water diesel submarine threat. A 2012 approved Capabilities Development Document established requirements for follow-on APB 5 and APB 6/ TI-1 software and hardware upgrades for which APB 5 software is in developmental testing in 2017 and will enter operational testing in FY 2018, with an expected initial operating capability (IOC) in FY 2020. APB 6/TI-1 development began in FY 2016 with a projected IOC of FY 2024. Both APB 5 and APB 6/TI-1 upgrades will receive and field valuable capability improvements developed jointly with the Office of Naval Research.

Developers

Lockheed Martin Sippican Marion, Massachusetts

* * * * * * * * * * * *

UGM-133A Trident II/D5 Submarine-Launched Ballistic Missile (SLBM)

Description

The Trident II/D5 is the sixth generation of the Navy's Fleet Ballistic Missile program, which started in 1955. The D5 is a three-stage, solid-propellant, inertial-guided submarine-launched ballistic missile with a range greater than 4,000 nautical miles and accuracy measured in hundreds of feet. Trident II/D5 missiles are carried by all 14 Ohio-class fleet ballistic-missile submarines, nuclear (SSBNs). Under the New Strategic Arms Reduction Treaty (New START) requirements, each SSBN is capable of carrying 20 SLBMs. The Navy continues to address future deterrence requirements, and the Trident II/D5 will ensure that the United States has a modern, survivable strategic deterrent. In that regard, the Navy has embarked on a Trident II/D5 Life Extension (D5LE) Program that upgrades missile systems and maintains Trident II/D5s in the Fleet into the 2040s, bridging the transition from Ohio-class SSBNs to Ohio Replacement (OR) SSBNs. The Trident II/D5LE SLBM will be the initial OR payload.

Status

Full missile procurement ended in FY 2012, with a total acquisition of 108 additional missiles. Life extension kits and replacement solid-propellant rocket motors are procured throughout and beyond the FY 2017 future years defense program to refurbish obsolete electronics and expiring rocket motors.

Developers

Lockheed Martin Sunnyvale, California

* * * * * * * * * * * *

SUBMARINE SENSORS AND SYSTEMS

BQQ-10 Submarine Acoustic Systems

Description

Submarine acoustic systems modernization enables rapid warfighting capability enhancements at reduced costs and for affordable sustainment. Acoustic Rapid Commercial Off-the Shelf (COTS) Insertion (ARCI) upgrades legacy sonar systems and significantly expands processing capability for existing sensors and enables future sensors through upgrades/modernizations. During the last 19 years, there have been four phases of A-RCI implementation spanning more than 180 modernizations. Phase I initially upgraded processing for towed arrays and the conformal hull array and Phase IV systems processed all acoustic sensors, including relatively new sensors such as the TB-34 towed array and the BQS-25 Flow Cost Conformal Array being installed on the Improved Los Angeles (SSN 688I)-class submarines. Additionally, the open architecture design of the ARCI system allows for the rapid insertion at minimal cost of new processing techniques and sensor systems such as the hull mounted Large Vertical Array.

Status

BQQ-10 ARCI is common across all submarine classes: Los Angeles/ Improved Los Angeles (SSN 688/688I), Seawolf (SSN 21), and Virginia (SSN 774) attack submarines, and Ohio-class guided-missile and fleet ballistic-missile submarines

(SSGN/SSBN). Submarines receive periodic improvements through hardware technology insertions (TIs) and software advanced processor builds (APBs). While TI upgrades are designed and produced biennially, individual submarines nominally receive a TI every-other cycle. This nominal four to six-year refresh of hardware keeps each submarine's processing power on pace with the commercial computing industry while, in turn, ensuring that the COTS components are upgraded before obsolescence. Biennial APBs permit rapid insertion of improved processing algorithms and increased capabilities requested by Navy type commanders to address emerging challenges. Navy research, development, testing, and evaluation will continue to develop processing algorithms from the surveillance, tactical, and advanced R&D communities, as well as to perform laboratory and at-sea testing.

Developers

Applied Research Lab,

University of Texas at Austin Austin, Texas

General Dynamics Advanced

Information Systems Fairfax, Virginia

Lockheed Martin Manassas, Virginia

Progeny Systems Corporation Manassas, Virginia

* * * * * * * * * * * *

BYG-1 Submarine Combat Control System

Description

BYG-1 is a Commercial Off-the-Shelf (COTS), Open-Systems Architecture (OSA) system that incorporates organic sensor fusion, target solution development, common tactical picture, weapon control, and tactical local-area network functions. The use of COTS/OSA technologies and systems enables frequent updates to both software and hardware with little or no impact on submarine scheduling. COTS-

117

based processors allow computer power growth at a rate commensurate with that of commercial industry. Additionally, the open-architecture design of the BYG-1 system allows for the rapid integration of new sensors and processing techniques at minimal cost. BYG-1 allows the submarine force to update the ship safety tactical picture rapidly, improves torpedo interfaces, and provides Tactical Tomahawk Land-Attack cruise missile capability.

Status

BYG-1 has been installed on all U.S. attack and guided-missile submarines and is scheduled to be installed on the Ohio-class fleet ballistic-missile submarines, with the first installation occurring in FY 2017. Submarines receive periodic improvements through hardware technology insertions (TIs) and software advanced processor builds (APBs). While TI upgrades are designed and produced biennially, individual submarines nominally receive a TI every other cycle. This nominal four-to-six year refresh of hardware keeps each submarine's processing power on pace with the commercial computing industry while, in turn, ensuring that the COTS components are upgraded before obsolescence. Biennial APBs permit rapid insertion of improved processing algorithms and increased capabilities requested by Navy type commanders to address emerging challenges. Navy research, development, testing, and evaluation will continue to develop processing algorithms from the surveillance, tactical, and advanced R&D communities, as well as to perform laboratory and at-sea testing.

Developers

General Dynamics Advanced Information Systems Fair Lakes, Virginia

Pittsfield, Massachusetts

Lockheed Martin Eagan, Minnesota

Progeny Manassas, Virginia

* * * * * * * * * * *

SUBMARINE EQUIPMENT AND SYSTEMS

Submarine Survivability

Description

Today's submariners use passive means to remove carbon dioxide from a disabled submarine's atmosphere, enabling survival up to seven days. Oxygen-generating chlorate candles and atmosphere-monitoring equipment are also used for submarine survivability. Survival improvements include introduction of new "flat-sheet" lithium hydroxide (LiOH) canisters for high-performance passive scrubbing.

Status

Passive carbon dioxide scrubbing curtains, granular lithium hydroxide, oxygen-generating chlorate candles and atmosphere monitoring equipment are installed on all submarines. Phased outfitting of flat-sheet LiOH canisters on all in-service Virginia (SSN 774)-class submarines is complete.

Developers

Analox Sensor Technology, Ltd. Stokesley, United Kingdom

Casco Manufacturing Solutions, Inc. Cincinnati, Ohio

Micropore, Inc. Newark, Delaware

Tangram Company, LLC Holtsville, New York

* * * * * * * * * * * *

119

Naval expeditionary warfare forces embody the flexibility, agility, and readiness that we need for today's and tomorrow's operations. Expeditionary forces can project power deep inland to disrupt the enemy, destroy enemy forces, and seize terrain in support of a joint campaign. The capability to operate from the sea base is a "crown jewel" of our forward presence, sea control, and power-projection posture. Marines embarked in amphibious warships, enabled by mine warfare forces, Seabees, and SEALs, enable us to go there, stay there, and fight and win there.

EXPEDITIONARY FORCES

Coastal Riverine Force

Description

In 2012, the Navy Expeditionary Combat Command (NECC) merged the Riverine Force and the Maritime Expeditionary Security Force (MESF) to form the Coastal Riverine Force (CRF). The CRF comprises the Coastal Riverine Group (CRG) 1 and CRG 2. The CRG forces are organized into three active squadrons with three companies each, and four reserve squadrons with four companies each. The primary unit of action for the CRF is the squadron, but the force maintains the capability to disaggregate into companies. The CRF operates in harbors, rivers, bays, across the littoral, and ashore. The CRF mission sets bridge the maritime gap between land forces and the Navy's blue-water forces. The primary mission of the

CRF is to conduct maritime security operations across all phases of military operations, around the clock and in all weather conditions and climates. CRF units are manned, trained, and equipped to defend high-value assets, critical maritime infrastructure, ports and harbors inland and on coastal waterways. They can also conduct offensive combat operations—surveillance and reconnaissance, insertion and extraction of small units, and command and control for supporting units. The CRF delivers task-organized units that are effective, flexible, and responsive to fleet and combatant commander littoral demands and seamlessly operate with other Navy, joint, interagency, and coalition partners.

Status

In 2015, the Navy Capabilities Board approved a CRF capabilities-based assessment to inform the update of the Maritime Expeditionary Force Initial Capability Document; this reflected the FY 2013 merger of the Maritime Expeditionary Security Force and Riverine Squadrons. The assessment informed an analysis of alternatives regarding CRF mission sets and the equipment needed to support them. The Navy has procured 12 Mk VI patrol boats; six are deployed, and the twelfth is scheduled for fleet delivery in the third quarter FY 2018. In late 2016, the Navy resource sponsor (OPNAV N957) is working with the NECC on a phased patrol boat recapitalization effort to replace the aging 34-foot patrol boat with a new Patrol Boat-X.

Developers

Multiple sources.

* * * * * * * * * * * *

Explosive Ordnance Disposal (EOD) / Mobile Diving and Salvage (MDS) Description

The Explosive Ordnance Disposal community is organized into two deploying EOD groups, each headed by a Navy captain (O-6). Each group comprises multiple EOD mobile units, a mobile diving and salvage unit (MDSU), training and evaluation unit, and an expeditionary support unit.

EOD units provide the Fleet, joint services, and the interagency community with the capability to detect, identify, render safe, recover, exploit, and dispose of ordnance that has been fired, dropped, launched, projected, or placed in such a manner as to constitute a hazard to operations, installations, people, or materiel. Commonly operating in platoons and smaller elements, EOD units assure access to battlespace by opening lines of communication in the sea-to-shore interface as well as blue-water and land-based operations. This can require diving operations, parachute insertion, or helicopter insertion and extraction. These mobility skills, along with responsibility for all underwater ordnance, make Navy EOD unique in the joint force. The Secretary of the Navy is the Single Manager for EOD Technology and Training, carrying out these duties primarily through the Navy EOD Technology Center and the Naval School Explosive Ordnance Disposal, where all U.S. and select foreign-partner military EOD technicians receive the same initial training to defeat conventional ordnance as well as improvised explosive devices. Navy EOD also has capabilities to render safe chemical, biological, radiological, nuclear, and enhanced-explosive weapons, including terrorist "dirty" bombs.

MDSUs conduct planning, coordinating, and directing combat harbor-clearance, anti-terrorism and force-protection diving missions, salvage and recovery operations, and other assigned tasks. MDSUs operate in direct support of naval, joint, and combined task forces, conducting operations afloat or ashore during combat or national emergencies worldwide, including climate extremes—Arctic, tropical, or desert environments. In addition to expeditionary salvage, search, and recovery operations, they perform harbor clearance to remove obstructions restricting access to ports, piers, and waterways; assist vessels in distress; de-beaching and salvaging of ships, submarines and aircraft; locate and recover other high-value objects; underwater cutting and welding; limited underwater ship repair; ship husbandry; and ATFP dive support for ships in port and port facilities.

Status

In late 2016, the EOD and MDS communities recapitalized their authorized equipment inventories with new tables of allowance (ToA). Based on a complete review of their mission requirements, each ToA aligned with force structures and standardized equipment across the Navy Expeditionary Combat Enterprise. Specialty equipment—e.g. man-transportable robotic systems, unmanned underwater vehicles, and Mk-16 underwater breathing apparatus/ multi-mission underwater breathing apparatus—were included for EOD units.

Developers

Multiple sources

* * * * * * * * * * * *

Naval Beach Group

Description

The Two Naval Beach Group Commanders—Naval Beach Group One (NBG 1) and Naval Beach Group Two (NBG 2)—serve as the immediate higher command for all amphibious enabling forces: assault craft units (ACUs) for displacement landing craft and non-displacement assault craft; beach master units (BMUs); and amphibious construction battalions (ACBs). Components of each of these commands can be embarked in amphibious ships in support of landing-force operations or can be deployed on strategic airlift and sealift platforms to support other operations. Naval Beach Groups also provide advocacy for amphibious assault, ship-to-shore movement, and logistics-over-the-shore units, and provide required unit level training and readiness assessments for all amphibious ships. Naval Beach Group 1 is also responsible for this function for all forward-deployed amphibious forces in Sasebo, Japan. The NBG missions, in single or multiple geographic locations, include wartime forward littoral operations supporting Marine Corps amphibious assault and follow-on USMC and joint combat missions, as well as peacetime forward littoral and humanitarian assistance. Each Naval Beach Group Commander can rapidly deploy worldwide to serve as Navy logistics-over-the-shore commander supporting the offload of Navy/ Military Sealift Command maritime prepositioned squadron ships and the offload-in-stream offloading of maritime shipping.

Status

NBG 1 is located in Coronado, California, and has oversight of ACU 1, ACU 5, BMU 1, and ACB 1. NBG 1 also supports NBU 7 in Sasebo, Japan. NBG 2 is located in Little Creek, Virginia, and has oversight of ACU 2, ACU 4, BMU 2, and ACB 2.

Developers

Multiple sources.

* * * * * * * * * * * *

Naval Mobile Construction Battalion (NMCB) "Seabees"

Description

Naval Construction Forces—"Seabees"—are the Navy's deploy-able engineer and construction force providing support to Marine Air-Ground Task Force (MAGTF), Navy commanders, and other joint forces, and combatant commanders. The force comprises naval construction groups, naval construction regiments, naval mobile construction battalions, construction battalion maintenance units, and underwater construction teams. In support of sea-strike and sea-basing missions, the Navy/Marine Corps Team projects power from the sea with a rapid flow of maneuver forces ashore, using roads, expeditionary airfields, force-protection structures, intermediate-staging bases, and advanced logistics bases. Forward-deployed Seabees enable the surge of task-tailored engineer forces and equipment sets to enhance the MAGTF and other naval and joint forces on land. Seabee capabilities include bridge erection, roadway clearing and construction, pier and wharf repair, forward operating base construction, airfield repair and construction, water well installation, and such civilian construction as schools and medical clinics. In operations other than war, forward-deployed naval mobile combat battalions (NMCB) hone construction skills through humanitarian-assistance and disaster-recovery operations, participate in foreign engagement exercises, and complete construction projects that support sustainment, restoration, and modernization of Navy and Marine Corps forward bases and facilities.

Status

The Navy has developed a long-range plan to recapitalize the tables of allowance of all Seabee units. The initial priority is to correct existing inventory deficiencies and replace aging tools and equipment that are no longer parts-supportable. During the next several years, NMCB tables of allowance will be outfitted with modern and recapitalized tactical vehicles, construction and maintenance equipment, communications gear, infantry items, and field-support equipment.

Developers

Multiple sources.

* * * * * * * * * * * *

Naval Special Warfare (NSW) "SEALs"

Description

The Naval Special Warfare community—Navy Sea, Air, Land ("SEALs") forces—is the maritime component of the U.S. Special Operations Command and the U.S. Navy Special Operations Component. The Commander, Naval Special Warfare Command is responsible for strategic vision, doctrinal, operational, and tactical guidance, as well as training, organizing, and equipping operational-support components. NSW forces provide a highly effective option across the spectrum of hostilities, from peacetime to global combat operations. Principal NSW operations include counter-terrorism, counter-proliferation, unconventional warfare, direct action, special reconnaissance, military information support operations, and security force assistance and civil affairs. NSW forces also conduct collateral missions, such as counter-drug activities, humanitarian assistance, and personnel recovery.

The NSW community is organized under several major commands, which include five operational commands, one training command, one tactics and technology development command, and one reserve component command. The major NSW operational components are: Naval Special Warfare Groups (NSWGs) One and Eleven in San Diego, California; NSWG Three in Pearl Harbor, Hawaii; and NSWGs Two, Four, and Ten in Little Creek, Virginia. The NSWG mission is to man, train, equip, support, and provide command and control elements as well as trained and ready SEAL platoons/troops, SEAL delivery vehicle platoons, special boat team combatant craft detachments, and other forces to the geographical combatant commanders. Two of the NSWGs also provide administrative control to five NSW units that are home-ported forward, and are under operational control of a theater special operations command. The primary deployable operational component of the community is the NSW task group (NSWTG).

A NSWTG is task-organized and unit-centered on a SEAL team and led by a SEAL team commanding officer. NSWTGs comprise three NSW task units, which are further broken into two-to-three SEAL platoons, or NSW task elements when supplemented with combat support or combat service support enablers. When a NSWTG is provisionally established, the deploying SEAL team will normally be augmented by combatant craft, combat support and combat service support enablers, and special detachments to execute assigned missions.

Status

Resources to support the NSW community are principally provided by U.S. Special Operations Command, but the Navy retains resourcing of responsibilities for service common capabilities.

Developers

Multiple sources.

* * * * * * * * * * * *

126

Navy Expeditionary Intelligence Command (NEIC)

Description

Navy Expeditionary Combat Command (NECC) established the Navy Expeditionary Intelligence Command to provide tactical indications and warning, force protection intelligence, sensitive site exploitation, and intelligence preparation of the operational environment, enabling Navy and joint commanders to conduct missions across the full spectrum of expeditionary operations and win decisively in major combat operations. NEIC activities are framed around its overall function to man, train, and equip intelligence exploitation teams (IETs) in support of naval combatant command and joint forces command operational requirements. NEIC components include a command element, command support staff, active component operational units, and reserve units. IETs are multi-intelligence, surveillance, and reconnaissance (ISR)-collection platforms that operate at the tactical level, with unique access to areas and environments— from "blue" to "green"' water, the coastal littoral, and far inland— that constrain more traditional ISR assets. NEIC capabilities give expeditionary, maritime, joint, and combined forces timely, relevant, and actionable intelligence to deny the enemy sanctuary, freedom of movement, and use of waterborne lines of communication while enabling friendly forces to find, fix, and destroy the enemy.

Status

The Commander, NECC approved NEIC's reorganization into integrated teams and, approved NEIC's updated table of allowance. NEIC continues to support the expeditionary and intelligence communities.

Status

Multiple sources.

* * * * * * * * * * *

Navy Expeditionary Logistics Support Group (NAVELSG)

Description

The Navy Expeditionary Logistics Support Group comprises Navy expeditionary logistics regiments (NELRs), Navy cargo handling battalions (NCHBs), a training and evaluation unit, and expeditionary support units. NAVELSG is responsible for providing expeditionary logistics capabilities for the Navy, primarily within the littoral maritime domain. The NELRs and NCHBs are capable of rapid, worldwide deployment and are trained and equipped to provide shore-based logistical support to Navy, Marine Corps, and joint force commanders for peacetime support, humanitarian and crisis response, and combat-service support missions. NCHBs can assume control of pier and terminal operations, surface and air cargo handling, and ordnance handling and management. Specialized capabilities include expeditionary fuel operations, pier and air terminal operations, weapons handling, cargo processing (including bulk mail), heavy-lift crane operations, customs inspections, expeditionary communications, short-haul trucking, and expeditionary warehousing.

Status

The ELSG table of allowance (ToA) was approved March 2010. The Navy has developed a long-range plan to recapitalize the ToAs of all expeditionary logistics units. The initial priority is to correct existing inventory deficiencies and replace aging tools and equipment that are no longer parts supportable.

Developers

Multiple sources.

* * * * * * * * * * * *

EXPEDITIONARY AND SPECIAL MISSION SHIPS AND CRAFT

Expeditionary Sea Base (ESB)

Description

The Expeditionary Sea Base (ESB) is a variant of the Expeditionary Transfer Dock (ESD) Program (formerly known as the Mobile Landing Platform Program), using the same hull and commercial technology. The ESB will fulfill critical strategic needs to support airborne mine countermeasures (AMCM) and support to Special Operations Forces (SOF) by enabling global access, reach, and persistence. The ESB (formally known as the Afloat Forward Staging Base, AFSB) adds new capability to include a forward deck house with berthing for 250 personnel; command spaces to support command and control, operations and logistics functions; a light deck with four operating spots for several types of aircraft including AH-6, CH-47, MH-53, MH-60, and MV-22; a hangar and ordnance magazines; underway replenishment capability; and deck space for AMCM and SOF boats, sleds, and equipment.

Status

The USNS Lewis B. Puller (ESB-3) was delivered to the Navy in June 2015 and will join the Fleet in 2017. The USNS Hershel Williams (ESB-4) will be delivered to the Navy in March 2018. The yet-unnamed ESB-5 was procured in FY 2016 and will start construction in June 2017. The ship is scheduled to deliver in summer 2019.

Developers

General Dynamics NASSCO San Diego, California

Expeditionary Transfer Dock (ESD)

Description

The Expeditionary Transfer Dock (ESD) program (formerly known as the Mobile Landing Platform, MLP) enhances the maritime prepositioning force throughput capability by providing a surface interface between large, medium speed roll-on/roll-off (LMSR) prepositioning ships and surface connectors including landing craft air cushion vehicle (LCAC), amphibious assault vehicle (AAV), and the future ship-to-shore connector (SSC). With further testing and development, the ESD could also provide surface interface with landing craft utility and the improved Navy lighterage system. The ESD is a highly flexible ship that provides logistics movement from sea to shore supporting a broad range of military operations. The vessel is the catalyst to integrating with amphibious assault assets, such as LCAC, and providing the capability to configure at sea. Although not a forcible-entry operation, the ability to move equipment and supplies rapidly through the T-ESD is a force enabler. The ESD's open, reconfigurable mission deck is outfitted with an elevated vehicle staging area and three LCAC lanes including barriers, lighting, washdown, and fueling services. Numerous skin-to-skin operations have been conducted with LMSR vessels, demonstrating the transfer of vehicles between the two vessels including loading the cargo in LCACs for transfer ashore. With a 9,500 nautical mile range at a sustained speed of 15 knots, these approximately 80,000-ton, 785-foot long ships leverage float-on/float-off technology and are capable of ballasting down. Additionally, the ships' size allows for 25,000 square feet of vehicle and equipment stowage space and 380,000 gallons of JP-5 fuel storage.

Status

The USNS Montford Point (ESD 1) and USNS John Glenn (ESD 2) were delivered to the Navy in May 2013 and March 2014, respectively. Military Sealift Command personnel operate these versatile ships.

Developers

General Dynamics NASSCO San Diego, California

* * * * * * * * * * * *

Landing Craft Air Cushion (LCAC) Description

This high-speed, fully amphibious landing craft is capable of carrying a 60-ton payload at speeds of 35 knots. Range is load- and sea state-dependent, but can approach 200 nautical miles. Its ability to ride on a cushion of air allows it to operate directly from the well decks of amphibious warships. Carrying equipment, troops, and supplies, the LCAC launches from the well deck, transits at high speed, traverses the surf zone, and lands at a suitable place ashore where it quickly offloads and returns to amphibious shipping for follow-on sorties. LCACs provide amphibious task force commanders flexibility in selecting landing sites, permitting access to more than 70 percent of the world's shores, as compared with 17 percent for conventional displacement landing craft. LCACs deliver vehicles and cargo directly onto dry land rather than to the surf zone, and have proved invaluable in support of humanitarian-assistance/disaster-relief missions, including Operation Tomodachi Tsunami Relief in Japan, Hurricane Katrina, and Operation Unified Response in Haiti. Some multi-mission LCACs have been outfitted with radar and radio system upgrades prior to entry into their service-life extension program (SLEP). A SLEP to extend service life from 20 to 30 years for 64 LCACs will be completed by FY 2018. As part of the LCAC SLEP, the Navy will incorporate the following enhancements: (1) hull (buoyancy box) upgrades, improvements, and improved corrosion control; (2) an open-architecture framework, relying on modern commercial off-the shelf equipment that will allow much easier incorporation of technology changes-such as precision navigation and communications systems; (3) engine upgrades (ETF-40B configuration) that will provide additional power and lift, particularly in hot (100° Fahrenheit and higher) environments and reduce fuel consumption and maintenance requirements; and (4) a new deep skirt to reduce drag, increase performance over water and land, and reduce maintenance requirements.

Status

LCAC initial operational capability was achieved in 1986. Contracts for 91 LCACs were approved in FY 1997, with all 91 craft delivered by the end of FY 2001. Disposal of 18 LCACs occurred in FY 2006 for cost reasons; two LCACs are dedicated research and development craft. The LCAC SLEP program began in 2000, and four SLEPs are planned each year through FY 2018.

Developers

Avondale Marine Gulfport, Mississippi

Gryphon Technologies LC Panama City, Florida

Textron Marine & Land Systems New Orleans, Louisiana

* * * * * * * * * * * *

LCU 1610 Landing Craft Utility Vessels

Description

The Landing Craft Utility (LCU 1610)-class vessels are a self-sustaining craft complete with living accommodations and messing facilities for a crew of 14. An adaptation of the designs pioneered during the Second World War, the LCU 1610 class replaced the venerable Landing Craft Tank (LCT) Mk V starting in 1959. The LCU provides a persistent, long-range and high-capacity landing craft to complement the high-speed, over-the-beach delivery capacity of the LCAC. This steel-hulled and diesel-propelled craft is capable of carrying a 125-ton payload to a nominal range of 1,200 nautical miles. These vessels have bow ramps for onload/ offload, and can be linked from their bow to the stern gate of amphibious ships to create a temporary causeway structure for at sea offload of vehicles and equipment. Its welded steel hull provides high durability, accommodating deck loads of 800 pounds per square foot. Arrangement of machinery and equipment has taken into account built-in redundancy in the event of battle damage. The craft features two engine rooms separated by a watertight bulkhead to permit limited operation in the event that one engine room is disabled. An anchor system is installed on the starboard side aft to assist in retracting from the beach.

The LCU's ability to transit intra-theater distances and operate independent of well-deck amphibious warships for up to ten days provides additional operational flexibility and a level of persistence that no other asset smaller than an amphibious warship can provide to the operational commander. Carrying equipment, troops, and supplies in any variation up to its maximum capacity, the LCU launches from a well deck-equipped amphibious warfare ship, transits to the surf zone and lands vehicles and cargo to provide organic mobility for naval forces from the sea base to the shore. LCUs have been adapted for many uses, including salvage operations, ferry boats for vehicles and passengers and underwater test platforms, and have proven invaluable in support of humanitarian-assistance/disaster-relief missions, including Operation Tomodachi Tsunami Relief in Japan, Hurricane Katrina, and Operation Unified Response in Haiti. They have been critical to non-combatant evacuation operations, such as the evacuation of more than 14,000 Americans from Lebanon in 2006. LCUs are multi-mission craft that can also conduct offload of Military Sea-lift Command maritime prepositioned squadron ships via crane loading, and they interoperate with joint-logistics-over-the-shore operations to sustain forces operating inland.

Status

LCU 1610 craft entered service in 1959; the average age of the operational vessel in 2016 is 45 years. Rugged steel hulls and diesel engines have allowed these craft to serve effectively well beyond their initial design service lives of 25 years. There are 32 LCU 1610 vessels stationed at Little Creek, Virginia; Coronado, California; and Sasebo, Japan.

Developers

Multiple sources.

* * * * * * * * * * * *

LHA 6 America-Class Amphibious Assault Ship

Description

America-class general-purpose amphibious assault ships—previously designated the LHA Replacement LHA(R) program— provide forward-presence and power-projection capabilities as elements of U.S. expeditionary strike groups. With elements of a Marine landing force, these warships will embark, deploy, land, control, support, and operate helicopters and MV-22 Osprey and F-35B Lightning II aircraft for sustained periods. The LHA 6-class will also support contingency-response and forcible-entry operations as an integral element of joint, interagency, and multinational maritime expeditionary forces. The USS America (LHA 6) is the first of the America class and is a variant of the USS Makin Island (LHD 8). The LHA 6 design includes an LHD 8 gas turbine and hybrid-electric propulsion plant, diesel generators, and all-electric auxiliary enhancements. These improvements represent a significant increase in aviation lift, sustainment, and maintenance capabilities. The Flight 0 (LHA 6 and LHA 7) ship optimization to support Osprey and F-35B aircraft includes: significantly increased JP-5 fuel capacity (1.3 million gallons, compared to

133

600,000 gallons for the Flight 1 (LHA 8) warships); space to support elements of a marine expeditionary unit or small-scale joint task force staff; an increase in service-life allowances for new-generation Marine Corps systems; and substantial survivability upgrades. The Flight 1 LHA 8 will modify the LHA 6 design to incorporate a well deck capable of supporting two landing craft air cushion vehicles and a reduced-island light deck to unlock seven F-35B spots and include a topside MV-22 maintenance spot. This will increase light deck space, thus retaining aviation capability on par with Flight 0 ships, which were optimized for aviation capability in lieu of a well deck.

Status

LHA 6 was launched June 4, 2012, delivered on April 10, 2014, and commissioned on October 11, 2014 in San Francisco during Fleet Week. The Navy awarded the contract for LHA 7 on May 31, 2012, the keel was laid on June 20, 2012, and the ship will deliver in December 2018. LHA 8 is programmed as a FY 2017 ship with planned delivery in FY 2025.

Developers

Avondale Marine Gulfport, Mississippi

Gryphon Technologies LC Panama City, Florida

Huntington Ingalls Industries, Ingalls Shipbuilding Pascagoula, Mississippi

* * * * * * * * * * * *

LHD 1 Wasp-Class Amphibious Assault Ship

Description

The Wasp class comprises eight 40,650-ton (full load) multipurpose amphibious assault ships whose primary mission is to provide embarked commanders with command and control capabilities for sea-based maneuver/assault operations as well as employing elements of a landing force through a combination of helicopters and amphibious vehicles. The Wasp-class also has several secondary missions, including power projection and sea control. LHD 1-class ships increase total lift capacity by providing both a light deck for helicopters and vertical/short takeoff and landing aircraft (AV-8B Harrier and the MV-22 Osprey), and a well deck for both air-cushioned and conventional landing craft. Each ship can embark 1,877 troops and has 125,000 cubic feet of cargo for stores and ammunition, and 20,900 square feet for vehicles. Medical facilities include six operating rooms, an intensive-care unit, and a 47-bed ward. LHDs 5 through 7 are modified variants of the class. Design changes include increased JP-5 fuel capacity, fire-fighting and damage-control enhancements, and women-at-sea accommodations. The USS Makin Island (LHD 8) incorporates significant design changes including gas-turbine propulsion, hybrid-electric drive, diesel generators, and all-electric equipment. Two gas turbines, providing 70,000 shaft-horsepower, replace the two steam plants found on earlier ships in the class, and the electric drive propels the ship while operating at flow speeds to increase fuel efficiency. All ships in the class will be modified to support F-35B Lightning II Joint Strike Fighter operations.

Status

Eight LHDs have been delivered to the Fleet. The USS Makin Island (LHD 8), the eighth and final ship of the class, commissioned on October 24, 2009 in San Diego, California. In FY 2014, the USS Wasp (LHD 1) completed modifications to support F-35B operations. The LHD mid-life program is scheduled to begin in FY 2016 with the USS Essex (LHD 2) and will enable LHDs to meet amphibious mission requirements and a 40-year expected service life starting in FY 2029 through FY 2049. The mid-life program is a key component to achieve LHD 1 "Class Wholeness" and includes hull, mechanical and electrical upgrades and C5I (command, control, communications, computers, collaboration, and intelligence); aviation; and training improvements.

Developers

Huntington Ingalls Industries, Ingalls Shipbuilding Pascagoula, Mississippi

* * * * * * * * * * * *

LPD 17 San Antonio-Class Amphibious Transport Dock Ship

Description

The San Antonio LPD is an amphibious transport dock ship optimized for operational flexibility and satisfying Marine Air-Ground Task Force (MAGTF) lift requirements in support of the expeditionary maneuver warfare concept of operations. The San Antonio-class LPDs are 684 feet in length, with a beam of 105 feet, a maximum displacement of 25,000 long tons, and a crew of approximately 380. Four turbocharged diesels with two shafts and two outboard-rotating controllable-pitch propellers generate a sustained speed of greater than 22 knots. Other ship characteristics include 20,000 square feet of space for vehicles—about twice that of the Austin-class (LPD 4), which LPD 17 replaces—34,000 cubic feet for cargo, accommodations for approximately 700 troops (800 surge), and a medical facility comprising 24 beds and four operating rooms (two medical and two dental). The well deck can launch and recover traditional surface assault craft as well as two landing craft air cushion vehicles capable of transporting cargo, personnel, Marine tracked and wheeled vehicles, and tanks. The LPD 17 aviation facilities include a hangar and light deck (33 percent larger than the LPD 4-class) to operate and maintain a variety of aircraft, including current and future fixed- and rotary-wing aircraft. Other advanced features include the advanced enclosed mast/sensor for reduced signature/sensor maintenance, reduced-signature composite-material enclosed masts, other stealth enhancements, state-of-the-art C4ISR (command, control, communications, computers, intelligence, surveillance, and reconnaissance) and self-defense systems, a shipboard wide-area network linking shipboard systems with embarked Marine Corps platforms, and significant quality of life improvements.

Status

The initial contract award to design and build the lead ship of the class was awarded to the Avondale-Bath Alliance in December 1996. The Navy transferred LPD 17 class workload from Bath Iron Works to Northrop Grumman Ship Systems (NGSS, now Huntington Ingalls Industries, Ingalls Shipbuilding) in June 2002. LPDs 17 through 26 have been delivered. Pre-Commissioning Unit Portland (LPD 27) will deliver in FY 2017. An additional ship, Fort Lauderdale (LPD 28), has been authorized and funded. Construction will begin in FY 2017 and delivery is scheduled for FY 2021.

Developers

Huntington Ingalls Industries,

Ingalls Shipbuilding Pascagoula, Mississippi

Raytheon San Diego, California

LSD 41 / 49 Whidbey Island / Harpers Ferry-Class Dock Landing Ships

Description

The mission of Whidbey Island/Harpers Ferry dock landing ships is to transport and launch amphibious assault vehicles and landing craft with their crews and embarked personnel. The key difference between the LSD 49-class and the LSD 41-class is that the LSD 49-class cargo variants have significantly expanded cargo and ammunition stowage facilities over those of the LSD 41-class at the cost of decreased landing craft air cushion (LCAC) capacity, from four to two. The LSD 41 Whidbey Island class is the primary support and operating platform for LCACs and can also provide limited docking and repair services as a boat haven for small ships and craft. Both LSD classes have two primary helicopter spots and can support Navy and Marine Corps helicopters as well as MV-22 Osprey tilt-rotor operations. Neither class is configured with a helicopter hangar, with aircraft fueling and rearming conducted on the light deck. LSDs are equipped with a vehicle turning area and tactical logistics communication spaces to facilitate and coordinate troop/vehicle movement and logistics. These ships have a doctor and dentist assigned as ship's company, two dental examination rooms, and one medical operating room.

Status

In late 2016, 12 LSDs were in the fleet: eight LSD 41-class and four LSD 49-class. Mid-life programs are designed around a 52-week maintenance availability with 11 ships already completed or in progress. The USS Tortuga (LSD 46) will receive her mid-life availability during a four-year deep-maintenance and modernization period (2016-2020). The mid-life program will enable both ship classes to meet amphibious mission requirements and a 40-year expected service life (ESL), with the first ship reaching ESL in FY 2025. The mid-life program improves material condition readiness, replaces obsolete equipment, and provides hull, mechanical and electrical systems upgrades. All ships have completed their mid-life availabilities with the exception of the USS Tortuga.

Developers

Avondale Industries, Inc. New Orleans, Louisiana

Lockheed Martin Seattle, Washington

Raytheon San Diego, California

* * * * * * * * * * *

Image courtesy of Huntington Ingalls Industries,
Ingalls Shipbuilding.

LX(R) Dock Landing Ship Replacement

Description

LX(R) is intended to replace the LSD 41 Whidbey Island and LSD 49 Harpers Ferry classes of dock landing ships when they begin reaching end of service life in 2025.

Status

The Navy's long-range shipbuilding plan associated with the FY 2013 President's Budget identified the LX(R) as an 11-ship program with lead ship procurement in FY 2018. LX(R) will be a recapitalization of the LSD 41/49 class. Planning for a replacement is well underway to ensure necessary lead-time for program development. The LX(R) initial capabilities have been defined, and initial contract design awards were issued to Huntington Ingalls Industries and General Dynamics NASSCO (the two competing shipyards) in June 2016. In September 2016 the Joint Staff approved the LX(R) capabilities development document. Following contract award in 2018, lead ship start of construction is scheduled for FY 2021 and delivery in FY 2025.

Developers

To be determined.

* * * * * * * * * * * *

MCM 1 Avenger-Class Mine Countermeasures Ship Modernization (MCM MOD)

Description

The Avenger-class surface mine countermeasures ships are used to detect, classify, and neutralize or sweep mines in sea lines of communication and naval operating areas. These ships are one leg of the mine countermeasures "triad" comprising surface and airborne MCM and explosive ordnance disposal forces.

MCM modernization improvement corrected the most significant maintenance and obsolescence issues in order to maintain the ships through their full 30-year service lives. The modernization package included: product improvement program upgraded the Isotta Fraschini main engines and generators for MCM 3 through MCM 14; replacement of the SLQ-48 mine neutralization vehicle on select hulls, addressed obsolete components; upgraded the SQQ-32 sonar with high-frequency wide-band capabilities; and replaced the acoustic sweep system with the advanced acoustic generator/infrasonic advanced acoustic generator system.

Status

Ship decommissionings have commenced and the entire class will be decommissioned by FY 2024.

Developers

Raytheon Portsmouth, Rhode Island

* * * * * * * * * * * *

Ship-to-Shore Connector (SSC) / LCAC 100

Description

The Ship-to-Shore Connector/Landing Craft Air Cushion 100 will provide high-speed, heavy-lift for over-the-horizon maneuver, surface lift, and shipping. The SSC/LCAC-100 is addressing the gap in heavy sea-to-shore lift that will emerge as the upgraded in-service LCAC reach their end of extended service lives after FY 2015. The SSC/LCAC-100 payload design will exceed the legacy LCAC payload of 74 short tons. The SSC design improves upon high failure rate and maintenance intensive systems to increase reliability and reduce life cycle costs. SSC/LCAC-100 will also employ enhanced lift fans, propellers, and greater use of composite materials.

Status

The Joint Requirements Oversight Council approved the initial capabilities document in October 2006. An analysis of alternatives was approved in early FY 2008, the capability development document (CDD) was approved in June 2010, and the CDD was accepted in lieu of the capability production document in October 2014. Initial operational capability is scheduled for FY 2020. A contract for the detailed design and construction of the first craft with options to build eight additional craft was awarded in July 2012. The first craft is funded by research, development, test and evaluation funds to serve as an operational test and evaluation platform, as well as a crew-transition training platform to allow for LCAC crews to become familiar with LCAC 100. The options included in the contract enable the Navy to begin flow-rate initial procurement of the first test and training craft plus eight option craft to support fleet introduction in the FY 2020 timeframe. Fabrication of the first SSC/LCAC 100 began in November 2014.

Developers

Alcoa Defense Pittsburgh, Pennsylvania

L-3 Communications New York, New York

Textron Marine & Land Systems New Orleans, Louisiana

* * * * * * * * * * *

Surface Connector (X) Replacement (SC(X)R)

Description

The Surface Connector (X) Replacement will recapitalize the capabilities provided by the long-serving LCU-1610 craft. SC(X) R will be a self-sustaining craft complete with living accommodations and messing facilities for the crew to enable persistent operations for up to ten days or intra-theater transit of up to 1,200 nautical miles. Like the venerable LCU, the SC(X)R will provide operational flexibility and a level of persistence no other asset smaller than an amphibious warfare ship provides to the operational commander. Carrying equipment, troops, and supplies in any variation up to its maximum capacity of 170 tons, the SC(X)R will launch from a well deck-equipped amphibious warfare ship, transit to the surf zone, and land vehicles and cargo to provide organic mobility for naval forces from the sea base to the shore. The SC(X)R is intended to address the gap in heavy sea-to-shore lift that will emerge as a result of the advanced age and long service of the LCU-1610 craft.

Status

The SC(X)R/LCU 1700 completed the Navy Requirements/ Acquisition Gate Review 1 in 2013. The analysis of alternatives to identify the suitable candidates to replace the LCU-1610 was completed in May 2014 and approved in September 2014. Navy Gate 2 was completed in October 2014, and the capability development document was approved and validated in July 2016.

Developers

To be determined.

* * * * * * * * * * * *

EXPEDITIONARY SYSTEMS

AES-1 Airborne Laser Mine Detection System (ALMDS)

Description

The Airborne Laser Mine Detection System is a light-detection and -ranging airborne mine countermeasures (AMCM) high-area coverage system that detects, classifies, and localizes floating and near-surface moored sea mines. The system is deployed in the MH-60S helicopter and will provide organic AMCM defense to the battle force.

Status

ALMDS completed operational assessment as part of the Littoral Combat Ship mine countermeasure mission package in FY 2015. Pre-planned product improvement delivers in 2018. Initial operational capability is scheduled for FY 2017.

Developers

Arete Associates Tucson, Arizona

Northrop Grumman Melbourne, Florida

* * * * * * * * * * *

Airborne Mine Neutralization System (AMNS)

Description

The Airborne Mine Neutralization System is deployed from the MH-60S helicopters using an expendable mine neutralization device, the Archerfish, with the capability to neutralize bottom and moored mines. The AMNS will be deployed from the littoral combat ship (LCS) as a key element of the LCS mine countermeasures mission module. This capability will be of critical importance in littoral zones, confined straits, choke points, near shore, and amphibious objective areas.

Status

AMNS successfully completed integrated test in May 2013 and demonstrated operational assessment as part of the LCS mine countermeasure mission package in FY 2015. Initial operational capability is scheduled for FY 2017.

Developers

BAE Systems Portsmouth, England

Raytheon Portsmouth, Rhode Island

* * * * * * * * * * * *

AQS-20A Sonar

Description

The AQS-20A is an underwater mine-detection side- and forward-looking sonar suite that also employs an electro-optic Identification sensor capable of locating and identifying bottom, close-tethered, and moored sea mines. The AQS-20A system will serve as a mine-hunting sensor subsystem of the Littoral Combat Ship mine countermeasures mission package.

Status

Improvements to the computer-aided detection/computer-aided classification and environmental data-collection capabilities are being implemented via enhanced research and development efforts. AQS-20A initial operational capability is projected for FY 2020.

Developers

Raytheon Portsmouth, Rhode Island

* * * * * * * * * * * *

Assault Breaching System (ABS)

Description

The Assault Breaching System program focuses on development of standoff systems to locate and neutralize mine and obstacle threats in the surf and beach zones. The program uses a system-of-systems approach that includes incremental development of the Coastal Battlefield Reconnaissance and Analysis (COBRA) mine/obstacle detection system and precision craft navigation and lane marking. The Joint Direct-Attack Munition Assault Breaching System (JABS) provides in-service neutralization capability against "proud" (i.e., not buried) bottom mines and obstacles in the beach and surf zone. The platform for the COBRA system is the Fire Scout vertical take-off unmanned aerial vehicle. Platforms for deploying neutralization systems include Navy strike aircraft and Air Force bombers.

Status

The COBRA Block I system achieved Milestone C in FY 2009, and initial operational capability is scheduled for FY 2017. JABS is a fielded capability in the beach and surf zone with ongoing testing to expand its capability into the very-shallow water zone.

Developers

Arete Tucson, Arizona

144

The Boeing Company St. Louis, Missouri

* * * * * * * * * * *

Joint Counter Radio-Controlled Improvised Explosive Device (RCIED) Electronic Warfare (JCREW)

Description

Improvised explosive devices (IEDs) continue to present a significant threat to U.S. and coalition forces throughout the world. The Counter Radio-Controlled IED Electronic Warfare (CREW) program encompasses mobile, man-portable, and fixed-site protection systems employed to counter IEDs that are either armed or initiated by radio signals. Fielded first- and second-generation CREW systems were acquired largely by non-developmental urgent operational need initiatives to address immediate warfighter requirements. Joint CREW (JCREW) is a Navy-led program to develop the next generation of joint-service CREW systems. JCREW will correct deficiencies in existing CREW systems and address emerging worldwide RCIED threats. Additionally, JCREW has an open architecture, facilitating the system's evolution as new threats, advances in technology, and new vehicle requirements are introduced.

Status

JCREW Increment 1 Block 1 (I1B1) program management remains with the Navy through the program life cycle, integrating joint service requirements. Milestone C was approved on September 9, 2014 and the acquisition program baseline was approved on October 5, 2014. The Navy and Air Force combined flow-rate initial production contract was awarded September 30, 2015. The Navy is responsible to upgrade JCREW techniques to defeat evolving global threats and improved capability is developed and fielded through a technology insertion program.

Developers

Northrop Grumman Systems Corporation San Diego, California

* * * * * * * * * * * *

KSQ-1 Amphibious Assault Direction System (AADS)

Description

The Amphibious Assault Direction System, with Enhanced Position Location Reporting System, integrates the NAVSTAR global positioning system to form a jam/intercept-resistant, friendly force-tracking and command and control system that supports the surface assault ship-to-shore movement in amphibious operations. It provides the capability to launch, monitor, track, record, and control landing craft air cushion (LCAC), landing craft utility (LCU) vessels, Naval Beach Group/seabasing craft conducting amphibious assaults from up to 100 nautical miles over the horizon (OTH) via radio relay group configuration. It integrates with the Marine Corps tactical radio (PRC-117G) and the Global Command and Control System-Maritime during ship-to-objective-maneuver operations.

Status

AADS satisfies operational requirements for an OTH amphibious assault command and control system. AADS is installed in 32 amphibious ships, 78 LCACs and 32 LCUs, in addition to Assault Craft Units 4 and 5 control towers, and Expeditionary Warfare Training Group (Atlantic and Pacific) Amphibious Boat Control Team Trainer (ABCTT) classrooms. ABCTT upgraded with AADS Simulator to properly train Amphibious Boat Control Team as per fielded boat control configurations. The AADS program Office is executing the AADS modernization plan, which addresses program IT risk assessment issues, Windows XP to Windows 7 migration and other upgrades to improve system integrity. The AADS program Office is also working to provide a coalition common operating picture with Australian and Canadian Forces using the KOK-23 Crypto Key Generator.

Developers

Naval Surface Warfare Center - Panama City Division Panama City, Florida

* * * * * * * * * * * *

Mk 62/63/65 Naval Quickstrike Mines

Description

The in-service Quickstrike family of aircraft-delivered bottom mines is being enhanced significantly by procurement of the programmable Target Detection Device (TDD) Mk 71. Engineering development efforts include new advanced algorithms for ship detection, classification, and localization against likely threats, including quiet diesel-electric submarines, mini-subs, fast patrol boats, and air-cushioned vehicles. The Quickstrike mines include one dedicated thin-wall mine—the 2,300-pound Mk 65 weapon—and two mines converted from conventional bombs using the Conversion Kit Mk 197: the Mk 62 500-pound and Mk 63 1,000-pound mines.

Status

In-service support continues for current inventories, and funding is in place for algorithm development and procurement of the TDD Mk 71 and associated hardware for Conversion Kit Mk 197. Aircraft integration and testing are ongoing to certify this new configuration for use on various Air Force and Navy aircraft.

Developers

SECHAN Electronics, Inc. Lititz, Pennsylvania

* * * * * * * * * * *

Submarine Launched Mobile Mine (SLMM) Description

The submarine launched mobile mine is a bottom influence mine that is launched from Los Angeles/Improved Los Angeles (SSN 688/688I)-class submarines, using a Mk 37 torpedo propulsion system and the Target Detection Device (TDD) Mk 57 as its sensing mechanism. SLMM provides the Navy's only clandestine mining capability. The SLMM has been in-service since 1983 and was originally scheduled to be phased out by the end of 2012. However, in December 2012, the Chief of Naval Operations directed retention of a specific quantity of SLMMs in a Ready for Issue status—the exact number is classified.

Status

SLMM support and maintenance continues, provided by the Naval Munitions Command Unit Guam. All in-service weapons are maintained in an all-up round status and as Ammunition Condition Code A: Ready for Issue. Future efforts will certify the Navy's advanced Mk 71 TDD into the weapon system to add greater targeting flexibility.

Developers

Multiple sources.

* * * * * * * * * * *

WLD-1 Remote Minehunting System (RMS)

Description

The WLD-1 Remote Minehunting System consists of one remote multi-mission vehicle and one AQS-20A variable-depth sonar. RMS is a high-endurance, semi-submersible, unmanned, off-board, flow-observable vehicle operated from the littoral combat ship (LCS). RMS is launched with a pre-programmed search pattern and will search detect, classify, and identify non-mine objects and mine threats. RMS is capable of line-of-sight and over-the-horizon operations. Once the mission is completed, RMS will return to the ship and data will be downloaded for post-mission analysis in which targets classified as mines are passed to follow-on systems for neutralization.

Status

To support LCS integration, RMS is being used as a surrogate tow platform for the AQS-20 sensor until the common unmanned surface vehicle has completed development and testing for LCS mine countermeasure mission package integration in FY 2020.

Developers

Lockheed Martin Riviera Beach, Florida

* * * * * * * * * * * *

SECTION 5

INFORMATION WARFARE

149

The Navy's Information Warfare Force comprises cryptologic warfare, meteorology and oceanography, intelligence, and information professionals. By combining those elements the Navy has aligned the Information Warfare Force with Air Warfare, Surface Warfare, and Undersea Warfare, and underscores efforts to identify information warfare as one of four predominant naval warfare areas. That alignment will help the Navy achieve mastery in the "information age" warfighting arena. Capabilities and programs include Consolidated Afloat Networks and Enterprise Services (CANES), Global Command and Control System-Maritime, and various unmanned aircraft systems, advanced data links, decoys, and more that contribute to broad-spectrum maritime domain awareness.

ASSURED COMMAND AND CONTROL

Afloat Electromagnetic Spectrum Operations Program (AESOP)

Description

The U.S. Navy's Afloat Electromagnetic Spectrum Operations Program is the only fielded operational spectrum planning tool that integrates surface radars, combat systems, and communications frequencies to de-conflict and reduce the electromagnetic interference (EMI) impacts for ships and strike groups. AESOP also develops the Operational Tasking Communication (OPTASK COMM) and OPTASK Electronic Warfare (EW) Annex K Radar Frequency Plans that support strike groups and coalition navies in joint exercises and operations, to ensure all systems interoperate and missions are successful. AESOP uses U.S. Navy-approved propagation models that include all strike group emitters—Navy and coalition partners—to identify and mitigate potential interoperability issues. In addition, AESOP helps to ensure that systems are in compliance with both national and international spectrum allocations and regulations. AESOP provides many benefits and enables the warfighter to maximize the performance of their systems by reducing system susceptibilities to interference or unintentional jamming, resulting in clear communications, increased detection ranges and intercepts, and enhanced awareness for emission control. AESOP is a man-in-the-loop fleet capability. Using sophisticated models and algorithms, the program creates OPTASK plans in minutes versus a manual process that would require days to complete.

Status

In 2016 196 ships were using AESOP 3.2 and 194 ashore commands. Accompanying the AESOP software programs are the EMC Criteria for Navy Systems Revision 3 and the Littoral Spectrum Restrictions Revision 4.The next progression for AESOP is to integrate and automate this capability with shipboard sensors to develop a real-time spectrum operations (RTSO) capability, a key tenet and enabler of electro-magnetic maneuver warfare (EMW). It is foundational to the EMW framework: electromagnetic resource control and allocation, EM awareness, EM agility, signature control, and EM engagement. RTSO will provide ships and strike groups the ability to sense, control, and plan the use of spectrum, detect electromagnetic interference, notify the operators of spectrum issues, and provide recommended actions allowing for command and control of the spectrum. It will be a networked collection of firmware, software, and hardware that continuously monitors the spectrum via direct connections to existing shipboard systems as well as antennas receiving the external environment. Once deployed, it will share this information across the strike group and be cognizant of global frequency restrictions. RTSO will execute the Navy's vision for information warfare and EMW by controlling the electromagnetic spectrum terrain and mitigating EMI. RTSO will enable the Navy to transition from its legacy static spectrum operations through three major incremental improvements embracing a dynamic, automated, real-time spectrum operations approach. RTSO will provide real-time dynamic command and control of the spectrum terrain. This transition from a static, assignment-based spectrum management system to a fully automated, real-time system is outlined in the Navy's Information Warfare Roadmap for Electromagnetic Spectrum (EMS) Usage. The EMS Usage Roadmap provides plans of action with timelines to drive Navy policy, engagement, and investment decisions regarding the operationalization of the electromagnetic spectrum.

Developers

EOIR Corporation Dahlgren, Virginia

Naval Surface Warfare Center

Dahlgren Division Dahlgren, Virginia

SENTEL Corporation Dahlgren, Virginia

* * * * * * * * * * * *

Automated Digital Network System (ADNS)

Description

The Automated Digital Network System is the key enabler for delivering net-centric capabilities that depend upon robust, dynamic, adaptable, survivable, and secure communications. ADNS is the shipboard network interface that enables connectivity between the ship's internal network and the outside world via radio frequency (RF) spectrum and landline when pier side. ADNS is also installed in Navy network operations centers (NOCs), enabling the NOCs to transmit and receive voice and data to and from ships. ADNS provides capability that enables unclassified, secret, top secret, and various joint, allied, and coalition services to interconnect to the Defense Information Systems Network.

ADNS Increment I combined data from different enclaves for transmission across available communications paths. ADNS Increment II added the capability to manage traffic from multiple enclaves simultaneously over multiple transit paths, including RF and terrestrial links, but still did not satisfy the Fleet's need for higher throughput. Increased throughput and converged internet protocol (voice, video, and data) capabilities were delivered to the Fleet with the deployment of Increment IIa/IIb. ADNS Increment III brings a protected core, reducing the exposure to cyber warfare network infiltration. It supports 25 megabits per second (mbps) aggregate throughput for submarines and unit-level ships and 50 mbps aggregate throughput for force-level ships. ADNS Increment III is a key enabler of the Navy's maritime security posture.

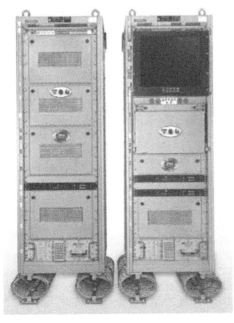

Status

ADNS is fully deployed and is undergoing sustainment and improvement efforts while migrating legacy increments are being migrated to ADNS Increment III. ADNS Increment III reached initial operational capability in FY 2010; ashore NOC installs were completed in FY 2010. Increment III will be installed on all ships and submarines and their respective shore facilities. ADNS Increment III is planned to reach full operational capability in FY 2020 and is synchronized with Consolidated Afloat Networks Enterprise Services deployment.

Developers

PEO C4I San Diego, California

Science Applications

International Corporation Arlington, Virginia

Space and Naval Warfare Systems

Center Pacific San Diego, California

* * * * * * * * * * *

Automatic Identification System (AIS)

Description

The Automatic Identification System is a maritime digital broadcast system that continually exchanges voyage and vessel data among network participants over very-high-frequency radio in support of regional and global maritime domain awareness (MDA) requirements. The data include vessel identity, position, speed, course, destination, and other information of critical interest for navigation safety and maritime security. The International Maritime Organization and the 1974 International Convention for the Safety of Life at Sea require commercial vessels greater than 300 gross tons and all passenger ships to use AIS. Warships are exempt. The Navy AIS program collects open-source AIS data broadcast from AIS transceivers on commercial vessels. Open-source AIS data, combined with other government intelligence and surveillance data, is used by Navy ships and submarines to improve safety of navigation and is integrated into the common

153

operational picture to enhance situational awareness. The AIS data collected by Navy platforms is also aggregated within the MDA/AIS Sensor/Server (MASS) capability at several operational shore sites. The MASS then provides the data to unclassified and classified users in support of MDA efforts, with particular focus on improving the Nation's maritime security.

Status

Navy AIS began as a rapid deployment capability, transitioned to a program of record on December 24, 2008, and was designated as an Acquisition Category IV program. The Space and Naval Warfare Systems Command Program Executive Office C4I is the milestone decision authority. As of October 2016, Increment I AIS systems were installed on 170 unit-level and group-level ships (e.g., patrol craft, cruisers and destroyers), 20 force-level ships (e.g., aircraft carriers and large-deck amphibious assault ships), 37 submarines, and four shore sites (Third Fleet, Fifth Fleet, Pacific Fleet, and Fleet Forces Command). The systems include a laptop computer display on the bridge and connectivity to send unclassified AIS data to shore sites. They also enable the direct transfer of AIS track information. The Navy is implementing a firmware upgrade to add encrypted capability on submarine AIS systems to improve safety of navigation for submarines operating in close proximity to Coast Guard vessels that routinely encrypt their AIS position reports.

Developers

L-3 Communications Orlando, Florida

SAAB Transponder Technologies Sterling, Virginia

Base Communications Office (BCO)

Description

Base Communications Office provides: (1) operations and maintenance—manage telephone switching networks and outside cable plant infrastructure; (2) telephone services—operate, maintain, and manage government and commercial service delivery points providing connectivity to Defense Switch Network (DSN), Public Switched Telephone Network (PSTN), and General Services Administration commercial long-distance service; (3) audio conferencing services—operate and maintain ad-hoc unclassified audio conferencing services; (4) billing support—provide telephone invoice validation and customer billing, and process customer requests for services; (5) voicemail services—operate and maintain standard business-class voicemail services; (6) customer support; (7) requirements definition and planning; (8) review of military construction and special projects; and (9) move, add, and change telephone services. The Fleet Cyber Command/Tenth Fleet manages the program, and the PEO-C4I/PMW790 Shore Telephony Program Office provides acquisition support to the BCO program, which serves more than 350,000 Navy personnel worldwide. Lifecycle switch replacement provides voice over internet protocol capability.

Status

Naval Computer and Telecommunications Area Master Stations BCOs provide base communications services and support to approximately 3,890 Navy and non-Navy shore activities and deployable units. BCOs operate, maintain, and manage the communications infrastructure supporting the transport of switched voice, video, and data in support of 49 BCOs worldwide. BCOs provide services at 114 campuses (base/station/other) and manage 109 government-owned telephone switches and 13 commercial dial-tone central exchange switches. This program responds to about 70,000 customer service requests worldwide each year, and its operators and automated attendants handle some 320,000 calls per month.

Developers

Science Applications

International Corporation Arlington, Virginia

Space and Naval Warfare Systems

Center Pacific San Diego, California

* * * * * * * * * * *

Base Level Information Infrastructure (BLII)

Description

Base Level Information Infrastructure provides a fully integrated, interoperable, and secure information technology (IT) infrastructure that enables the rapid and reliable transfer of voice, video, and data to bases, stations, homeports, and piers outside of the continental United States (OCONUS). BLII area of responsibility includes 14 major OCONUS fleet bases, stations, and other remote locations. BLII provides the infrastructure, hardware, and software for the Fleet Cyber Command/Tenth Fleet-managed

* * * * * * * * * * *

OCONUS Navy Enterprise Network (ONE-NET) Operations.

BLII also sustains Navy CONUS/OCONUS pier IT infrastructure capability, which includes maintaining pier fiber runs, conduits, junction boxes, brow umbilicals, and associated electronics. Modern pier IT infrastructure enables forward-deployed ships to maintain situational awareness, receive operational and intelligence traffic, and perform maintenance or training on their radio frequency systems while pier-side.

Status

This program provides IT services to 28,000 BLII/ONE-NET seats, supporting approximately 51,000 forward-deployed OCONUS Navy users. Additionally, all piers/maintenance will be brought under a single program manager to centralize maintenance functions and accountability. This program is expected to transition into the Next-Generation Enterprise Network follow-on contract by the end of FY 2018. This merger will realize standardization and efficiencies associated with a centrally managed program.

Developers

Booz Allen Hamilton San Diego, California

Computer Sciences Corporation San Diego, California

Deloitte San Diego, California Science Applications International

Corporation San Diego, California

* * * * * * * * * * *

Battle Force Tactical Network (BFTN)

Description

The Battle Force Tactical Network is the Navy's program of record for high-frequency internet protocol (HFIP) and subnet relay (SNR) communications, providing command and control in a satellite communications-denied environment and serves as a primary backup for SIPRNET (Secret Internet Protocol Router Network) in the absence of satellite communications. The HF component of BFTN is HFIP, which is capable of data rates of 9.6 kilobits per second (kbps) in single side band and 19.2 kbps in independent side band. The UHF component of BFTN is SNR, which is capable of data rates up to 64 kbps. BFTN also provides critical non-satellite line of sight and beyond line of sight transmission control protocol/internet protocol intra-aircraft carrier strike group connectivity among U.S. and coalition ships, submarines, and aircraft.

Status

BFTN is installed on 65 ships, 24 aircraft (aHFIP), and four submarines in late 2016. Baseline program strategies refocused efforts toward completing the initial operational testing and evaluation in FY 2017, adhering to fleet operational requirements to procure and install an additional eight baseline systems in FY 2016-2017 to support the forward-deployed naval forces and enhancements to the baseline system with higher data rates and shore reach-back capability. The program is also conducting market research for BFTN-Enhanced to accommodate fleet-requested baseline system enhancements.

Developers

Quatech Hudson, Ohio

Rockwell-Collins Cedar Rapids, Iowa

Space and Naval Warfare

Systems Center Pacific San Diego, California

* * * * * * * * * * *

Commercial Satellite Communications (COMSATCOM)

Description

The Commercial Satellite Communications program augments military satellite communications capabilities in support of surface combatants and includes two elements: the new Commercial Broadband Satellite Program (CBSP) and the legacy Commercial Wideband Satellite Program (CWSP). CWSP will continue in the Fleet until replaced by CBSP. The CBSP terminal is the USC-69; the CWSP terminal is the WSC-8. The CBSP

USC-69 terminal has three variants for force-level, unit-level, and small ships. All terminal groups transport voice, video and data, e.g. NIPRNET (Non-secure Internet Protocol), SIPRNET (Secret Internet Protocol Router Network), JWICS (Joint Worldwide Intelligence Communications System), DCGS-N (Distributed Common Ground System-Navy), and other requirements. The CBSP program also includes the worldwide space segment and end-to-end architecture. The Navy use of Iridium on surface combatants is for emergency communications. Separate from the emergency communications requirement on ships, the Navy has more than 15,000 Iridium devices total that are used for various purposes at shore command locations and afloat to meet flow-bandwidth voice and video requirements.

Status

CBSP was established as a rapid deployment capability in March 2007, achieved program Milestone C September 2009, initial operational capability in June 2010,

158

and full rate production in September 2011. The Navy expects full operational capability will be achieved in FY 2020. As of December 31, 2011, all ships reliant on INMARSAT transitioned to CBSP. The approved CBSP terminal objective is 177 ships. As of the end of FY 2016, 85 ships were operational with the CBSP terminal. The legacy CWSP WSC-8 will continue in the Fleet until replaced by the CBSP terminal in the FY 2019 timeframe.

Developers

CBSP: CVG, Inc. Chantilly, Virginia

CBSP/CWSP: Harris Corporation Melbourne, Florida

IRIDIUM: IRIDIUM, LLC McLean, Virginia

JEOD VSAT: L3 Communications Victor, New York

* * * * * * * * * * * *

Consolidated Afloat Networks and Enterprise Services (CANES)

Description

Consolidated Afloat Networks and Enterprise Services is the Navy's program of record to replace existing afloat networks and provide the necessary infrastructure for applications, systems, and services required for the Navy to dominate the cyber warfare domain. CANES is the technical and infrastructure consolidation of existing, separately managed afloat networks including Integrated Shipboard Network Systems (ISNS), Combined Enterprise Regional Information Exchange System-Maritime (CENTRIXS-M), Sensitive Compartmented Information (SCI) Networks, and Submarine Local Area Network (SubLAN). CANES is replacing these legacy, obsolete afloat network designs. CANES provide capacity for enterprise information assurance management. It also reduces total ownership cost through consolidation and normalization of products and services while employing constant competition to enable efficient acquisition of new fleet requirements and capabilities.

The fundamental goal of CANES is to bring "Infrastructure as a Service" (IaaS) and "Platform as a Service" (PaaS), within which in-service and future iterations of Navy Tactical Network computing and storage capabilities will reside. CANES will provide complete infrastructure inclusive of hardware, software (including Agile Core Services for the Navy Tactical Cloud), processing, storage, and end-user devices for unclassified, coalition, secret, and sensitive compartmented information for all basic network services (email, web, chat, and collaboration) to a wide variety of Navy surface combatants, submarines, aircraft, maritime operations centers, and regional network operations and security centers. CANES will develop updates on a rolling four-year hardware baseline and a two-year software baseline.

CANES is based on the overarching concept of reducing the number of afloat network baselines and providing enhanced efficiency through a single engineering focus on integrated technical solutions. Navy-validated applications, systems, and services that use the CANES infrastructure and services include the Distributed Common Ground System-Navy, Global Command and Control System-Maritime, Naval Tactical Command Support System, and Undersea Warfare Decision Support System.

Status

CANES full deployment decision was achieved October 2015, authorizing the program to field the remainder of its target inventory objective. At the full deployment decision, milestone decision authority was delegated to the Assistant Secretary of the Navy for Research, Development and Acquisition, and the program was designated as an Acquisition Category IAC program. This decision was granted based on a successful initial operational test and evaluation on a unit level platform, and the system was declared as operationally effective, suitable, and survivable by Director, Operational Test and Evaluation. In late 2016, follow-on force-level plat

form test and evaluation was in progress on board the USS John C. Stennis (CVN 74) and expected to be completed in FY 2017. CANES is planned to reach full operational capability in FY 2023.

Developers

Naval Undersea Warfare Center Newport, Rhode Island

Space and Naval Warfare Systems

Center Atlantic Charleston, South Carolina

Space and Naval Warfare Systems

Center Pacific San Diego, California

* * * * * * * * * * * *

Defense Red Switch Network (DRSN)

Description

The Defense Red Switch Network is the secure circuit-switched element of the Defense Information System Network, providing reliable and high-quality secure voice, data, and conferencing capabilities to senior national, combatant commander, and fleet commander decision-makers. The DRSN program ensures that operational commanders have immediate access to a flash-precedence, robust, multi-level secure, physically diverse, and survivable voice network. The Department of Defense and select federal agencies have a continuing operational requirement for a separate, controlled, and interoperable multi-level secure communications and conferencing network to support command, control, and crisis-management activities. The DRSN capability satisfies that requirement and comprises a network of circuit switches interconnected by the DISN backbone and commercial transmission links as well as gateway access to the voice over secure internet protocol network.

Status

As assigned by the Joint Staff, the Navy has responsibility for operations and maintenance of five switches in the DRSN network: (1) Joint Staff Detachment (Former Commander, Joint Forces Command, Norfolk, Virginia); (2) Commander, Pacific Command (Camp H.M. Smith, Hawaii); (3) Commander, Pacific Fleet (Pearl Harbor, Hawaii); (4) Commander, Naval Forces Europe (Naples, Italy); and (5) Commander, U.S. Naval Forces Central Command (Manama, Bahrain). The Fleet Cyber Command is responsible for personnel, training, logistics, security and accreditation, and command policy for DRSN assets under Navy operational control.

Developers

Raytheon Waltham, Massachusetts

* * * * * * * * * * * *

Deployable Joint Command and Control Capability (DJC2)

Description

The Deployable Joint Command and Control program provides a standardized, rapidly deployable, scalable, and reconfigurable C2 and collaboration capable combat operations center that can be set up anywhere in the world in six-to-24 hours after arrival in theater to support geographic combatant commanders and their joint component commands in the rapid standup of a joint task force (JTF) headquarters. DJC2 can be employed when executing operations ranging in scale from a first responder or small early-entry, forward-component operations center to a full JTF headquarters. DJC2 extends the joint sea base ashore for rapid, dynamic joint operations.

DJC2 has been used for humanitarian-assistance and disaster-response operations, including: Operation Damayan after Typhoon Haiyan in the Philippines; Superstorm Sandy relief in New Jersey and New York; Operation Tomodachi after the earthquake and tsunami in Japan; JTF Unified Response after the earthquake in Haiti; JTF Caring Response after Cyclone Nargis in Myanmar; and JTF Katrina after

Hurricane Katrina in New Orleans, Louisiana. Additionally, the systems are used extensively for JTF headquarters joint exercises and training.

The DJC2 system has three modular tent/mobile shelter configurations, which iteratively build up C2 capability during the phases of a joint operation. Configurations include: an autonomous Rapid-Response Kit (five to 15 seats); Early Entry (20 to 40 seats); and Core (60 seats). An Early Entry configuration can be set up and operational with three networks and communications in less than six hours. The fully fielded DJC2 configuration in a footprint of approximately 40,000 square feet can be set up and operational with five networks in less than 24 hours. The number of users supported can be expanded by lashing together two or more Cores, or by adding Core Expansion Kits (three available, adding 60-seats each, 180 total). A fully fielded DJC2 includes self-generated power, environmental control, shelters (tents), infrastructure, limited communications equipment, C2 applications, and Office automation and collaboration software applications with operator workstations (laptop computers, chairs, and tables), displays, intercommunications, local-area networks, and access to wide-area networks.

Status

In September 2008, the DJC2 program attained full operational capability with the delivery of six operational Core systems to: the U.S. Southern Command (SOUTHCOM), two Core systems, with one transferred to U.S. Army South; U.S. European Command (EUCOM); U.S. Pacific Command (PACOM), two Core systems, with one transferred to III Marine Expeditionary Force; and U.S. Africa Command (AFRICOM). A seventh system was provided to Naval Forces Central Command (CENTCOM) in support of an urgent operational needs statement and their continuity of operations plan requirements. In October 2016, three of the six DJC2s transferred custody to Joint Communications Support Element, U.S. Transportation Command, from SOUTHCOM, AFRICOM, and EUCOM. Two are held at MacDill Air Force Base and one at Ramstein AFB. Programmed funding supports hardware sustainment, information technology refresh, and technology-insertion efforts (based on warfighter input as technologies mature) across the future years defense program. The DJC2 program is in the operations and support phase and has successfully fielded several cycles of technology insertion (delivered in "spirals") since September 2008. Because of its open architecture and modular design, the DJC2 system can be reconfigured to meet a wide variety of form/fit/functions.

Developers

ARINC Panama City, Florida

Georgia Tech Research Institute Atlanta, Georgia

ISPA Technology Panama City, Florida

Naval Surface Warfare Center Panama City, Florida

* * * * * * * * * * * *

Digital Modular Radio (DMR)

Description

The USC-61(C) Digital Modular Radio is the Navy's first software-defined radio to have become a communications system standard for the U.S. military. DMR has four independent, full-duplex channels that provide surface ships, submarines, and shore commands with multiple waveforms and associated internal multilevel information security for voice and data communications. A single DMR is capable of replacing numerous existing Navy and Coast Guard legacy radios in the high frequency, very high frequency, and ultra-high frequency (UHF) line-of-sight and UHF satellite communications (SATCOM) frequency bands. The DMR is software configurable and programmable with an open system architecture using commercial off-the-shelf/non-developmental item hardware. DMR is the Navy's primary solution for providing the UHF SATCOM Integrated Waveform (IW) and Mobile User Objective System (MUOS) waveform to the Fleet.

Status

The Navy has procured 645 DMR systems through FY 2016. The DMR is installed on various platforms, including the Nimitz (CVN 68)-class aircraft carriers, Arleigh Burke (DDG 51)-class guided missile destroyers, the Makin Island (LHD 8) and America (LHA 6) amphibious assault ships, San Antonio (LPD 17)-class amphibious transport dock ships, Lewis and Clark (T-AKE)-class ships, submarines as part of the common submarine radio room, and select shore communications stations. DMR is the Navy and Coast Guard's radio/terminal solution for implementing the IW and MUOS waveforms. For Navy new construction, DMR is also used to provide an HF capability as part of the High-Frequency Distribution Amplifier Group (HFDAG). With the introduction of IW, MUOS and HFDAG, DMR is the Navy's complete tactical communication solution for the radio-frequency spectrum from 2 MHz through 2 GHz. IW/MUOS-capable DMRs are planned to start fielding in FY 2017.

Developers

General Dynamics Scottsdale, Arizona

* * * * * * * * * * *

E-6B Mercury

Description

Derived from the Boeing 707, the E-6B platform provides the Commander, U.S. Strategic Command (USSTRATCOM), with the command, control, and communications capability needed for execution and direction of strategic-nuclear forces. Designed to support a robust and flexible nuclear deterrent posture well into the 21st Century, the E-6B performs very flow frequency (VLF) emergency communications, the U. S. Strategic Command airborne command post mission, and airborne launch control of ground-based inter-continental ballistic missiles. It is the Navy's only survivable means of nuclear command and control (C2).

Status

The Block I modification program will sustain and improve E-6B capability and is focused on several aircraft deficiencies identified by USSTRATCOM. The contract for Block I was awarded to Rockwell Collins in March 2004, and became operational in 2013 with the last Block I modification scheduled for completion in 2019. In March 2012, the Navy awarded to Northrop Grumman the contract for Multi-Role Tactical Common Data Link (MR-TCDL) integration and installation into one E-6B aircraft and the E-6B Systems Integration Lab. The Internet Protocol and Bandwidth Expansion (IP/BE), MR-TCDL, and Family of Advanced Beyond Line-of-Sight Terminal/Presidential National Voice Conferencing (FAB-T/PNVC) programs will support USSTRATCOM's migration of nuclear C2 to a distributed, network/internet protocol-based global C2 system as an airborne node. Planned initial operational capabilities for MR-TCDL and FAB-T/PNVC programs are in 2018 and 2019, respectively.

Developers

The Boeing Company Wichita, Kansas

Northrop Grumman Herndon, Virginia

Rockwell Collins Richardson, Texas

* * * * * * * * * * *

Enterprise Services

Description

Enterprise Services establish Navy's enterprise-level information technology (IT) services that provide opportunities and enhance user capabilities to meet Navy needs while increasing security and achieving cost efficiencies. Enterprise Services provide the capabilities to manage and deliver the Navy's IT services centrally, enabling it to: reduce total ownership costs; promote information sharing and interoperability in the Department of the Navy (DoN) and Department of Defense (DoD); ensure compliance with DoD and congressional IT mandates; and significantly improve the Navy's information assurance posture. This allows seamless access to resources no matter where they connect to the Navy or DoD. Initial efforts in Enterprise Services focus on consolidating data centers, as well as establishing enterprise software licensing agreements. Managing services at the enterprise level provides an opportunity to eliminate stovepipe systems that do not communicate with each other and enhances the Navy warfighters' capability to access mission-critical information. The DoN has made significant progress eliminating legacy networks, servers, systems, applications, and duplicative data environments. These Enterprise Services will be leveraged across the DoN and joint partners to provide seamless connectivity to mission-critical information. Future technological demands warrant higher levels of interoperability with our joint partners and allies to achieve operational efficiency and success. Enterprise Services are critical enablers to help the DoN achieve its information warfare strategy offering significant advantages operationally while enhancing our cyber security posture.

Status

The Navy is in the process of consolidating its data centers dispersed throughout the continental United States. The Navy Data Center Consolidation (DCC) initiative is leveraging DoN, Space and Naval Warfare Systems Command, Defense Information Systems Agency, commercial data centers and Cloud service providers to provide enterprise capabilities to satisfy system, application, and database hosting requirements for the Navy. The Navy is engaged in implementing various IT infrastructure modernization and cost saving consolidation initiatives in preparation for transitioning to the joint information environment. In addition to DCC, the Navy is actively engaged in other IT efficiency efforts, including enterprise software licensing (ESL), Navy portal consolidation, help desk consolidation, and application rationalization. The Navy established enterprise service license agreements with major software manufacturers and continues to analyze requirements for software applications used throughout the DoN to generate further efficiencies. ESL is a strategic effort to leverage the combined buying power of the Navy and Marine Corps to improve the DoN's IT/cyberspace investment decision practices by providing DoN enterprise-level evaluation and management.

Developers

Multiple sources.

* * * * * * * * * * * *

Global Broadcast Service (GBS)

Description

The Global Broadcast Service is a military satellite communications (MILSATCOM) extension of the global information grid that provides worldwide, high-capacity, one-way transmission of voice, data, and video supporting fleet command centers and joint combat forces in garrison, in transit, and deployed to global crisis and combat zones. Specific products include unmanned aerial vehicle feeds, imagery, intelligence, missile-warning, weather, joint and service-unique news, education, training, video, and various other high-bandwidth services. GBS is a joint Acquisition Category (ACAT) 1 program overseen by the Air Force, and Navy GBS is an ACAT 3 program that aligns to joint development. GBS interfaces with other communications systems in order to relieve overburdened and saturated satellite networks and provide information services to previously unsupportable (due to flow

167

bandwidth) users. It provides fleet and strike group commanders the highest broadband data rate available afloat, up to 23.5 megabits per second (mbps) per channel on ultra-high-frequency follow-on satellites and 45 mbps with the Wideband Global SATCOM constellation. GBS also enables critical delivery of information products required to provide assured command and control in crisis and combat environments.

Status

Navy GBS is fully deployed and is undergoing sustainment and improvement efforts. Architectural enhancements permit improved sharing and reallocation of broadcast coverage and bandwidth between users, information products, media types, and security levels. Worldwide SIPRNET (Secret Internet Protocol Router Network) Split Internet Protocol capability was established on all GBS-equipped platforms in FY 2011, enabling users to request real-time data via an alternate off-ship system for delivery via GBS and significantly enhancing the warfighter's situational awareness. Sustainment efforts include the upgrade of the Receive Broadcast Manager GBS application software and the shift to a Digital Video Broadcasting-Satellite-Second Generation (DVB-S2) transmission security-enabled broadcast architecture using a standardized modem to replace in-service integrated receiver decoders. All cruisers and destroyers will be equipped with GBS by FY 2021, with installations concurrent with the AN/W SC-9 Navy Multiband Terminal that will provide the antenna for GBS.

Developers

Raytheon Reston, Virginia

Space and Naval Warfare Systems Command

PEO C4I and PMW/A 170 San Diego, California

USAF Space and Missile Systems Center El Segundo, California

* * * * * * * * * * * *

Global Command and Control System-Maritime (GCCS-M)

Description

Global Command and Control System-Maritime is the maritime implementation of the Department of Defense GCCS family of systems. It supports decision making at all echelons of command with a single, integrated, scalable C4I (command, control, communications, computers, and intelligence) system. The C4I system fuses, correlates, filters, maintains, and displays location and attribute information on friendly, hostile, and neutral land, sea, and air forces, integrated with available intelligence and environmental information. It operates in near real-time and constantly updates unit positions and other situational-awareness data. GCCS-M also records data in databases and maintains a history of changes to those records. System users can then use the data to construct relevant tactical pictures using maps, charts, topography overlays, oceanographic overlays, meteorological overlays, imagery, and all-source intelligence information coordinated into a common operational picture that can be shared locally and with other sites. Navy commanders review and evaluate the general tactical situation, plan actions and operations, direct forces, synchronize tactical movements, and integrate force maneuver with firepower. The system operates in a variety of environments and supports joint, coalition, allied, and multinational forces. GCCS-M is implemented afloat and at select ashore fixed command centers.

Status

The GCCS-M program is designated an Acquisition Category IAC evolutionary acquisition program, with development and implementation progressing in increments. The acquisition strategy calls for each GCCS-M increment (major release) to proceed through acquisition milestone reviews prior to fielding. The program is operating in two simultaneous acquisition increments: Increment 1 (GCCS-M Version 4.0 and prior) is in sustainment; and Increment 2 (GCCS-M Version 4.1) completed a fielding decision review (FDR) on August 16, 2011, resulting in authorization of full fielding of Increment 2 force-level (e.g., aircraft carriers) and unit-level (e.g., guided-missile cruiser) configurations. The Increment 2 group-level configuration completed FDR in December 2014 and full fielding is in progress. Full operational capability is expected in 2023. As of August 2016, the following software variants are in the Fleet: 3.x (1 ship); 4.0.2 (10 ships/9 shore); 4.0.3 (87 ships/44 subs/4 shore); and 4.1 (64 ships/28 subs/9 shore). GCCS-M includes efforts necessary to ensure synchronization and interoperability with the GCCS family of systems.

Developers

Space and Naval Warfare

Systems Center San Diego, California

* * * * * * * * * * * *

Information Systems Security Program (ISSP)

Description

The Navy's Information Systems Security Program ensures protection of Navy and joint cyberspace systems from exploitation and attack. Products and capabilities are provided through development, testing, certification, procurement, installation, and lifecycle support of network and host-based security products and systems. ISSP includes computer network defense (CND), communication security/cryptography, key management infrastructure (KMI), public key infrastructure, cybersecurity services, SHARKCAGE, and Navy cyber situational awareness. Cyberspace systems include wired and wireless telecommunications systems, information technology systems, and the content processed, stored, or transmitted therein. The ISSP includes protection of the Navy's National Security Systems and Information implementation, and provides for procurement of secure communications equipment for Navy and Military Sealift Command ships, shore sites, and aircraft, and Marine Corps and Coast Guard assets. This program also provides cybersecurity capabilities to protect information systems from unauthorized access or unauthorized modification and against the denial of service to authorized users.

Technologies provide greatly improved cyber threat intelligence and situational awareness from external boundaries to tactical edge infrastructures while reducing the complexities of monitoring, assessing, and detecting adversary activities across multiple enclaves. Cybersecurity programs comprise a layered protection strategy using commercial off-the-shelf and government off-the-shelf hardware and soft-ware products that collectively provide multiple levels of security mechanisms to detect and react to intrusions and assure the confidentiality and integrity of information. Cybersecurity is critical in protecting our ability to wage network-centric warfare and in protecting the entire naval cyberspace domain that includes mobile forward-deployed subscribers, shore information infrastructures, and interconnections with other cyberspace domains. Effective cybersecurity capabilities must evolve quickly to meet rapidly evolving advanced threats and new vulnerabilities. The Navy's ISSP will continue to provide tools, technology, cryptographic equipment, security products, operations, people, and services in alignment with the Department of Defense Cybersecurity Program.

Status

The Navy's ISSP is a collection of related abbreviated acquisition programs and projects that provide the full spectrum of cyber-security capabilities. These programs are in various phases of the acquisition process, from concept development through capability sustainment. The ISSP provides Navy warfighters the essential information security characteristics of availability, confidentiality, integrity, authentication, and non-repudiation. CND Increment 2 reached initial operational capability (IOC) in FY 2012 and full operational capability (FOC) in FY 2016. KMI Spiral 2 reached IOC in FY 2016, with FOC scheduled for FY 2018. VINSON/ANDVT (Advanced Narrowband Digital Voice Terminal) Cryptographic Modernization (VACM) reached IOC in FY 2016.

Developers

Georgia Tech Research Institute San Diego, California

MITRE San Diego, California

Raytheon Largo, Florida Space and Naval Warfare

Systems Center Atlantic Charleston, South Carolina

* * * * * * * * * * * *

Integrated Broadcast Service / Joint Tactical Terminal (IBS/JTT)

Description

The Integrated Broadcast Service is an integrated, interactive dissemination system that provides Navy commanders and forces with real-time/near-real-time all-source, multiple-intelligence, intelligence, information, and data allowing for continuous prior-to-mission execution; indications and warning, strategic and threat warning/intelligence, tactical warning and intelligence, time-sensitive targeting, and situational awareness during mission execution; and post-mission assessment and analysis. Legacy IBS will migrate into the Joint Service IBS Common Interactive Broadcast (CIB) waveform incorporating the Common Message Format (CMF). The IBS will send data via communications paths such as ultra-high frequency satellite communications and networks over super-high-frequency, extremely high-frequency, and Global Broadcast Service. The JTT is a multi-channel transmit and receive radio with onboard capabilities to encrypt/ decrypt, filter, process, and translate the IBS data for shipboard use on tactical data processors. The Navy is upgrading in-service fleet inventory of JTT-Maritime systems to implement the CIB waveform and CMF, and demand assigned multiple access integrated waveform capabilities for improved bandwidth use.

Status

The Navy commenced initial shipboard installations of JTT in FY 2001, and 133 JTT-M systems have been fielded as of the end of CY 2016. In order to support the addition of new ships requiring access to near-real-time over-the-air IBS special intelligence, the Navy contracted with Raytheon Space and Airborne Systems to reopen the JTT-Senior production line. This met the increasing fleet, Aegis ballistic missile defense, and Aegis Ashore requirements before ending in FY 2016. The transition to the next-generation Common Interactive Broadcast services began in FY 2013 with the installation of JTT Upgrade Kits for legacy systems, procured from Raytheon via a joint-service contract.

Developers

IBS: L-3 Communications Fairfax, Virginia

JTT: Raytheon Systems St. Petersburg, Florida

* * * * * * * * * * *

Maritime Operations Center (MOC)

Description

Navy maritime operations centers are a warfighting capability of the Navy component commander (NCC) and numbered fleet commander (NFC), organized, trained, manned, and equipped to support commanders' decision-making and set conditions for operational command and control (C2) of naval, joint, interagency, and combined forces. MOCs ensure the Navy's C2 capabilities at the operational level are manned by individuals proficient in joint and naval operational-level staff processes and equipped to provide globally networked, standardized, scalable, and flexible capability across the spectrum of operations. MOCs provide organizational consistency, scalability, and flexibility to transition between various command roles, and enhanced global networking among Navy-maritime organizations. The MOC construct sustains effective, agile, networked, and scalable staffs, employing a standardized system of command, control, communications, computers, intelligence, surveillance, and reconnaissance systems, in accordance with common doctrine and processes. Each MOC supports its NCC/NFC tasked with command and control of Navy and joint forces in joint, interagency, and combined roles. The global network and standardized Core Baseline with Mission Build (CB/MB) systems and applications that enable both reach-back and load sharing between MOCs. Education provided via the Maritime Staff Operators Course provides foundational knowledge in joint and naval operational-level processes and prepares personnel to perform Navy operational-level MOC functions. Training and assist teams from U.S. Fleet Forces Command and the Naval War College provide MOCs with on-site training and assessment and share best practices in order to maintain proficiency in and ability to execute critical staff processes.

Status

Eight Navy operational-level headquarters at nine locations are equipped with the initial MOC CB/MB material baseline. Key MOC baseline systems hardware and software capabilities have been fielded to U.S. Fleet Forces Command, Pacific Fleet, Third Fleet, Naval Forces Southern Command/Fourth Fleet, Naval Forces Central Command/Fifth Fleet, Naval Forces Europe/Africa/ Sixth Fleet (ashore and afloat), Seventh Fleet, and Fleet Cyber Command/ Tenth Fleet. Systems fielded to these MOC locations include the Combined Enterprise Regional Information Exchange System-Maritime, Air Defense System Integrator and Link Monitoring and Management Tool, Radiant Mercury, Maritime Integrated Air and Missile Defense Planning System, Command and Control Battle Management and Communications System, Command and Control Personal Computer, Distributed Common Ground System-Navy, Joint Automated Deep Operations Co-ordination System, Theater Battle Management Core System, and Global Command and Control System-Joint. Support and program wholeness depend on multiple suppliers, joint and Navy programs of record across several interconnected requirements and resource seams.

Developers

DRS Tinker AFB, Oklahoma

Rockwell Collins Richardson, Texas

* * * * * * * * * * * *

Maritime Tactical Command and Control (MTC2)

Description

Maritime Tactical Command and Control is the next generation maritime command and control (C2) software-only solution and the follow-on to the Global Command and Control System-Maritime (GCCS-M) program of record. It provides tactical C2 capabilities and maritime unique operational level of war capabilities not supported by the joint C2 effort. MTC2 will leverage the Integrated Shipboard Network System (ISNS), Consolidated Afloat Networks Enterprise Services (CANES), Afloat Core Services (ACS), Next-Generation Enterprise Network (NGEN), and the Navy Tactical Cloud (NTC). MTC2 will retain capability of GCCS-M 4.1 system while ultimately providing a suite of C2 maritime applications as part of an "application store" concept that enables enhanced situational awareness, planning, execution, monitoring, and assessment of unit mission tasking and requirements. MTC2 will greatly expand the scope of C2 functions across all Navy echelons, from the MOC level to maritime tactical units, afloat and ashore.

Status

MTC2 completed an analysis of alternatives in the third quarter of FY 2013, with the recommendation to satisfy maritime C2 requirements, as defined in the MTC2 Initial Capabilities Document, with the addition of leveraging NTC as an expanded data source. In FY 2014, MTC2 was directed to realign the development and implementation strategy to field in alignment with CANES, Distributed Common Ground System-Navy Inc.2, and Naval Integrated Tactical Environmental System Next (NITES NEXT). An initial build decision is anticipated in FY 2017.

Developers

Space and Naval Warfare

Systems Center Pacific San Diego, California

* * * * * * * * * * *

Mobile User Objective System (MUOS)

Description

The Mobile User Objective System is a next-generation narrowband tactical communications system that improves communications for U.S. forces on the move. The Navy is responsible for providing narrowband satellite communication for the Department of Defense (DoD). Each Service is responsible for procurement of MUOS-capable terminals. In addition to providing reliable communication for all branches of the U.S. military, Navy-delivered space-based narrowband capability provided by MUOS also supports reliable worldwide coverage for national emergency assistance, disaster response, and humanitarian relief when these missions are properly equipped and operated within the bounds of information-assurance policies.

MUOS satellites have a legacy ultra-high-frequency (UHF) payload that provides replacement capability similar to legacy UHF satellites, as well as a new MUOS wideband code division multiple access payload that will provide a significant improvement to the number of simultaneous voice and data services required to meet growing warfighter needs.

The MUOS constellation will consist of five geo-synchronous satellites, one of which is an on-orbit spare. The system also includes four ground stations strategically located and interconnected around the globe to provide worldwide coverage and the ability to connect users to DSN (Defense Switch Network), NIPRNET (Non-secure Internet Protocol), and SIPRNET (Secret Internet Protocol Router Network) services. The ground system transports data, manages the worldwide network, and controls the satellites. The MUOS design leverages commercial technology, providing worldwide netted, point-to-point, and broadcast services of voice, video, and data. Target users are unified commands and joint task force components, DoD and non-DoD agency mobile users that require communications on the move, and allied and coalition legacy users. Legacy narrowband communication system users have to be stationary with an antenna up and pointed toward a satellite. MUOS will provide more than ten times the worldwide capacity and allow the warfighter to move around the battlespace while communicating.

Status

MUOS was designated a DoD major acquisition program in September 2004. Key decision point Milestone C occurred in August 2006, and build approval was granted in February 2008. The first satellite was launched in February 2012 and was accepted for initial operational use supporting legacy terminal users in November 2012. All satellites have been launched with four of five in their final orbital slots. MUOS completed the multi-service operational test and evaluation-2 in April 2016 and has entered an early use period. It provides military users simultaneous voice, video, and data capability by leveraging third-generation mobile communications technology. The MUOS constellation is expected to achieve full operational capability in FY 2019, extending narrowband availability beyond 2028.

Developers

Boeing El Segundo, California

General Dynamics Scottsdale, Arizona

Lockheed Martin Sunnyvale, California

* * * * * * * * * * * *

Navy Air Operations Command and Control (NAOC2)

Description

Navy Air Operations Command and Control program provides task force commanders the ability to plan, disseminate, monitor, and execute theater air battles. NAOC2 capability is provided by the Theater Battle Management Core Systems (TBMCS). TBMCS is an Air Force Acquisition Category III program of record with joint interest. TBMCS is integrated and fielded to enable the air planner to produce the joint air tasking order and air space control order, which give afloat battle staffs and maritime operations centers the capability to lead, monitor, and direct the activities of assigned or attached forces during large-scale combined joint service operations with a joint force air and space component commander (JFACC).

176

Status

TBMCS 1.1.3 is in the operations and sustainment phase. Software and security upgrades are fielded as they become available. The NAOC2 program is integrated and tested within the Navy operational environment for fielding to force-level ships (e.g., aircraft carriers, amphibious assault ships, and command ships), maritime operations centers, and selected training sites. The Air Force's Command and Control Air and Space Operations Suite and Command Control and Information Services programs of record will replace TBMCS. The Air Force will develop these programs in a service-oriented architecture environment, and the Navy will migrate into these programs, which will reside in the Consolidated Afloat Networks and Enterprise Services environment.

Developers

Lockheed Martin Colorado Springs, Colorado

Space and Naval Warfare Systems Center Pacific San Diego, California

* * * * * * * * * * * *

Navy Multi-band Terminal (NMT)

Description

The Navy Multi-band Terminal will be the Navy's primary means of transporting a variety of protected and wideband command, control, and communications (C3) application data (e.g., secure voice, imagery, data, and fleet broadcast systems). It is replacing the USC-38/Follow-on Terminal (FOT) and the WSC-6 super-high-frequency satellite communications (SHF SATCOM) terminals on Navy ships, submarines, and shore stations. It provides access to new MILSATCOM-protected and wideband services provided by the Advanced Extremely High Frequency (EHF) and Wideband Global SATCOM (WGS) satellites. It also increases the number of user accesses and offers increased protected and wideband throughput. NMT enhances space resiliency with improved protected SATCOM capabilities and an anti-jam path through the addition of an SHF wideband anti-jam modem to the program. It is a key element of the Navy's mitigation of warfighting C3 concerns and is an enabler of the ballistic missile defense mission.

The NMT is more reliable with a 22 percent greater designed reliability than predecessor systems. A completely redesigned user interface makes operator-use easier with 85 percent fewer steps in operator terminal interactions. The terminal lowers fleet operating cost by reducing number of parts and terminal footprint on board ships. NMT-equipped units will be able to access military EHF and SHF SATCOM satellites, including protected SATCOM services available on Advanced EHF, Milstar, EHF payloads on board ultra-high-frequency follow-on satellites, Interim and Enhanced Polar EHF payloads. It provides wideband service using the Wideband Global Service and Defense Satellite Communications System satellites. Three international partners—Canada, the Netherlands, and the United Kingdom—are procuring a variant of the NMT. In addition, the Department of Defense Teleport and Enhanced Polar SATCOM system programs have procured NMTs to provide fleet units with shore reach-back capabilities.

Status

On November 8, 2012, NMT entered full-rate production status. As of July 2016, 223 of an objective 250 terminals had been placed under contract. Installations began in February 2012 with 132 ship, submarine, and shore installations completed as of July 2016.

Developers

Raytheon Marlborough, Massachusetts

* * * * * * * * * * * *

Network Tactical Common Data Link (NTCDL)

Description

Navy Common Data Link systems on force-level ships (e.g., aircraft carriers and amphibious assault ships) include the Network Tactical Common Data Link and its predecessor, the Communications Data Link System (CDLS), with Hawklink on unit-level ships (e.g., cruisers and destroyers) and other configurations on Littoral Combat Ships. NTCDL provides the ability to exchange command and control information and transmit/receive realtime intelligence, surveillance, and reconnaissance (ISR) information (voice, data, imagery, and full motion video) simultaneously from multiple sources (air, surface, sub-surface, and man-portable) across dissimilar joint, service, coalition, and civil networks. NTCDL provides warfighters the capability to support multiple, simultaneous, networked operations with in-service common data link (CDL)-equipped aircraft (e.g., P-3 Orion, P-8 Poseidon, and MH-60R Seahawk) in addition to next-generation manned and unmanned platforms (e.g., F-35 Joint Strike Fighter, MQ-4 Triton, MQ-25A Stingray, Small Tactical Unmanned Aircraft Systems, and MQ-8 Fire Scout). NTCDL is a tiered capability providing modular, scalable, multiple-link networked communications. NTCDL benefits the Fleet by providing horizon extension for line-of-sight sensor systems for use in time-critical strike missions, supports maritime superiority requirements through relay capability, and enhances tasking collection processing exploitation dissemination (TCPED) via its ISR networking capability. NTCDL will support multi-simultaneous CDL missions; provide capability for ship-ship, ship-air and air-air communication; facilitate download of ISR information to multiple surface commands (ship/shore); support unmanned aerial vehicles; and support TCPED architecture. NTCDL also supports humanitarian-

179

assistance/disaster-relief efforts through its ability to share ISR data across dissimilar joint, service, coalition, and civil organizations.

Status

In December 2010, the Chief of Naval Operations directed a solution to address the Navy's requirement for multi-simultaneous CDL mission support within the future years defense program. The task was to replace the existing single, point-to-point shipboard CDLS with a multi-point networking system to support ISR transport. Initial investment in 2013 stood up the NTCDL program of record and funded the requirement for NTCDL on board aircraft carriers, with initial operational capability planned for 2019. Future investments will fund requirement for large-deck amphibious ships and develop multi-link NTCDL to meet requirements for use on aircraft, smaller ships, submarines, and shore-based handheld users and mobile platforms.

Developers

BAE Systems Arlington, Virginia

Cubic San Diego, California

Harris Corporation Melbourne, Florida

L3 Communications New York, New York

* * * * * * * * * * * *

Next-Generation Enterprise Network (NGEN)

Description

NGEN is the service contract to operate the Navy-Marine Corps Intranet (NMCI) under a government-owned/contractor-operated model for Navy. NMCI is DoD's largest single network, delivering some 300,000 seats to more than 700,000 Navy users. NGEN includes the existing NMCI network and services; improves operational control, governance, security posture, and integrated operations capabilities; and supports alignment with DoD's joint information environment (JIE). This construct provides enhanced network command and control (C2), improved cybersecurity, and more flexibility. The NGEN program supports user access to protected voice, video, and data services over continental United States (CONUS) Navy ashore unclassified and classified networks. This provides the secure net-centric data and information technology services to the Navy and Marine Corps.

Status

The NGEN contract ends in June 2018. The Department of the Navy is working on the follow-on ashore IT enterprise contract, NGEN Re-compete. Under the new contract the Navy's outside of the U.S. enterprise will be merged with CONUS to standardize the ashore enterprise globally.

Developers

HP Enterprise Services Plato, Texas

* * * * * * * * * * * *

OCONUS Navy Enterprise Network (ONE-NET)

Description

181

The outside of the continental United States (OCONUS) Navy Enterprise Network (ONE-NET) provides the manpower and administration services to operate the Base Level Information Infrastructure (BLII) architecture, a fully integrated and interoperable network that consists of standard hardware, software, and information-assurance suites governed by operational and administrative policies and procedures. ONE-NET is the OCONUS equivalent to the Navy's CONUS-based enterprise services and is the medium that enables the rapid and reliable transfer of official classified and unclassified messages, collaboration, e-mail, and data. ONE-NET manpower provides information technology (IT) operations including e-mail, print, storage, directory, and Internet services, as well as help desk and enterprise management for approximately 28,000 seats, delivering vast performance and security improvements compared to legacy networks. ONE-NET manages the enterprise through three Theater Network Operation and Security Centers (TNOSCs) at Yokosuka, Japan; Naples, Italy; and Bahrain; in addition to 11 Local Network Support Centers (LNSCs) within their respective regions.

Status

The program provides IT services to approximately 28,000 BLII/ ONE-NET seats, supporting approximately 51,000 forward-deployed OCONUS Navy users. Fleet Cyber Command operates the three TNOSCs and 11 LNSCs servicing ONE-NET customers. The network is operated and maintained by a blended workforce of active duty, civilian, and contractor personnel. This program is expected to transition into the Next-Generation Enterprise Network follow-on contract by the end of FY 2018. This merger will realize efficiencies and standardization associated with a centrally managed program.

Developers

Computer Sciences Corporation Falls Church, Virginia

* * * * * * * * * * * *

Submarine Communications Equipment

Description

The goal of the Submarine Communications Equipment program is to create a common, automated, open-system architecture radio room for all submarine classes. The program provides for the procurement and installation of systems incorporating the technical advances of network centric warfare to allow the submarine force to communicate as part of the strike group. It addresses the unique demands of submarine communications, obsolescence issues, and higher data rate requirements and includes two elements: common submarine radio room (CSRR) and submarine antennas.

CSRR is a network-centric communications gateway that supports interoperable communications and information warfare between on-board subsystems, external platforms, and land-based communications facilities and is interoperable with Department of Defense (DoD) infrastructure. CSRR comprises an open-architecture hardware and software approach for integrating government-off-the-shelf, commercial-off-the-shelf, and non-developmental item hardware and application-specific software into a common, centrally managed architecture. CSRR leverages existing Navy and DoD C4I (command, control, communications, computers, and intelligence) capability-based acquisition programs. CSRR allows common systems, software, and equipment to be installed on all submarine classes, use of common logistics products across all submarine classes, and the uniform training of personnel across all submarine classes, resulting in new capability at a reduced cost.

The submarine antennas programs support the development and sustainment of antennas designed to withstand the underwater environment. These antennas cover the frequency spectrum from very-flow-frequency to optical. Programs in the development phase include OE-538 Increment II Multi-function Mast, and Submarine High-Data-Rate (SubHDR) antenna. The improvements to the OE-538 Multi-Function Mast antenna support Mobile User Objective System, Link-16, Global Positioning System Anti-Jam, and Iridium capabilities. The SubHDR antenna is receiving improved radome and shock hardening.

Status

CSRR Increment I Version 3 began fielding in FY 2011 and is scheduled to complete in FY 2019. OE-538 Increment II achieved Milestone C decision in July 2015. SubHDR radome replacement began fielding in FY 2014.

Developers

Lockheed Martin Eagan, Minnesota

Lockheed Martin Sippican Marion, Massachusetts

Naval Undersea Warfare Center Newport, Rhode Island

Space and Naval Warfare Systems Center San Diego, California

* * * * * * * * * * * *

Super-High-Frequency Satellite Communications (SHF SATCOMS)

Description

The Super-High-Frequency Satellite Communications program includes: the WSC-6(V) 5, 7, and 9 terminals; the X-Band Kit Upgrade to the Extremely-High-Frequency Follow-On Terminal installed on submarines; and the enhanced bandwidth efficient modem installed on surface ships. The SHF SATCOM WSC-6 terminal is the primary SATCOM terminal in the Fleet, providing the bandwidth for voice, video, data, and imagery requirements for the warfighter, including NIPRNET (Non-secure Internet Protocol), SIPRNET (Secret Internet Protocol Router Network), JWICS (Joint Worldwide Intelligence Communications System), JCA (Joint Concentrator Architecture), video teleconferencing, and telephones. These SHF system terminals have been in the Fleet since the early 1990s and are in sustainment.

The Navy Multiband Terminal (NMT) WSC-9 is replacing the WSC-6 terminals. As of August 2016, 56 of 128 terminals have been replaced and an additional 55 terminals will be installed by 2024. Two of the terminals will not be replaced because their platforms will decommission prior to FY 2024. The remaining 15 terminals (LCS 02-16) have not yet been added to the NMT inventory objective for replacement.

Status

Program is in sustainment.

Developers

WSC-6(V) 5, 7: Raytheon Marlborough, Massachusetts

184

WSC-6(V) 9: Harris Melbourne, Florida

X-Band Kit Upgrade: Raytheon Marlborough, Massachusetts

* * * * * * * * * * *

Tactical Messaging Description

Command and Control Official Information Exchange (C2OIX) provides the Navy with organizational messaging services and interfaces with the worldwide Department of Defense consumers, such as tactical deployed users, designated federal government organizations, and allies. C2OIX Afloat consists of the Navy Modular Automated Communications System (NAVMACS), a shipboard message processing system that guards broadcast channels and provides the only General Service Top Secret level communications path on and off the ship. C2OIX Shore provides the shore-messaging infrastructure via C2OIX Version 3.x at the Naval Computer and Telecommunications Area Master Stations (NCTAMS).

Status

The C2OIX project combined the Tactical Messaging (ACAT IVT) and the Defense Message System (DMS) (ACAT IVM) into a single service life extension project supporting all Navy messaging requirements, providing organizational C2 messages to shore, afloat, and mobile Navy users. Afloat component NAVMACS II is in the operations and sustainment phase to technically refresh all shipboard systems that lack support and adherence to in-place cyber security requirements. Shore components are in the operations and sustainment phase, and C2OIX is fielded on three enclaves (NIPR, SIPR and TS) at the NCTAMS, Atlantic and Pacific.

Developers

General Dynamics Taunton, Massachusetts

Scientific Research Corporation Charleston, South Carolina

* * * * * * * * * * * *

Tactical Mobile (TacMobile)

Description

The Navy Tactical Mobile program provides systems to support maritime commanders with the capability to plan, direct, and control the tactical operations of maritime patrol and reconnaissance forces (MPRF), joint and naval expeditionary forces, and other assigned units within their respective areas of responsibility. The TacMobile systems that support these missions are the tactical operations centers (TOCs) and mobile tactical operations centers (MTOCS). TOCs and MTOCs provide MPRF and aircraft (MPRA) operational support ashore at main operating bases, primary deployment sites and forward-operating bases that are similar to support provided on board an aircraft carrier to embarked tactical air wings. Support includes persistent situational operational and tactical awareness, MPRA pre-mission coordination and planning, mission and target briefings, tactical in-light support, post-mission analysis of collected sensor data, data dissemination, and feedback to aircraft sensor operators and supported commanders. Services provided include: analysis and correlation of diverse sensor information; data management support; command decision aids; data communication; mission planning, evaluation, and dissemination of surveillance data; and threat alerts to operational users ashore and afloat. As advances in sensor technology are fielded on MPRF/MPRA, TOC and MTOC sensor analysis equipment will evolve to support the new sensor capabilities.

Status

TacMobile Increment 2.1 full-rate production and fielding were authorized in November 2012 to field new capabilities incorporating P-8A Poseidon multi-mission maritime aircraft mission support, applications and systems interfaces as well as critical communications upgrades needed for TOCs and MTOCs to support P-8A intelligence surveillance and reconnaissance operations. Increment 2.1 achieved initial operational capability in October 2013 and reached full operational capability in FY 2016. Development is ongoing, and fielding is commencing to support P-8A Increment 2 engineering change proposals and MQ-4C Triton unmanned aircraft system to achieve more efficient information flow across the Navy's sensor grid through implementation of tactical service-oriented architecture enabled by the global information grid. Joint Capabilities Integration and Development System documentation will identify requirements for Increment 3 to support P-8A and MQ-4C multi-intelligence-upgrade.

Developers

Northrop Grumman Hollywood, Maryland

Science Applications

International Corporation Charleston, South Carolina

Space and Naval Warfare

Systems Center Atlantic Charleston, South Carolina

* * * * * * * * * * *

Telephony

Description

The Department of Defense (DoD), Chief Information Officer (CIO) Memorandum of November 5, 2015 "DoD CIO Capability Priorities for Fiscal Years 2018-2022" lists as a priority the modernization of network infrastructure to be regionally based, centrally managed, and cyber secure. This includes migrating existing infrastructure from time division multiplexing (TDM) to internet protocol (IP) based communications to enable unified capabilities. Telephony procures and integrates commercial-off-the-shelf (COTS) hardware and software to meet the DoD-CIO TDM-to-IP mandate for the Navy. These IP-capable switches will service TDM systems and facilitate connectivity to Public Switched Telephone Network, Navy Marine Corps Intranet, and outside the continental United States (OCONUS) Navy Enterprise Network. All efforts are performed in accordance with policy and procedures articulated in Department of Defense Instruction (DoDI) 8100.03, Chairman of the Joint Chiefs of Staff Instruction

(CJCSI) 6212.01 and CJCSI 6215.01D and DoD Unified Capabilities Requirement 2013. Specific Telephony capabilities include: Voice over Internet Protocol; Voice over Secure Internet Protocol; Video Teleconferencing over Secure Internet Protocol; Telephony unified Messaging System; Regional Telephony Management System; Navy Video Conferencing System and NVCS Coalition; IP Trunking; Aegis Ashore; Telephony systems infrastructure (e.g. cable plant); C2 voice communications to the Navy warfighter, including multi-level precedence and preemption; Telecommunications engineering support for Base Communications Office locations; and C2 shore-to-ship dial tone "Plain Old Telephone Service" and pier side lines via tactical networks and infrastructure. Telephony system installations and/or upgrades are being implemented at facilities in accordance with requirements as identified by Navy Information Warfare Forces, Office of the Chief of Naval Operations, and Missile Defense Agency (e.g., fleet network operations centers, fleet telecommunications sites, and Aegis Ashore sites).

Status

Telephony is modernizing the CONUS/OCONUS infrastructure from legacy TDM to IP capability to support unified capabilities requirements. As Telephony capabilities migrate to IP-based transport, telephony services will become increasingly dependent on Navy Enterprise Services.

Developers - Space and Naval Warfare Systems; Command, PEO C4I and PMW790 San Diego, California

BATTLESPACE AWARENESS

Airborne ASW Intelligence (AAI)

Description

Airborne anti-submarine warfare (ASW) intelligence rapidly develops and fields prototype ASW acoustic intelligence (ACINT) systems that collect, process, exploit, and disseminate intelligence in order to exploit threat submarine vulnerabilities. AAI is responsible for 70 percent of the Navy's acoustic intelligence collections, 100 percent of active target strength measurement (ATSM) collections, and 100 percent of submarine electromagnetic collections. Additionally, AAI enables environmental characterization as well as rapid prototyping and deployment of advanced ASW capabilities. AAI collections provide input to the Navy's ASW tactical decision aids, oceanographic prediction models, strategic simulations, fleet ASW training, and the development of future ASW sensors. The program additionally supports emergent and special ASW operations. In-service AAI collection platforms in late 2016 include the P-3C Orion and P-8A Poseidon. AAI will also equip the MH-60R Seahawk helicopter for ACINT collections. AAI provides rapid turn-around of tactical intelligence products to Theater ASW commanders for inclusion into tactical decision aids and for all ASW engineering disciplines for performance improvements and development of next-generation ASW weapons systems.

Status

The Airborne ASW Intelligence program maintains calibration of all P-8A and P-3C systems in support of acoustic collections. The program is recapitalizing the Navy Underwater Active Multiple Ping (NUAMP) family of sonobuoys that enables calibrated active sonar measurement of threat submarines for the improvement of

ASW modeling, simulations, and weapons systems. In FY 2016, the program designed, developed, and conducted engineering analysis for certification of NUAMP F4/5 sonobuoy and the Acoustic Intelligence Collection Suite (ACS) Block II to be used onboard P-8A, P-3C, and other platforms. NUAMP F1 design and development began in FY 2016 and will complete engineering analysis for certification in FY 2017. AAI will analyze the MH-60R acoustic system for platform certification. The program will continue to make improvements to the Tactical Acoustic Processing Suite used to conduct detailed analysis and mission reconstruction of collected acoustic intelligence data against real-world submarines.

Developers

EAGLE Systems Lexington Park, Maryland

ERAPSCO Columbia City, Indiana

* * * * * * * * * * * *

EP-3E ARIES II Spiral 3

Description

The EP-3E ARIES II aircraft is the Navy's manned airborne intelligence, surveillance, reconnaissance, and targeting (AISR&T) platform supporting naval and joint commanders. EP-3Es provide long-range, high-endurance support to carrier strike groups and amphibious readiness groups, in addition to performing independent maritime operations. The late 2016 force consists of one active-duty squadron based at Naval Air Station Whidbey Island, Washington. Although optimized for the maritime and littoral environments, capability upgrades have ensured EP-3E mission effectiveness in support of global contingency operations. The fusion of internet protocol (IP) connectivity, the incorporation of imagery intelligence capability, and completion of significant signals intelligence (SIGINT) upgrades enables continued alignment with the Intelligence Community and the early implementation of a distributed SIGINT concept of operations. Multi-INT sensors, robust communication and data links, and employment on the flexible and dependable P-3C Orion aircraft ensure effective AISR&T support to conventional and non-conventional warfare forces across the range of military operations. With the EP-3E scheduled for retirement after meeting operational requirements through FY 2020, the Navy is focused on sustainment and modernization to pace emerging threats until transitioning the capabilities across the spectrum of manned and unmanned platforms.

Status

EP-3E aircraft are being sustained through a series of special structural inspections (SSIs) and replacement of outer wing assemblies (OWAs). SSIs and OWAs provide the inspections and repairs necessary to ensure safety of light until more comprehensive maintenance can be performed. The pre-emptive modification and replacement of critical structural components allows up to 7,000 additional light hours. These programs ensure sustainment of the EP-3E fleet until the capability is recapitalized across the spectrum of manned and unmanned platforms.

The EP-3E Joint Airborne SIGINT Architecture Modification Common Configuration (JCC) program accelerates the introduction of advanced capabilities to the AISR&T Fleet. The resultant program aligns mission systems to meet the challenges of rapidly emerging threat technology and addresses obsolescence issues. Spiral developments have modernized the aircraft systems. The aircraft is also equipped with forward-looking infrared and remote reach-back capabilities. Recapitalization capabilities migration will allow continued development of the EP-3E and vital testing of equipment designed for use in the next generation of intelligence, surveillance, reconnaissance, and targeting platforms. The final EP-3E will complete the latest JCC upgrade, JCC Spiral 3, in third quarter FY 2017. JCC Spiral 3 enables the EP-3E to pace the enemy threat by providing faster, more precise geo-location capability for better precision targeting, indications and warning, and direct threat warning that can match rapidly developing threat technology.

Developers

Aeronixs Melbourne, Florida

Argon-ST / Boeing Fairfax, Virginia

L3 Communications Waco, Texas

Ticom Geomatics Austin, Texas

* * * * * * * * * * * *

Fixed Surveillance Systems (FSS)

Description

The Fixed Surveillance Systems program consists of the Sound Surveillance System (SOSUS), the Fixed Distributed System (FDS), and the FDS-Commercial (FDS-C), a commercial off-the-shelf version of FDS. FSS provides threat location information to tactical forces and contributes to an accurate operational maritime picture for the joint force commander. FSS comprises a series of arrays deployed on the ocean floor in deep-ocean areas and strategic locations. Due to its long in-situ lifetime, it provides indications and warning of hostile maritime activity before

191

conflicts begin. The system consists of two segments: the integrated common processor (ICP), which handles the processing, display, and communication functions; and the underwater segment, which consists of SOSUS, a long array of hydrophones, and FDS or FDS-C. FSS leverages advances made in the commercial industry to provide a more cost-effective FDS caliber system to meet the Fleet's ongoing needs for long-term undersea surveillance.

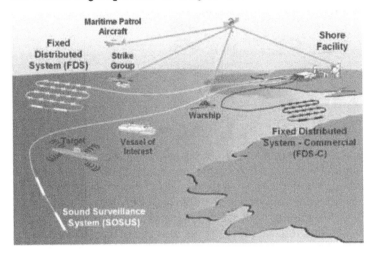

Status

ICP technical refreshes are installed as required to provide increased operator efficiency, functionality, and savings in logistics support and software maintenance.

Developers

Multiple sources.

Large Displacement Unmanned Undersea Vehicle (LDUUV)

Description

The Large Displacement Unmanned Undersea Vehicle will provide a robust, long-endurance, persistent, multi-mission, unmanned undersea vehicle capability for the Navy. Like all unmanned undersea systems, LDUUV will expand the undersea forces' operating envelope. LDUUV will complement and augment manned undersea platforms by conducting "dull, dirty, dangerous, and distant" operations, freeing up manned platforms to perform higher-complexity missions. Subsurface and surface platforms will launch and recover the LDUUV. The LDUUV strategy leverages our investments and development efforts across industry, academia and the naval research and development establishment, specifically the efforts by the Office of Naval Research (ONR) LDUUV Innovative Naval Prototype program that started in FY 2011.

Status

The LDUUV completed Milestone A in the fall 2015, after the service capability development document and concept of operations were approved. In 2016, ONR redirected program efforts from award of a contract to industry for engineering development models to a government-led systems integration of prototypes. The prototypes will be delivered in two phases, with industry contributing key enabling technologies.

Developers

To be determined.

* * * * * * * * * * *

MQ-4C Triton Unmanned Aircraft System (UAS)

Description

The MQ-4C Triton UAS is a key element in the recapitalization of the Navy's maritime patrol and reconnaissance force (MPRF) airborne intelligence, surveillance, and reconnaissance (ISR) capability. Triton will be a force multiplier for joint force and fleet commanders, enhancing their situational awareness and shortening the sensor-to-shooter kill chain by providing a multiple-sensor, persistent maritime ISR capability. Triton's persistent-sensor dwell and ability to network its data, deliver a capability that will enable the MPRF family of systems to meet the Navy's maritime ISR requirements. A single Triton orbit provides continuous surveillance capability at a maximum mission radius of 2,000 nautical miles for a minimum of 24 hours. At full operational capability, the system will provide up to five simultaneous orbits worldwide.

Status

The MQ-4C Triton UAS achieved Milestone B in April 2008 and critical design review completed February 2011. Triton's first flight occurred on May 23, 2013, and initial envelope-expansion lights completed in March 2014. Sensor integration began in December 2014 at Naval Air Station Patuxent River, Maryland. The operational assessment completed November 2015. Milestone C is expected in 2016 along with entry into the production and deployment phase. A baseline Triton early operational capability (EOC) is planned for FY 2018 to be replaced by a Multi-INT Triton EOC in FY 2020. Initial operation test and evaluation begins in FY 2020, and initial operational capability is planned for FY 2021.

Developers

Exelis Baltimore, Maryland

L3COM Salt Lake, Utah

Northrop Grumman Bethpage, New York

Rolls Royce Indianapolis, Indiana

* * * * * * * * * * * *

MQ-8B/C Fire Scout Vertical Takeoff and Landing Tactical UAV (VTUAV) System

Description

The MQ-8B/C Fire Scout VTUAV System is a component of the Navy's airborne intelligence, surveillance, and reconnaissance (ISR) family of systems. The MQ-8 provides day and night real-time ISR target acquisition—using the Brite Star II turret electro-optical/infrared/laser designator-range finder payload and maritime search radar—along with other modular mission-specific payloads for voice communications relay and battlefield management support to the tactical commander. Fielded in two variants (B and C), Fire Scout can operate at a maximum range of up to 150 nautical miles with an endurance of some 12 hours, depending on payload, environment, and air vehicle variant. The VTUAV System comprises one or more air vehicles, a mission control station, UAV common automatic recovery system, tactical common data link, and tactical control system software interface for operator control of the air vehicle. Dual-qualified (MH-60R/S helicopter and MQ-8 VTUAV) members of an aviation detachment from the expeditionary rotary-wing communities operate and maintain the system. The system will conduct launch, recovery, and mission command and-control functions from the Littoral Combat Ship (LCS) or any suitably equipped air-capable ship; it can also be flown from sites ashore to support land-based expeditionary operations. Fire Scout will complement the LCS surface warfare and mine countermeasures mission modules of the LCS or other surface platforms. Additionally, the air vehicle's open architecture will accommodate modular payloads and facilitate integrating future capabilities to support other warfare areas as technologies mature.

Status

The Navy terminated production of the MQ-8B in FY 2011 in favor of a more capable airframe. The decision to terminate MQ-8B production was in response to a joint emergent operational need and payload, range, and endurance upgrades to the Bell 407 (MQ-8C) platform to replace the Schweizer 333-based model (MQ-8B). Flight-testing the MQ-8C began in October 2013 in preparation for its fleet introduction. Additionally, integration and developmental testing of radar and an advanced precision-kill systems continue. Through FY 2016 Fire Scout logged more than 15,000 total light hours, including ten deployments on board Oliver Hazard Perry (FFG 7)-class frigates and two on Littoral Combat Ships.

Developers

Bell Helicopter Ozark, Alabama

Northrop Grumman San Diego, California

Raytheon Falls Church, Virginia

Sikorsky Aircraft Corporation Stratford, Connecticut

* * * * * * * * * * * *

RQ-7B Shadow Unmanned Air System (STUAS)

Description

The RQ-7B Shadow provides intelligence, surveillance, and reconnaissance (ISR) for Marine Corps forces. By partnering with the Army, the Marine Corps realizes fiscal and programmatic efficiencies. Shadow provides day/night full motion video, laser designation, and radio relay to USMC and other ground combat forces, and is fielded to four Marine unmanned aerial vehicle (VMU) squadrons, each of which has three systems.

Status

The RQ-7B is a Group 3 UAS Army ACAT 1C program. It is in its sustainment phase and is completing the Tactical Common Data Link upgrade. This modification not only incorporates the encrypted data link, but it also upgrades many other parts of the system for improved efficiency and increased capability. Two of the VMU squadrons have received the updated systems and a third VMU begins transition in FY 2018. In 2016, Shadow systems surpassed 1 million light hours in combined Army and Marine Corps service.

Developers

Textron Systems Unmanned Systems Hunt Valley, Maryland

* * * * * * * * * * * *

RQ-21 Blackjack Small Tactical Unmanned Air System (STUAS)

Description

The Blackjack system is an asset organic to Navy Special Warfare, Navy Expeditionary Combat Command, and Whidbey Island (LSD 41)-class ships to provide tactical intelligence, surveillance, and reconnaissance capability. Blackjack vehicles are equipped with electro-optic/infrared sensors, laser range finders and illuminators, automatic Identification system (AIS), and a communications relay. A system consists of five air vehicles, one (ship) or two (shore ground) control stations, launch and recovery system, spare parts, and government furnished equipment. The Blackjack is a 75-pound/16-foot wingspan vehicle (135 pounds fully loaded) capable of 15 hours endurance at 55 knots at altitudes higher than 15,000 feet.

Status

Marine Corps initial operational capability (IOC) was declared in the second quarter FY 2016. Navy IOC is expected in the fourth quarter FY 2017.

Developers

HoodTech Hood River, Oregon

Insitu, Inc. Bingen, Washington

Northwest UAV Propulsion Systems Portland, Oregon

Quatro Composites Poway, California

UQQ-2 Surveillance Towed Array Sensor System (SURTASS)

Description

The UQQ-2 Surveillance Towed Array Sensor System consists of a fleet of five ships that provide passive detection of nuclear and diesel-electric powered submarines, and real-time reporting to theater commanders and operational units. SURTASS employs the TL-29A twin-line acoustic towed array, which offers passive detection capability for undersea surveillance operations in both deep-ocean and shallow-water littoral environments using directional noise rejection and a bearing ambiguity resolution capability.

Status

Five SURTASS vessels are operational in the Pacific Fleet. All have TL-29A twin-line arrays and have been upgraded with the integrated common processor (ICP), which will result in increased operator proficiency, functionality, and savings in logistics support and software maintenance. Technical refreshes to ICP hardware will be installed to meet future requirements.

Developers

Lockheed Martin Manassas, Virginia

Syracuse, New York

* * * * * * * * * * *

WQT-2 Surveillance Towed Array Sensor System (SURTASS) / Flow Frequency Active (LFA)

Description

The Flow Frequency Active system is the active adjunct to the Surveillance Towed Array Sensor System sonar system. LFA consists of a vertical source array with active transducers, power amplifiers, and an array-handling system. The LFA transmit array is deployed through a center well hatch of T-AGOS oceanographic survey ships. It uses the SURTASS passive array as the receiver and is capable of long-range detections of submarine and surface ship contacts. A mobile system, SURTASS LFA can be employed as a force-protection sensor wherever the force commander directs, including forward operating areas or in support of carrier strike group and amphibious ready group operations.

Status

One LFA array system is installed on board the USNS Impeccable (T-AGOS 23). The Compact LFA (CLFA) system, employing smaller and lighter sources, has been installed on the USNS Victorious (T-AGOS 19), USNS Able (T-AGOS 20), and USNS Effective (T-AGOS 21). Technical refreshes to the integrated common processor are installed to maintain increased operator proficiency and functionality.

Developers

BAE Systems Manchester, New Hampshire

198

Lockheed Martin Manassas, Virginia

* * * * * * * * * * * *

INTEGRATED FIRES

Advanced Tactical Data Link Systems (ATDLS)

Description

The ATDLS program provides tactical data link (TDL) command and control (C2) for U.S. forces, allies, and coalition partners in accordance with the Joint Tactical Data Enterprise Services Migration Plan (JTMP). ATDLS sustains and improves existing networks while developing future networks. Joint TDLs (Link-11, Link-16, and Link-22) include terminals, gateways, networks, and support initiatives that improve connectivity, interoperability, training, and support. Link-16 is the Department of Defense's (DoD) primary TDL implemented to most TDL-capable platforms and some munitions for specific applications. Link-22 is a multi-national development effort replacing Link-11 with a more suitable high-frequency protocol using a message format similar to Link-16. Terminals include the Joint Tactical Information Distribution System (JTIDS) and Multi-functional Information Distribution System (MIDS), which provide a Link-16 capability for C2 of aircraft, ships, and ground sites. Gateways include the Command and Control Processor (C2P), the Air Defense System Integrator (ADSI), and the Link Monitoring and Management Tool (LMMT).

MIDS-Flow Volume Terminal (MIDS-LVT): The MIDS-LVT is smaller and lighter than Joint Tactical Information Distribution System (JTIDS) terminals. The MIDS-LVT is managed by the MIDS International Program Office (IPO). The IPO is governed by a Steering Committee with a five-country program memorandum of understanding signed by France, Germany, Italy, Spain and the United States. More than 10,000 MIDS-LVTs are in use by the United States and more than 40 allies and partners.

MIDS Joint Tactical Radio System (JTRS): The MIDS JTRS terminal was built as a multi-channel, software-defined variant of MIDS-LVT, and includes Link-16 Enhanced Throughput (LET), Frequency Remapping (FR), and Crypto Modernization (CM). MIDS JTRS adds capacity for three waveforms in addition to Link-16. Command and Control Processor (C2P)/Common Data Link Management

System (CDLMS) is a TDL communication processor associated with host combat systems, such as Aegis or the Ship Self-Defense System.

The in-service system (often called the Next-Generation C2P) provides extended-range capabilities and improved operator interfaces through an incremental approach for capability enhancements and technology refresh. C2P is adding Link-22 capability through its next major upgrade. ADSI is a time-sensitive tactical C2, commercial off-the-shelf system providing for processing and display of multiple TDL interfaces, data forwarding, and TDL information to the Global Command and Control System-Maritime (GCCS-M). LMMT is a network monitoring management and communications system to meet emerging maritime operations center (MOC) C2 multi-mission TDL requirements and address the shortcomings of existing systems, such as ADSI.

Status

JTIDS/MIDS on Ships (MOS): Planned updates to JTIDS/MOS terminals will satisfy National Security Agency (NSA) cryptographic modernization and DoD/Department of Transportation (DoT) frequency remapping mandates, with an initial operational capability (IOC) planned for FY 2018. Program management and acquisition authority for JTIDS/MOS is under the Link-16 Network Program.

DNM: Time Slot Reallocation (TSR) achieved IOC on ships in the C2P and JTIDS programs in FY 2007. TSR fielded on E-2C, EA-6B, and H-60 aircraft in FY 2009, and is scheduled to field on other joint platforms such as E-3 and E-8. DNM achieved Milestone C in 2014 and is scheduled for full-deployment decision review/IOC in FY 2017, and full operational capability (FOC) in FY 2018.

MIDS-LVT: Block Upgrade 2 (BU2) to MIDS-LVT, planned for completion in 2017-2018, will add three major features through retrofits to existing terminals. First, BU2 will include a LET mode that will increase data rates available to platforms from three to ten times the existing waveform capacity. Second, the built-in cryptography is being modernized to implement next-generation NSA algorithms, keys, and security features, including field-upgradability of crypto logic. Third, BU2 will implement FR to satisfy a DoD and DoT agreement to more easily share part of Link-16's radio spectrum with planned civil aviation systems by 2025. The maturity of the MIDS architecture makes it possible to implement these features without requiring changes to host platform interfaces and while maintaining interoperability with other Link-16 radios.

MIDS JTRS: The more modular design of MIDS JTRS has facilitated the rapid incorporation of new technology, such as Four Net Concurrent Multi-Netting (CMN-4) with Concurrent Contention Receive (CCR). CMN-4 consists of two capabilities, CMN and CCR, which dramatically expand the number of platforms and network-enabled systems that can be reliably included in a Link-16 network. These enhancements allow a single MIDS JTRS terminal to receive up to four messages (compared with just one today) within a single Link-16 time slot, allowing a user to "hear" messages from up to three additional sources at once. The fielding of this capability, planned for 2017, will support Naval Integrated Fire Control-Counter Air (NIFC-CA). The flexibility of the MIDS JTRS design has been demonstrated through the application of several capability enhancements, including the addition of a new waveform, Tactical Targeting Network Technology (TTNT), which is planned for fielding in 2021. MIDS JTRS will realize its multi-channel potential with the addition of TTNT, a high-bandwidth, flow-latency, internet protocol-capable waveform. The TTNT waveform augments existing Link-16 CMN-4 capability to provide increased capacity to support NIFC-CA and offensive anti-surface warfare mission capabilities.

C2P: C2P Legacy, C2P Rehost, and C2P Increment 1 have completed fielding and are in the operations and support phase. C2P Increment 2 achieved full rate production in July 2008 and will achieve full operational capability and transition to the operations and sustainment phase by FY 2016 as per the in-service shipboard architecture upgrade plan. C2P Increment 3 began development in FY 2013.

North Atlantic Treaty Organization Improved Link Eleven (NILE): NILE partner countries have fielded Link-22 in a limited number of ships and shore sites. Link-22 capability will be implemented in NGC2P as Increment 3, with development work having commenced in FY 2013 and IOC planned for FY 2019.

ADSI: ADSI Version 14 is in fielding in late 2016. ADSI Version 15 testing is complete and limited fielding commenced in FY 2014. The program intends to supplement/replace certain ADSI systems with the Link Monitoring and Management Tool capability.

Developers

Data Link Solutions Wayne, New Jersey

Northrop Grumman San Diego, California

Rockwell Collings Cedar Rapids, Iowa

ViaSat Carlsbad, California

* * * * * * * * * * * *

Cooperative Engagement Capability (CEC)

Description

Cooperative Engagement Capability provides improved battle force air-defense capabilities by integrating sensor data of each cooperating ship, aircraft and ground station into a single, real-time, fire-control-quality, composite track picture. CEC is a critical pillar of the Naval Integrated Fire Control-Counter Air (NIFC-CA) capability and provides a significant contribution to the Joint Integrated Fire Control (JIFC) operational architecture. CEC interfaces the weapons and sensor capabilities of each CEC-equipped ship and aircraft in the strike group, as well as ground mobile units in support of integrated engagement capability. By simultaneously distributing sensor data on airborne threats to each ship within a strike group, CEC extends the range at which a ship can engage hostile tracks to beyond the radar horizon, significantly improving area, local, and self-defense capabilities. CEC enables a strike group or joint task force to act as a single, geographically distributed combat system. CEC provides the Fleet with greater defense in-depth and the mutual support required to confront evolving anti-ship cruise missile and theater ballistic missile threats.

Status

The Defense Acquisition Board approved full-rate production for CEC shipboard and flow-rate initial production for E-2C Hawkeye airborne equipment in April 2002. In September 2003, the Defense Department approved FY 2004/2005 follow-on production for the USG-3 and full-rate production in April 2014 for the airborne version. There are 160 installations (76 ships, 52 aircraft, eight JLENS, ten USMC composite tracking networks, and 14 land-based test sites) as of August 2016. Total future CEC installation is planned for 283 ships, aircraft, and land units. Successful operational testing on the most recent CEC shipboard system was completed on board the USS Princeton (CG 59) in December 2015. Testing has commenced on the USS John Paul Jones (DDG 53) and is expected to be complete by late FY 2017. Live-fire NIFC-CA From-The-Sea testing is scheduled to continue with approximately one event every six-to-nine months through FY 2022.

Developers

Johns Hopkins University Applied

Physics Laboratory Laurel, Maryland

Raytheon Systems Company St. Petersburg, Florida

Sechan Electronics Inc. Lititz, Pennsylvania

* * * * * * * * * * *

Distributed Common Ground System-Navy (DCGS-N)

Description

Distributed Common Ground System-Navy is the Navy component of the Department of Defense (DoD) DCGS family of systems. It is the Service's primary intelligence, surveillance, reconnaissance, and targeting (ISR&T) support system, and provides processing, exploitation, and dissemination services at the operational and tactical levels of war. DCGS-N operates at the secret and sensitive compartmented information (SCI) security levels. DCGS-N makes maximum use of commercial-off-the-shelf (COTS) and mature government-off-the-shelf (GOTS) hardware and software along with joint services software, tools, and standards to provide a scalable, modular, extensible multi-source capability that is interoperable with the other service and agency DCGS systems.

DCGS-N Increment 1 (Inc 1) replaces all legacy Joint Service Imagery Processing System-Navy and SCI Global Command and Control Maritime systems. The DCGS-N Inc 1 Block 2 capability will be hosted by Consolidated Afloat Networks and Enterprise Services and provide users with an integrated ISR suite.

DCGS-N Increment 2 (Inc 2) will provide an enterprise solution to fulfill specific capability gaps. This includes the ability to integrate and automate all-source fusion and analysis capabilities; enhance tasking, collection, processing, exploitation, and dissemination (TCPED) capabilities via automation of workflow processes; and sustain and enhance maritime domain awareness capabilities. Inc 2 will share information across commands, services, and agencies to improve situational awareness in accordance with emerging joint information environment and intelligence community information technology enterprise concepts. Inc 2 will be a robust, integrated ISR&T capability that is a scalable, modular, and extensible multi-source capability and interoperable with Navy and joint ISR, sensor and infrastructure capabilities. Ashore, DCGS-N Inc 2 will provide maritime operations centers and intelligence organizations the ability to collaborate in the exploitation, analysis, production, and dissemination of intelligence at the ashore enterprise node. The enterprise node will provide an all-source cross-cueing capability that improves the workflow automation for TCPED for Navy Intelligence analysts. Additionally, Inc 2 will provide all-source exploitation afloat and fuse organic TCPED with intelligence produced by strategic and theater intelligence production organizations to address time sensitive, dynamic tactical planning, and execution decisions afloat.

The Intelligence Carry-On Program (ICOP) fulfills fleet requirements and urgent operational needs for a subset of DCGS-N intelligence capabilities on Navy cruisers and destroyers. The ICOP suite includes an integrated 3-D operational display of intelligence and other data sources to provide a complete picture of the battlespace. The system supports a full-motion video receive, process, exploit, and disseminate capability as well as the ability to process and correlate electronic intelligence and communications externals. It integrates mature COTS and GOTS applications with shared storage and communication paths to reach back to the DCGS-N Enterprise Node and national ISR systems, making the tactical user a part of the larger ISR enterprise. The ICOP prototype received positive feedback from fleet users and won both the Department of Navy Acquisition Excellence Award for Technology Transition and the Office for Naval Research Rapid Technology Transition Achievement Award.

Status

The DCGS-N installation plan includes aircraft carriers, large-deck amphibious assault ships, fleet command ships, intelligence training centers, schoolhouse facilities, and shore-based numbered fleet maritime operations centers. Inc 1 fielded to its total inventory objective and achieved full operational capability in 2014. ICOP development began in FY 2014 with delivery commencing in FY 2015. Inc 2 is scheduled to reach initial operational capability in the second quarter FY 2021. Fleet Capability Release 1 (FCR-1) will field in FY 2018 and develops shore node infrastructure and core analytic tools. FCR-2 will deliver afloat capabilities in FY 2021.

Developers

BAE Systems Rancho Bernardo, California

* * * * * * * * * * *

E-2C/D Hawkeye Airborne Early Warning Aircraft

Description

The E-2 Hawkeye is the Navy's airborne surveillance and battle management command and control platform, providing support of decisive power projection at sea and over land for the carrier strike group and joint force commanders. In addition to in-service capabilities, the E-2 has an extensive upgrade and development program to continue improving the capability of the aircraft.

The E-2C Hawkeye2000, with the APS-145 radar, features a mission computer upgrade (MCU), Cooperative Engagement Capability (CEC), improved electronic support measures, Link-16, global positioning system, and satellite data and voice capability. The MCU greatly improves weapons systems processing power, enabling incorporation of CEC. In turn, CEC-equipped Hawkeye 2000s significantly extend the engagement capability of air-defense warships. They are key to early cueing of the Aegis Weapons System, dramatically extending the lethal range of the surface-to-air Standard Missiles.

The E-2D Advanced Hawkeye, with the APY-9 radar, is a two-generation leap in radar performance from the E-2C, which brings an improved over-the-horizon, over-land, and littoral detection and tracking capability to the carrier strike group and joint force commanders. The APY-9, coupled with CEC, Link-16, and the Advanced Tactical Data Link, fully integrates the E-2D Advanced Hawkeye into the joint integrated air and missile-defense (IAMD) role. The APY-9's advanced detection and tracking capability, in conjunction with Aegis and the upgraded Standard Missiles, as well as the F/A-18 Hornet and its upgraded AIM-120 Advanced Medium Range Air-to-Air Missile, will allow strike groups to deploy an organic, theater-wide air and cruise missile defense capability to protect high-priority areas and U.S. and coalition forces ashore and afloat. The E-2D is the key enabler for the Naval Integrated Fire Control-Counter Air capability and will continue as the airborne "eyes" of the Fleet.

Status

As of August 2016, there were 43 E-2C aircraft in the Fleet, and 25 E-2Ds have been delivered. The Navy signed a 25-aircraft multi-year procurement contract on

June 30, 2014 covering FY 2014 through FY 2018. The E-2D developmental test program and initial operational test and evaluation completed in October 2012 and reported the E-2D as effective and suitable. The first fleet squadron completed transitioning to the E-2D in January 2014, achieved initial operational capability in October 2014, and completed its first deployment in November 2015.

Developers

Lockheed Martin Syracuse, New York

Northrop Grumman Melbourne, Florida

St. Augustine, Florida

* * * * * * * * * * * *

Joint Automated Deep Operations Coordination System (JADOCS)

Description

Joint Automated Deep Operations Coordination System is the principal tool for joint time-sensitive targeting (TST) and maritime dynamic targeting (MDT) collaboration, information sharing, targeting situational awareness plus command and control. JADOCS is an Army Acquisition Category III program of record with joint interest supporting TST/MDT fire-support management for Navy tactical and operational-level forces, targeting coordination, and common operational picture capabilities.

Status

JADOCS is pre-Milestone C with an acquisition decision memorandum approved by the Army in April 2013. JADOCS is delivered to the Navy as a software-only capability. JADOCS 1.0.5 is in the operations and sustainment phase, with the stand-up of a Navy project Office in FY 2014. JADOCS is tested within the Navy operational environment for fielding to force-level ships (e.g., aircraft carriers, amphibious assault ships, and command ships), maritime operations centers, and selected training sites. The Army is developing JADOCS 2.0 with additional capabilities that will be fielded to Navy sites in a Consolidated Afloat Networks and Enterprise Services environment.

Developers

Communications-Electronics Command Fort Sill, Oklahoma Raytheon Waltham, Massachusetts

* * * * * * * * * * *

Mk XIIA, Mode 5 Identification Friend or Foe (IFF) Combat ID

Description

The Mk XIIA Mode 5 Identification Friend or Foe is a secure, real-time, cooperative "blue-force" combat Identification system designed to inform commanders' "Shoot/No-Shoot" decisions. Advanced technology, coding, and cryptographic techniques are incorporated into IFF Mode 5 to provide reliable, secure and improved performance. The Mode 5 waveform is defined in Standard NATO Agreement (STANAG) 4193 and is compatible with all U.S. and international civil IFF requirements. This Navy Acquisition Category II program is based on the improved Mk XII Cooperative IFF Operational Requirements Document dated April 27, 2001. Transponders will be installed on more than 3,000 ships and Navy/Marine Corps aircraft. Mode 5 interrogator equipment will be fielded on aviation ships, air-capable ships, and selected aircraft, including MH-60R Seahawk helicopters, E-2D Advanced Hawkeye, F/A-18C/D/E/F Hornet/Super Hornet and E/A-18G Growler. Mode 5 is a key enabler in the Joint Concept for Access and Maneuver in the Global Commons (JAM-GC, formerly the Air-Sea-Battle) concept, including Naval Integrated Fire Control-Counter Air, bringing the tactical advantage of cooperative target Identification.

Status

Navy initial operational capability and full-rate production were approved in 2012. Interoperability and valid IFF Mode 5 responses were demonstrated with E-2C, P-3C, MH-60R and UH-1Y aircraft, DDG 51-class destroyers, and CG 47-class cruisers during Bold Quest 13-01/Joint Operational Test Approach event 2 in June 2013. Operational testing of the combined interrogator/transponder on the F/A-18E/F and EA-18G aircraft completed in 2014. The program is on track to meet the operational requirements specified for joint full operational capability by 2020.

Developers

BAE Systems Greenlawn, New York

The Boeing Company St. Louis, Missouri

General Dynamics C4 Systems Scottsdale, Arizona

Northrop Grumman Woodland Hills, California

* * * * * * * * * * *

Nulka Radar Decoy System

Description

Nulka is an active, off-board, ship-launched decoy developed in cooperation with Australia to counter a wide spectrum of present and future radar-guided anti-ship cruise missiles (ASCMs). The Nulka decoy employs a broadband radio frequency repeater mounted on a hovering rocket platform. After launch, the Nulka decoy radiates a large, ship-like radar cross-section and lies a trajectory that seduces incoming ASCMs away from their intended targets. Australia developed the hovering rocket, launcher, and launcher interface unit. The Navy developed the electronic payload and fire control system. The in-service Mk 36 Decoy Launching System (DLS) has been modified to support Nulka decoys, and the mod is designated the Mk 53 DLS.

Status

Nulka received Milestone C approval for full-rate production in January 1999. Installation began on U.S. and Australian warships in September 1999. The system is installed on U.S. Coast Guard cutters and more than 120 U.S. Navy ships. Installation on aircraft carriers began in the fourth quarter of FY 2013. Additional installations will continue throughout FY 2017.

Developers

BAE Systems Edinburgh, Australia

Lockheed Martin Sippican Marion, Massachusetts

208

SECHAN Electronics Inc. Lititz, Pennsylvania

* * * * * * * * * * *

SSQ-130 Ship Signal Exploitation Equipment (SSEE) Increment F

Description

The SSQ-130 SSEE Increment F is a shipboard combat systems suite that provides area commanders with automatic target acquisition, geo-location, and non-kinetic fires capabilities. SSEE Increment F incorporates counterintelligence, surveillance, and reconnaissance capabilities that improve situational awareness and enhances integrated fires. SSEE Increment F provides a standardized information operations weapon system across multiple naval platforms. SSEE uses modular commercial-off-the-shelf/ non-developmental technology, which allows the system to be easily reconfigured and respond rapidly to emergent tasking and evolving threats. SEEE's hardware and software are scalable and tailorable, enabling the rapid insertion of new and emerging technologies with minimal integration efforts. A modular SSEE Increment F small-footprint variant will further enable mission-specific configurations and rapid deployment of new technology. It will provide a permanent cryptologic capability for Flight I Arleigh Burke (DDG 51) guided missile destroyers and accelerate removal of SSEE Increment E from the Fleet.

Status

SSEE Increment F entered full-rate production in July 2011, and 77 units will be delivered by FY 2019, with full operational capability estimated for FY 2023. At the end of FY 2016, 46 units had been delivered and 26 units completely installed.

Developers

Argon-ST / The Boeing Company Fairfax, Virginia

* * * * * * * * * * *

209

Surface Electronic Warfare Improvement Program (SEWIP)

Description

The Surface Electronic Warfare Improvement Program is an evolutionary development block upgrade program for the SLQ-32 electronic warfare system. Block 1A replaces the SLQ-32 processor with an electronic surveillance enhancement processor and the UYQ-70 display console. Block 1B also improves the human-machine interface of the SLQ-32 and adds specific emitter Identification capability that provides platform Identification. The high-gain, high-sensitivity receiver (Block 1B3) provides improved situational awareness through non-cooperative detection and Identification of platforms beyond the radar horizon. Block 2 provides improvements to the electronic support receiver. Upgrades to the antenna, receiver, and combat system interface allow the SLQ-32 system to pace new threats; improve signal detection, measurement accuracies, and classification; and mitigate electromagnetic interference. Block 3 will provide improvements for the electronic attack transmitter by providing integrated countermeasures against radio frequency-guided threats and extending frequency range coverage. SEWIP will also cue Nulka decoy launch.

Status

As of FY 2016, 181 SLQ-32 systems are installed on Navy aircraft carriers, surface combatants, and amphibious ships, and Coast Guard cutters. SEWIP was established as an Acquisition Category II program in July 2002 after cancellation of the Advanced Integrated Electronic Warfare System. The Navy awarded the SEWIP Block 2 development contract on September 30, 2009 and began delivery in 2014. Approximately 60 units are to be delivered within the future year's defense program. As of FY 2016, ten systems have been delivered with seven installed and three in the process of installation. SEWIP Block 3's advanced, active-Electronic Attack capabilities are in full development with a Milestone C decision in FY 2016. Block development completion and first procurement are expected in 2017, followed by first delivery in the 2018 timeframe.

Developers

General Dynamics Advanced

Information Systems Fairfax, Virginia

Lockheed Martin Eagan, Minnesota

Northrop Grumman PRB Systems Goleta, California

* * * * * * * * * * * *

UYQ-100 Undersea Warfare Decision Support System (USW-DSS)

Description

The Undersea Warfare Decision Support System (USW-DSS) enables the anti-submarine warfare (ASW) commander (ASWC) to plan, coordinate, establish, and maintain an undersea common tactical picture and execute tactical control. Employing net-centric decision-making tools in an open-architecture framework, it enables near-real-time sharing of key ASW tactical data and shortens the ASW kill chain. USW-DSS complements and interfaces with common operational picture (COP) systems such as Global Command and Control System-Maritime and Link-11/16. The SQQ-89 surface ship sonar system on cruisers and destroyers provides ship, sensor and track data to USW-DSS. The Tactical Support Center provides these data on board aircraft carriers. These data sources enable USW-DSS to generate a shared composite track picture for situational awareness. Integrated decision support tools provide the sea combat commander, theater ASW commander, and ASWC the ability to plan, conduct, and coordinate USW operations across all ASW platforms. USW-DSS provides highly detailed visualization, integrated platform sensor and distributed combat systems, reduced data entry, improved sensor performance predictions, and data fusion while reducing redundancy of USW tactical decision aids.

Status

USW-DSS Build 2 Release 3 (B2R3) completed initial operational test and evaluation (IOT&E) in FY 2013. As of late 2016, the Navy has delivered USW-DSS to 43 surface combatants, aircraft carriers, and shore commands. B2R3 fully leverages the Consolidated Afloat Networks and Enterprise Services (CANES) hardware and software-computing environment by installing as software-only on ships. Initial operating capability was fielded in the first quarter of FY 2010. A B2R3 software update commenced (as a result of the completed IOT&E) in FY 2015. B2R3 fielding is planned to continue through FY 2020 on a total of 107 ships and shore sites. USW-DSS Build 3 (B3) Fleet Capability Release (FCR 1) is currently in development and is scheduled for IOC ashore in the fourth quarter FY 2019. Developed with open, service oriented architecture and hosted on CANES, B3 will link to the Distributed Common Ground System Navy Increment 2 for "high-side" fusion and tactical-to-national integration of operational and intelligence information.

Developers

Adaptive Methods Inc. Centerville, Virginia

Naval Surface Warfare Center Division Carderock, Maryland

Naval Undersea Warfare Center Division Keyport, Washington

Progeny Systems Corporation Manassas, Virginia

* * * * * * * * * * *

OCEANOGRAPHY AND MARITIME DOMAIN AWARENESS

Hazardous Weather Detection and Display Capability (HWDDC)

Description

Hazardous Weather Detection and Display Capability passively extract data from the tactical scans of the SPS-48(E) and SPS-48(G) 3-D air-search radars to generate weather situational awareness products in near real-time. Within the radar field, HWDDC indicates operational impacts from precipitation intensity, storm cell movement, atmospheric refractivity (which effects electromagnetic propagation), and wind speed and direction. This is the first capability of its kind and dramatically increases safety of flight and reduces risk to other shipboard operations, to include: small boat operations, amphibious maneuver, and deck evolutions (refueling or ordnance handling). Not only is the data used on board aircraft carriers and large-deck amphibious assault ships by Aerographers to support light deck operations and navigation, but it is shared to every squadron ready room and embarked staff by close-circuit TV. Information is shared with other ships in company and theater maritime operations center with maritime headquarters using SIPRNET (Secret Internet Protocol Router Network). Hourly data is also transmitted to Fleet Numerical Meteorological and Oceanographic Command, Monterey California where it is assimilated into Coupled Ocean/Atmosphere Mesoscale Prediction System numerical environmental models, increasing the accuracy of tactical meteorological predictions.

Status

Designated an Abbreviated Acquisition Program by the Space and Naval Warfare Systems Command PEO C4I (Command, Control, Communication, Computers, and

Intelligence), HWDDC is installed on nine aircraft carriers and seven large-deck amphibious assault ships equipped with SPS-48(E) or SPS-48(G) air-search radars. HWDDC entered the Consolidated Afloat Networks Enterprise Services integration and testing in FY 2016, and full operational capability will be achieved when all aircraft carrier and amphibious assault platforms have received the SPS-48(G) upgrades. The Tactical Environmental Processor (TEP), which is a follow-on capability of HWDDC onboard destroyers equipped with the AN/SPY-1D(V) radars upgraded with a Multi-Mission Signal Processor, has been installed on the USS Arleigh Burke (DDG 51), USS Mitscher (DDG 57), and USS Milius (DDG 69), with two additional installs planned during FY 2017, nine in the future years defense program, up to 30 overall. Full operational capability will be achieved when all destroyers receiving the ACB12 and ACB16 modernization package have received TEP.

Developers

BCI Sensors Mt. Laurel, New Jersey

Space and Naval Warfare Systems Command, PEO (C4I) PMW-120 San Diego, California

* * * * * * * * * * * *

Littoral Battlespace Sensing-Unmanned Undersea Vehicles (LBS-UUV)

Description

The Littoral Battlespace Sensing-Unmanned Undersea Vehicle program provides a family of vehicles with a flow-observable, continuous capability to characterize ocean properties that influence sound and light propagation for acoustic and optical weapon and sensor performance predictions. Critical to realizing undersea dominance, the program has delivered buoyancy-driven undersea gliders (LBS-G);

electrically powered, autonomous undersea vehicles (LBS-AUV) launched from Pathfinder (T-AGS 60)-class oceanographic survey vessels; and autonomous undersea vehicles (LBS-AUV(S)) launched from submarines. All three systems provide persistent battlespace awareness and enable anti-submarine, mine countermeasures, expeditionary, and naval special warfare planning and execution and persistent intelligence preparation of the environment (IPOE). The relevant information collected from this system is integrated at the Glider Operations Center into naval C4ISR (command, control, communication, computer, intelligence, surveillance, and reconnaissance) systems as part of the global information grid enterprise services. These systems are a force multiplier for the T-AGS oceanographic survey ships, further expanding collection capabilities in contested areas to ensure access and reduce risk in fleet operations.

Status

LBS-G reached full operational capability in July 2012, and by August 2016 the program had delivered 137 gliders to the Naval Oceanographic Office with 25 more undergoing government acceptance testing. LBS-AUV reached and obtained full operational capability in February 2015 and by May 2014 had delivered a total of five AUVs, including two engineering design models to the Naval Oceanographic Office; a total of seven vehicles will be delivered by FY 2017. Both LBS-G and LBS-AUV are conducting real-world ocean-sensing missions in overseas locations in support of anti-submarine warfare, mine warfare, and intelligence preparation of the operational environment (IPOE). LBS-AUV(S) will reach initial operational capability in FY 2019 and support the Submarine Force in conducting IPOE and other undersea warfare operations.

Developers

Hydroid, Inc. Pocasset, Massachusetts

Teledyne Brown Engineering Huntsville, Alabama

Teledyne Webb Research East Falmouth, Massachusetts

* * * * * * * * * * *

Maritime Domain Awareness (MDA)

Description

Maritime Domain Awareness (MDA) facilitates timely decision-making that enables early actions to neutralize threats to U.S. national security interests. MDA results from the discovery, collection, sharing, fusion, analysis, and dissemination of mission-relevant data, information, and intelligence in the context of maritime political, social, economic, and environmental trends within geographic regions. MDA requires a collaborative and comprehensive information and intelligence-sharing environment, working across international and agency borders. The Navy MDA Concept signed in July 2011 emphasizes Navy maritime operations centers as the focal point for efforts to improve Navy MDA, leveraging reach-back intelligence hubs for analytical support. The Navy's MDA concept complements the 2012 Presidential Policy Directive (PPD)-18 on Maritime Security, the 2013 National MDA Plan, which directs integration of all-source intelligence, law-enforcement information, and open-source data, and the 2015 DoD Strategic Plan for MDA that provides overarching guidance focusing on enterprise-wide unity of effort mitigating MDA capability gaps and long-standing challenges. Navy funding also supports MDA/intelligence focused analytic capabilities across the Naval Intelligence Enterprise (including at the Office of Naval Intelligence), and other Navy activities to close validated capability gaps. By addressing the maritime challenges our Nation and its partners currently face, and promoting further progress in identifying and addressing MDA challenges, MDA seeks to enable decision-makers by strengthening and enhancing the information sharing environment. MDA will accomplish this through the continued development of policies, enhanced situational

215

awareness, intelligence integration, and information sharing and safeguarding capabilities to provide a maritime domain supporting prosperity and security within our domestic borders and around the world.

Status

In 2010, the Joint Requirements Oversight Council approved the MDA initial capabilities document, which identified 20 prioritized MDA capability gaps aimed at improving information access, analysis, and sharing to a wide range of interagency and international partners. For example, SeaVision is an unclassified, web-based maritime situational awareness tool that enables users to view, track, understand, and analyze vessel movements. SeaVision displays Automatic Identification System (AIS) data from the U.S. Department of Transportation's Volpe Center-developed Maritime Safety and Security Information System (MSSIS) network as well as other data sources, and ingests and displays a wide variety of maritime and geospatially referenced data. Future tools operating primarily at the classified—general services and sensitive compartmented information—levels will reside within Increment 2 of the Distributed Common Ground System-Navy program.

Developers

SPAWAR Systems Center San Diego, California

* * * * * * * * * * * *

Meteorological Mobile Facility (Replacement) Next Generation [MetMF(R) NEXGEN]

Description

The TMQ-56 Meteorological Mobile Facility (Replacement) (MetMF(R)) Next-Generation environmental collection and forecast system provides meteorological and oceanographic (METOC) support to Marine Corps and joint forces. The main functions of the system are to collect and analyze data, predict the future environment, tailor METOC products and information, and mitigate the impact of and exploit the future environment. Following evolutionary acquisition, MetMF(R) NEXGEN is a replacement of the Meteorological Mobile Facility (Replacement) and provides greater mobility and operational flexibility in response to identified meteorological capability gaps. The required capabilities are defined in two operational requirements documents.

Status

Two MetMF(R) NEXGEN prototypes were developed and the capability production document was approved in July 2010. MetMF(R) NEXGEN passed its operational evaluation in September 2011, and was approved at Milestone C for full rate production in October 2011. MetMF(R) NEXGEN Officially met all requirements for initial operational capability in July 2013.

Developers

Smiths Detection Edgewood, Maryland

Space and Naval Warfare

Systems Command San Diego, California

* * * * * * * * * * *

Naval Integrated Tactical Environmental System-Next Generation (NITES-Next)

Description

Naval Integrated Tactical Environmental System-Next Generation (NITES-Next) is a software-centric solution that leverages Consolidated Afloat Networks Enterprise Services infrastructure and services on force-level ships (e.g., aircraft carriers and large-deck amphibious assault ships) afloat, Amazon Web Services ashore, and a mobile variant for expeditionary warfare users. It is being developed to replace legacy meteorology and oceanography (METOC) capabilities in support of the Naval Meteorology and Oceanography Command's operating concept, fleet safety, integrated fires, and battlespace awareness. NITES-Next represents the core processing, exploitation, and dissemination tool of the METOC professional and provides a "one-stop shop" of tools and tactical decision aids required to generate decision products in support of full-spectrum naval operations. It is capable of consuming Open Geospatial Consortium (OGC)-compliant information and products, processed remotely sensed environmental information, as well as ocean and atmospheric models. Data are analyzed and fused with embedded tactical decision aids to expedite the METOC professional's forecasts of environmental conditions and impacts to fleet safety, weapons performance, sensor performance, and overall mission. NITES-Next is also capable of producing OGC-compliant products that can be shared/viewed on in-service and future Navy command and control systems—e.g., Command and Control Rapid Prototype Continuum, Maritime Tactical Command and Control, and Distributed Common Ground System-Navy— that will increase fleet-wide situational awareness.

Status

NITES-Next was designated an information technology streamlining pilot program in March 2012 and received a Fleet Capability Release (FCR)-1 build decision in May 2012. NITES-Next will be developed in five FCRs. Initial operational capability was achieved after successful operational test and evaluation of FCR-1 in February 2015. Full operational capability will be achieved in FY 2024 after FCR-5 is fielded.

Developers

Forward Slope, Inc. San Diego, California

General Dynamics Information Technology San Diego, California

Space and Naval Warfare Systems Center, Pacific San Diego, California

Space and Naval Warfare Systems Command, PEO C4I and PMW-120 San Diego, California

* * * * * * * * * * *

NAVSTAR Global Positioning System (GPS)

Description

The Navigation System using Timing and Ranging Global Positioning System (NAVSTAR GPS) program is a space-based, satellite radio navigation system that provides authorized users with "24/7," worldwide, all-weather, three-dimensional positioning, velocity, and precise time data. Navy responsibilities include the integration of GPS in 275 surface ships and submarines and more than 3,700 aircraft, integration of shipboard combat systems with the Navigation Sensor System Interface (NAVSSI) and the deployment of follow-on GPS-based Positioning, Navigation, and Timing Services (GPNTS) and anti-jam (A/J) protection for high-priority combat platforms through the navigation warfare (NAVWAR) program. NAVSSI is the in-service shipboard system that collects, processes, and disseminates position, velocity, and timing data to weapons systems, C4I (command, control, communication, computer, and intelligence), and combat-support systems on board surface warships. GPNTS will incorporate the next-generation of GPS receivers, initially the Selective Availability Anti-Spoofing Module (SAASM), to be followed by Military-Code (M-Code) receivers, to ensure that Navy ships can use the new GPS signals being broadcast from the latest GPS satellites. GPNTS also features A/J antennas and multiple atomic clocks to support assured position, navigation, and timing services. NAVWAR provides anti-jam antennas to protect air and sea naval platforms against GPS interference to ensure a continued high level of mission effectiveness in a GPS jamming environment. GPS plays a critical role not only in precise navigation, but also in providing precise time synchronization to precision-strike weapons, naval surface fire support systems, and ship C4I systems.

Status

All Navy platform GPS installations are complete. The Air NAVWAR program continues tests on suitable A/J antennas for Navy unmanned aerial vehicles such as Fire Scout. Installation of A/J antennas in F/A-18 E/F/G Super Hornet/Growler aircraft is ongoing with approximately 24 installs a year. Efforts to integrate GPS A/J antennas into E-2D Hawkeye aircraft and H-1 helicopters are ongoing. The Sea

NAVWAR program is installing GPS A/J antennas on major surface combatants and the Navy's submarine force. The Navy is completing installation of NAVSSIs on select Navy surface combatants. Installation of NAVSSI will continue on new construction ships until GPNTS is approved for all baselines. The GPNTS program's next major event is Milestone C, scheduled for June 2017. GPNTS initial operational capability is expected in March 2020.

Developers

Boeing Military Aircraft St. Louis, Missouri

Litton Data Systems San Diego, California

Raytheon Los Angeles, California

Rockwell-Collins Cedar Rapids, Iowa

* * * * * * * * * * * *

Precise Timing and Astrometry (PTA)

Description

The Navy Precise Timing and Astrometry program executes Department of Defense (DoD) tasking to develop, maintain, and assure precise timing and time interval services, earth orientation parameters, and the celestial reference frame for the DoD components. PTA is a critical component to the effective employment of a myriad DoD systems, including command and control, intelligence operations, network operations, and data fusion. It is essential to battlespace awareness, assured command and control, and integrated fires. Coordinated Universal Time as referenced to the U.S. Naval Observatory (UTC-USNO) is the DoD standard and the primary timing reference for the global positioning system (GPS) and numerous other military applications. The U.S. Naval Observatory (USNO) Master Clock, an ensemble of dozens of independent atomic clocks, is the most precise and accurate operational clock system in the world, and supports the stringent GPS III nanosecond timing precision requirement. The Navy, through USNO, also determines and predicts earth orientation parameters that are the time-varying alignment of the Earth's terrestrial reference frame to the celestial reference frame. USNO is the DoD lead for defining the celestial reference frame, which is the basis for the extremely precise and accurate positions and attitudes of positioning and targeting systems. PTA also supports relevant research conducted by USNO necessary to improve mission performance in clock development and time dissemination, determining and cataloging the positions and motions of celestial objects for the celestial reference frame, earth orientation parameters, and astronomical application production for navigation and operations.

Status

USNO's Navy Rubidium Fountain atomic clocks have met initial operational capability. Additional funding has been added toward a secure USNO network that is sustained through a program of record.

Developers

Naval Meteorology and Oceanography Command Stennis Space Center, Mississippi Navigator of the Navy Washington, D.C.

U.S. Naval Observatory Washington, D.C.

U.S. Naval Observatory Flagstaff Station Flagstaff, Arizona

* * * * * * * * * * * *

T-AGS Oceanographic Survey Ship

Description

The Pathfinder (T-AGS 60)-class oceanographic survey vessels comprise five 329-foot long, 5,000-ton vessels that provide multipurpose oceanographic capabilities in coastal and deep-ocean areas. Under the Military Survey restrictions of the United Nations Convention on the Law of the Sea, the T-AGS 60 represents an internationally recognized environmental information-collection capability that can operate within the exclusive economic zones of sovereign nations in support of DoD requirements without host-nation approval. Non-military ships conducting these collections may only do so with host-nation approval. T-AGS ships perform acoustic, biological, physical, and geophysical surveys, and gather data that provide much of DoD's information on the ocean environment as well as mapping the ocean floor to update nautical charts and promote safety of navigation. These data help to improve undersea warfare technology and enemy ship and submarine detection. The T-AGS ships are manned and operated for the Oceanographer of the Navy. Merchant mariner crews are provided by the Military Sealift Command, and the Naval Oceanographic Office provides mission scientists and technicians.

T-AGS 60-class ships are designed with a common-bus diesel-electric propulsion system consisting of twin-screw propellers driven through azimuth stern drive (Z-drives). The Z-drives, with 360-degree direction control, provide for precise and accurate position-keeping and track-line following. The Navy accepted delivery of the newest vessel to the T-AGS fleet, the USNS Maury (T-AGS 66), in FY 2016 to bring total T-AGS fleet to six vessels. A modified version of the Pathfinder-class vessels, the ship is named after Lieutenant Matthew Fontaine Maury, the father of modern oceanography and naval meteorology. T-AGS 66 is 24 feet longer than the in-service Pathfinder T-AGS vessels to accommodate the addition of an 18-foot by 18-foot inboard moon pool. The moon pool allows access to the water through the ship's hull for the deployment and retrieval of unmanned undersea vehicles. The increased ship length also provides 12 additional permanent berthing accommodations. As on previous T-AGS vessels, a hull-mounted mission system gondola will house the multi-beam sonar system.

Status

VT Halter Marine laid Maury's keel on February 1, 2011; the ship was christened and launched on March 27, 2013; the Navy accepted the ship in FY 2016; and final contract trials were scheduled for early FY 2017.

Developers

Naval Meteorology and Oceanography Command Stennis Space Center, Mississippi Oceanographer of the Navy Washington, D.C.

VT Halter Marine Pascagoula, Mississippi

* * * * * * * * * * * *

Task Force Climate Change (TFCC)

Description

Task Force Climate Change (TFCC) is supported by the Office of the Chief of Naval Operations (CNO) and the Office of Naval Research and engages with representatives from multiple governmental offices and staffs in an effort to gain a comprehensive and unambiguous understanding of the complex environment of the Arctic region and the impacts of climate change on naval readiness. TFCC's objective is to develop a comprehensive approach to guide future public, strategic, and policy discussions. The primary deliverable of TFCC is a holistic, chronological roadmap for future Navy action with respect to the Arctic that is synchronized with a science-based timeline, provides a framework for how the Navy discusses the Arctic, and includes a list of appropriate objectives tempered by fiscal realities. TFCC's subsequent focus will be other climate change implications, particularly the challenges associated with sea level rise and its effect on base infrastructure and mission readiness.

Status

Task Force Climate Change developed the initial Navy Arctic Roadmap in 2009 and released an update in 2014. Both roadmaps are signed by the CNO and are consistent with existing National, Joint, and Naval guidance, including National Security Presidential Directive-66 and Homeland Security Presidential Direc-tive-25, Department of Defense Arctic Strategy, Joint Vision 2020, a Cooperative Strategy for 21st Century Seapower (2015), and the 2016 Design for Maintaining Maritime Superiority. Both roadmaps provide plans of action with timelines intended to drive Navy policy, engagement, and investment decisions regarding the Arctic and global climate change, and the most recent release expands upon the previous roadmap's efforts and outlines actions needed in the near-term, mid-term, and far-term in order to balance potential investments with other Service priorities. Actions specified in the roadmap are underway, and TFCC provides regular updates to the CNO on their implementation status. Following the guidance in the 2014 Quadrennial Defense Review, the Navy's investments are focused on improvements in observation, prediction, and communication capabilities in high-latitude maritime regions, as well as vulnerability assessments, local sea level rise methodologies, and uncertainty management.

Developers

Chief of Naval Operations Staff Washington, D.C.

Naval Meteorology and Oceanography Command Stennis Space Center, Mississippi Office of Naval Research Arlington, Virginia

* * * * * * * * * * * *

SECTION 6

Admiral Hyman Rickover, the "father" of the nuclear Navy, understood that "Bitter experience in war has taught the maxim that the art of war is the art of the logistically feasible." All of America's naval forces depend upon supply and logistics to carry out the full spectrum of operations to protect our citizens, interests, and friends. Naval logistics bridges the gap between land bases and depots and forces at sea. The Combat Logistics Force is critical to that capability, and, coupled with the Navy Energy Plan, undergirds the reach and persistence of forces for forward presence, sea control, power projection, and extended combat across the range of military operations.

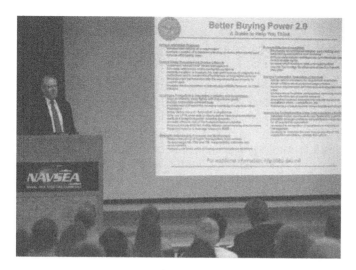

Navy Electronic Procurement System (EPS)

Description

The Electronic Procurement System is the Department of the Navy (DoN) end-to-end contract writing system. It will provide the Navy and Marine Corps contracting community with a full contract writing management capability and facilitate integration with federally mandated systems, DoN financial systems, and industry. The EPS will replace existing legacy contracting systems and resolve existing challenges of outdated architecture, limited capabilities, and scalability concerns.

The EPS will span the DoN enterprise buying activities that include small procurements, major weapon systems acquisitions, research and development, military construction, grants, Service buys, and cooperative agreements. The EPS will maximize automation through standardized, data-driven contracting processes, from requirements inception through award, administration, payment, and final closeout. An Enterprise Service Bus (ESB) will serve as a hub to relay procurement data to various financial and reporting systems of record. The ESB will enable interoperability using Department of Defense (DoD) data exchange standards, such as the Procurement Data Standard and Purchase Request Data Standard.

The EPS implementation will result in auditable processes and a contracting workforce that issues accurate and timely contracts in standard formats that comply with applicable DoD and federal laws, regulations, and policies. Vendors will have a means of submitting electronic proposals, connected financial systems will be able to generate timely and accurate financial accounting data, and distribution and reporting of contracts and modifications will occur automatically.

Status

The EPS Program is a tailored pre-Acquisition Category (ACAT) IAM Defense Business System. The program anticipates request for proposal release in December 2016, and contract award in January 2018.

Developers - To be determined.

Naval Operational Business Logistics Enterprise (NOBLE)

Description

Navy and Marine Corps operational forces require a comprehensive suite of maintenance, supply, and personnel administration capabilities to generate and sustain warfighter readiness. In late 2016 the Naval Tactical Command Support System (NTCSS) provides this information for all ships, submarines, aviation squadrons, expeditionary units, and other ashore operational sites. NTCSS however, is no longer capable of meeting fleet operating concepts and the in-service technical architecture is not fiscally supportable. NOBLE is the follow on to NTCSS.

The NOBLE family of programs comprises the Naval Operational Supply Systems (NOSS), Naval Aviation Maintenance System (NAMS), and Naval Maritime Operational Environment (NOME). Together, these systems will provide the required capabilities using an open architecture framework that incorporates business process reengineering allowing for the consolidation of more than 23 stand-alone application systems. These capabilities include enhanced situational awareness, planning, execution, and management of maintenance and supply logistics and business functions for a user base exceeding 150,000. The NOBLE family of programs will meet current and emerging demands for cyber, Financial Improvement and Audit Readiness, Navy logistics and maritime maintenance mission requirements. The NOBLE family of programs will deploy to Navy enterprise data centers ashore, the Consolidated Afloat Networks and Enterprise Services afloat, and Department of Navy commercial cloud computing environments.

Status

NOSS, NAMS, and NOME are in the pre-acquisition phase in late 2016, with an approved new start in FY 2018.

Developers

To be determined.

Naval Tactical Command Support System (NTCSS)

Description

The Naval Tactical Command Support System is the combat logistics support information system used by Navy and Marine Corps commanders to manage and assess unit and group material and personnel readiness. NTCSS provides intermediate and organizational maintenance, supply, and personnel administration management capabilities to aviation, surface, and sub-surface operational commanders. NTCSS also supports network-centric warfare by integrating logistics information to complement the tactical readiness picture for operational commanders. Business process improvements are developed and implemented under sponsorship of functional and fleet managers. Ongoing initiatives include:

• Migrating to an open service-oriented architecture

• Using Navy Enterprise Data Centers

• Converting Navy and Marine Corps aviation squadrons to an NTCSS Virtual Environment, significantly reducing hardware requirements

• Centralizing visibility of Navy assets (Operational Supply)

• Streamlining aviation maintenance repair operations (Beyond Capability Maintenance Interdiction and Global Individual Components Repair List management)

 As a result, both the Navy and Marine Corps will realize greater operational efficiency and lower total ownership costs.

Status

NTCSS continues to be the warfighters' system to maintain fleet readiness. Full operational capability (FOC) at Naval Air Stations, Marine Corps air logistics squadrons, and on board ships and submarines occurred in FY 2009. An optimized NTCSS capability, targeted for aircraft squadrons, began full-rate production in FY 2007 and achieved FOC in the first quarter of FY 2012. The "tech refresh" to replace legacy NTCSS hardware/software and maintain compliance with Department of Defense/Department of the Navy Information Assurance and Baseline Reduction mandates completed in FY 2016. NTCSS will remain in sustainment through the future years defense program (FYDP). Naval Operational Business Logistics Enterprise (NOBLE) is the "umbrella" nomenclature for Naval Operational Supply Systems (NOSS), Naval Aviation Maintenance System (NAMS), and Naval Maritime Operational Environment (NOME), and will be in acquisition and development through the FYDP.

Developers

Advanced Enterprise Systems Norfolk, Virginia

CACI Norfolk, Virginia

* * * * * * * * * * * *

Navy Energy Program

Description

The Navy Energy Program addresses energy as a strategic resource that is essential to the successful execution of Navy afloat and ashore missions. Our goal is to increase operational capability and shore resilience by decreasing the Navy's reliance on petroleum, while increasing the use of alternative energy in our operations and in our facilities. The Navy Energy Strategy encompasses strategic investments in people, technology, and programs across the aviation, expeditionary, maritime, and shore enterprises. To increase combat readiness and mission success, the Navy continues to make significant progress by adjusting policies to enable more energy efficient operations, ingraining awareness and energy-conscious behavior, optimizing existing technologies to reduce energy consumption, and accelerating the implementation of new technologies.

We are cultivating a new generation of "energy warriors" through incentives and education. The incentivized energy conservation program encourages ships' crews to apply energy efficient procedures and operations, whether underway or in port, resulting in estimated energy cost avoidance of greater than 13 percent. With the fleet-wide launch of the aircraft energy conservation program in 2014, progress is being made towards optimizing fuel consumption on the Navy's 3,700 aircraft through procedural improvements such as short-cycle mission and recovery tanking and ground truck refueling.

Education and behavior change efforts extend from the classroom to shipboard and aircraft applications. The Naval Postgraduate School offers four master's degree programs and graduate certificates with an energy focus for Navy and Marine Corps personnel: Master of Science in Operational Analysis; Naval/Mechanical Engineering; Electronic Systems Engineering; and Financial Management. The General Military Training (GMT) for energy was successfully deployed in FY 2016 and provides Navy personnel with the key lessons about the importance of energy as a combat enabler and the knowledge to adopt energy-conserving behaviors within their commands.

The Navy's maritime efficiency initiatives seek to reduce shipboard energy demands for propulsion and electric power through a combination of passive, active, and actionable technologies. Passive technologies, such as stern laps, improve hydrodynamic flow and reduce drag, which reduces fuel consumption regardless of the ship's operating speed. Active technologies, such as the hybrid-electric propulsion system onboard several Amphibious Assault Ships, are used when operationally appropriate to deliver savings when the technology is in use. Actionable technologies, such as the shipboard energy dashboard, provide real-time situational awareness and feedback to ships' crews of energy demands associated with onboard equipment to enable optimized energy performance. The installation of the shipboard energy dashboard on board the USS Kidd (DDG 100) demonstrated energy savings of more than 92,000 kilowatt hours. In FY 2016, the Navy continued installation of solid state lighting upgrades across the surface fleet with expected savings of more than 400 barrels of fuel per ship per year and reduced maintenance hours compared to traditional fluorescent lighting.

Navy aircraft engine research is focused on new turbine engine configurations using innovative materials and processes. This will produce improved components needed to decrease fuel consumption as well as acquisition and maintenance costs, while increasing aircraft operational availability and performance. This includes developing new high-temperature metal alloys and inter-metallic materials for lighter and more heat-resistant turbine blades and disks, and thermal/environmental barrier coatings systems to improve component heat resistance to obtain greater fuel efficiency. Additionally, increased use of aviation simulators in continental U.S. flight training is helping pilots decrease fuel usage while increasing readiness.

Alternative fuel research remains a high priority in order to diversify energy supply options, which offers a strategic logistics supply advantage. To meet Department of Navy (DoN) requirements for alternative fuels to be interchangeable with and capable of being fully blended with petroleum without any changes to current aircraft or ship systems, Navy completed testing, qualification, and military specifications updates for JP-5, JP-8, and F-76 for the hydrotreated esters and fatty acids and Fischer-Tropsch pathways. Qualifying these fuels enables operational use by Navy aircraft and ships when they become available through the Defense Logistics Agency's fuel procurement process at costs competitive with conventional fuels.

In January 2016, the Navy kicked off the Great Green Fleet (GGF) as one of the Secretary of Navy's five energy goals established in 2009. Through this keystone year-long event, Navy demonstrated its commitment to the use of alternative energy and the importance of energy efficiency as a combat capability enabler. The centerpiece of GGF was the deployment of the USS John C. Stennis (CVN 74) carrier strike group from San Diego with an accompaniment of ships steaming on advanced biofuel blends and employing energy-efficient technologies and best practices.

Ashore, the Navy continues to focus on increased efficiency with more than 70 percent of shore energy funding directed toward infrastructure and utility system upgrades. Navy has installed advanced meters to monitor energy consumption, has deployed alternative fuel vehicles to decrease the fuel consumption of the non-tactical vehicle fleet, and has established energy management systems to drive changes in culture and behavior. Renewable energy technologies are being implemented where viable. The Navy has a geothermal power plant at China Lake, wind power in the Bahamas and California, Landfill Gas-to-Energy in Hawaii, and solar-powered lighting and hot water heaters at installations across the world.

The DoN Renewable Energy Program Office (REPO) successfully implemented cost-effective, large-scale (defined as ten megawatt or greater) renewable energy projects that leveraged private sector financing for the production of renewable electricity. REPO also surpassed its goal to bring one gigawatt (GW) of renewable energy into procurement by the end of 2015. As of August 2016, the DoN had 150 megawatts (MW) of production capacity in operation, another 551 MW from projects with executed agreements in place, and 409 MW from other projects in procurement. The DoN will continue to support these projects through their planned initial operating dates in 2017 and 2018. The benefits of these projects went beyond increasing the diversity of the DoN's energy portfolio by increasing energy independence; potential energy savings to the DoN could total up to $400 million over the life of the contracts, and the DoN will receive $62 million in hardware upgrades via in-kind considerations. New areas of focus in 2017 and 2018 include identifying energy resiliency opportunities and enhancing energy security, such as battery storage, fuel cells, equipment electrification, and microgrids.

Status

The hybrid electric drive is on schedule for initial fielding and installation on two DDG-51 class ships in late 2016. Stern flaps are installed on all guided missile cruisers (CG) and destroyers (DDG), and certain amphibious ships (LHD, LPD, LSD). Energy dashboards have been installed on 21 DDGs and will be installed on an additional three DDGs in FY 2016 and five in FY 2017. Combustion trim loops are now installed on eight amphibious ships, including LHD 1-7, and LCC-19. Looking forward to FY 2018, the Navy's energy investment will maintain FY 2016 and FY 2017 operational and shore energy initiatives, including funds to address legislative requirements and tactical efforts that target energy efficiency, energy consumption reduction, and alternative fuel test and certification.

Developers

Naval Air Systems Command Patuxent River, Maryland

Naval Facilities Command Washington, District of Columbia Naval Postgraduate School Monterey, California

Naval Sea Systems Command Washington, District of Columbia Office of Naval Research Arlington, Virginia

Navy Enterprise Resource Planning (Navy ERP)

Description

Navy ERP is the tool chosen to meet congressional mandates to establish and maintain federal financially compliant management systems, federal accounting standards, and U.S. Government General Ledger procedures at the transaction level. The Navy ERP foundation to achieve enterprise-wide business transformation is accomplished through two integrated releases: the Financial/Acquisition Solution and the Single Supply Solution. In October 2008, the Assistant Secretary of the Navy (Financial Management and Comptroller) designated Navy ERP the Navy's Financial System of Record for all the major acquisition systems commands, including Naval Air Systems Command, Naval Supply Systems Command (NAVSUP), Space and Naval Warfare Systems Command, Naval Sea Systems Command, Office of Naval Research, and Strategic Systems Programs.

Status

The Navy has overcome a broad range of challenges to successfully deploy financial, acquisition, supply chain, and workforce management capabilities to up to 72,000 users. Navy ERP is used to manage $69 billion of the Navy's total obligation authority annually. Navy ERP has deployed the single supply solution covering all of Navy's Material Groups to the NAVSUP Headquarters, field activities, fleet logistic centers and partner sites. The program completed deployments in FY 2013 and entered sustainment in FY 2014. As of FY 2016, Navy ERP has supported the schedule of budgetary activity audits and Department of Defense Inspector General inquiries. This will require Navy ERP's continued participation in data collection activities, audit finding remediation, and adherence to risk management framework and financial compliance requirements.

Developers

SAP America, Inc. Newtown Square, Pennsylvania

T-AH 19 Mercy-Class Hospital Ship

Description

The Navy's two Mercy-class hospital ships—the USNS Mercy (T-AH 19) and USNS Comfort (T-AH 20)—are national strategic assets employed in support of combatant commander (COCOM) requirements. Hospital ships provide a mobile, highly capable medical facility and are configured and equipped to meet their primary mission as a large-scale trauma center for combat operations. Each ship has 12 operating rooms and up to 1,000 beds (100 acute care, 400 intermediate care, and 500 minor care). As powerful enablers of stability, security, and reconstruction efforts around the globe, hospital ships serve as cornerstones for peacetime shaping operations. Hospital ships provide a highly visible, engaged, and reassuring presence when deployed for theater security cooperation (TSC) or when called to respond to humanitarian-assistance or disaster-relief missions. Assigned to the Military Sealift Command (MSC), these ships are maintained in a reduced operating status (ROS) when not required for scheduled mission tasking or emergent COCOM requests. Generally, one hospital ship is scheduled for a 120-150 day TSC deployment per year. The MSC performs periodic maintenance to ensure both ships can meet full operational capability within a few days following activation from ROS. A civilian mariner crew, with military medical staff augmentation when activated, mans these ships.

Status

Comfort (homeported in Norfolk, Virginia) has an expected service life to 2021. The Navy has programmed service-life extension maintenance that will extend Mercy's (homeported in San Diego, California) service life to 2036.

Developers

National Steel and

Shipbuilding Company San Diego, California

* * * * * * * * * * * *

T-AKE 1 Lewis and Clark-Class Dry Cargo and Ammunition Ship

Description

The Navy has 12 Lewis and Clark (T-AKE 1)-class dry cargo and ammunition ships in the combat logistics force (CLF). Assigned to the Military Sealift Command, the T-AKEs are built to commercial standards and are manned by civilian mariners. Along with the T-AOs, they form the foundation of the Navy's ability to project power ashore. They provide the dry cargo and ammunition necessary to enable Navy carrier strike groups and amphibious ready groups to operate worldwide without the need to constantly return to port for supplies. Additionally, they have a limited capacity for providing fuel to support dispersed surface action groups. T-AKEs have large, easily reconfigurable cargo holds to support delivery of a variety of cargo, including refrigerated, frozen, dry cargo and ammunition. The T-AKEs replaced three previous classes of fleet auxiliaries with a single hull form. A Navy aviation detachment or contracted commercial equivalent embarked on board provides vertical-replenishment capability.

Status

Twelve T-AKEs support the CLF and two T-AKEs support maritime prepositioning force program requirements. The final ship in the class—the USNS Cesar Chavez (T-AKE 14)—delivered in October 2012.

Developers

National Steel and Shipbuilding Company San Diego, California

* * * * * * * * * * *

T-AO 187 Kaiser-Class and T-AO(X) Replenishment Oiler

Description

The Navy has 15 Henry J. Kaiser-class fleet replenishment oilers in the combat logistics force. Assigned to the Military Sealift Command, the T-AOs are built to commercial standards and are manned by civilian mariners. Along with the T-AKE, they form the foundation of the Navy's ability to project power ashore. They provide the fuel and dry cargo necessary to enable Navy carrier strike groups and amphibious ready groups to operate worldwide without the need to constantly return to port for supplies. The T-AO primarily provides bulk petroleum (diesel fuel marine and JP5 jet fuel) to forces afloat. Additionally, they have a limited capacity for providing dry stores and refrigerated cargo. The John Lewis (T-AO 205)-class fleet replenishment oiler is the Navy's next-generation oiler, featuring increased dry and refrigerated cargo capacity compared to the T-AO 187 class. The ships will be double-hulled to comply with the Oil Pollution Act of 1990 standards. They are scheduled to replace the in-service Kaiser class T-AOs and the Supply-class T-AOEs when they reach the ends of their expected service lives beginning in 2021.

Status

On 30 June 2016, the Navy awarded the National Steel and Shipbuilding Company a contract for the first six T-AO 205-class ships. Seventeen T-AO 205s are planned, with delivery of the first ship in FY 2020.

Developers

To be determined.

* * * * * * * * * * * *

T-AOE 6 Supply-Class Fast Combat Support Ship

Description

The Navy has two Supply (T-AOE 6)-class fast combat support ships in the combat logistics force. Assigned to the Military Sealift Command they are manned by civilian mariners. Capable of maintaining higher sustained speeds than other Navy replenishment ships and carrying the full spectrum of afloat replenishment requirements (fuel, ordnance, and dry cargo), these ships provide "one-stop shopping" to carrier strike groups and amphibious ready groups. Working in concert with Lewis and Clark (T-AKE 1)-class dry cargo and ammunition ships, as well as the in-service Kaiser (T-AO 187)-class and new John Lewis (T-AO 205)-class fleet replenishment oilers, the T-AOE is a key enabler of the Navy's ability to project power ashore through replenishment at sea. A Navy aviation detachment is embarked to provide vertical-replenishment capability.

Status

The USNS Bridge (T-AOE 10) was inactivated in FY 2014, and the USNS Rainier (T-AOE 7) was inactivated in FY 2016. The two remaining T-AOEs, USNS Supply (T-AOE 6) and USNS Arctic (T-AOE 8), have expected service lives to 2034 and 2035, respectively.

Developers

National Steel and Shipbuilding Company San Diego, California

* * * * * * * * * * *

T-ATS(X) Towing, Salvage and Rescue Ship

Description

The Navy has four Powhatan (T-ATF 168)-class fleet ocean tugs and four Safeguard (T-ARS 50)-class salvage ships to support towing, salvage, diving, and submarine rescue operations. These ships are reaching the ends of their service lives and require recapitalization. Due to changes in technology, the latest diving and submarine rescue systems are now modularized and can be embarked upon a variety of ships that meet certain minimum requirements. A dedicated purpose-built salvage and rescue ship is no longer required, and the T-ATF and T-ARS ships will be replaced with a single common-hull towing, salvage and rescue ship, T-ATS(X). The T-ATS(X) will be built to commercial standards and will be manned by civilian mariners and operated by the Military Sealift Command. They will be able to support Navy towing, salvage, diving and rescue missions.

Status

Two T-ARS and one T-ATF will be inactivated in FY 2017. Contract award for the first T-ATS(X) is expected in the summer 2017, with delivery of the first ship in FY 2020. Eight T-ATS(X)s are planned.

Developers

To be determined.

* * * * * * * * * * *

T-EPF 1 Spearhead-Class Expeditionary Fast Transport (formerly Joint High-Speed Vessel)

Description

The Expeditionary Fast Transport is a high-speed, shallow-draft surface vessel with an expansive open mission bay and ample reserve power and ships services capacity. Manned by Military Sealift Command civilian mariners, EPFs provide a persistent deployed presence in operational theaters around the world. Capable of speeds in excess of 35 knots and ranges of 1,200 nautical miles fully loaded, the EPF's shallow-draft allows it to operate effectively in littoral areas and small, austere ports. FY 2017 will see the continued deployments of EPFs, providing increased opportunities to integrate these new, highly adaptable platforms into the Fleet and evaluate the many ways the Navy can employ the vessels' unique combination of persistent forward presence, flexible payload capacity, and speed.

Status

The Navy will acquire 12 EPFs, seven of which have been delivered as of mid-2016 with the remaining five programmed to be delivered from FY 2017 through FY 2020. The USNS Spearhead

(T-EPF 1) delivered in October 2012 and was ready for fleet tasking in November 2013. The USNS Choctaw County (T-EPF 2) delivered in June 2013 and was ready for fleet tasking in July 2014. The USNS Millinocket (T-EPF 3) delivered to the Navy in March 2014 and was ready for fleet tasking in April 2015. The USNS Fall River (T-EPF 4) delivered in September 2014 and was ready for fleet tasking in August 2015. USNS Trenton (T-EPF 5) was delivered in April 2015 and was ready for fleet tasking in March 2016. USNS Brunswick (T-EPF 6) was delivered in January 2016 and will be ready for fleet tasking in October 2016. USNS Carson City (T-EPF 7) was delivered in June 2016 and will be ready for fleet tasking in July 2017. USNS Yuma (T-EPF 8) is programmed to be delivered in January 2017, and the USNS Bismarck (T-EPF 9) is programmed to be delivered in July 2017. The other ship in the class is USNS Burlington (T-EPF 10). T-EPF 11 and T-EPF 12 have not been named.

Developers

Austal USA Mobile, Alabama

* * * * * * * * * * * *

SECTION 7

Naval science and technology (S&T) is our "insurance policy" enabling the Navy and Marine Corps to stay ahead of any competitor. Focused in the Office of Naval Research, the S&T program—from the seabed to the stars—includes electromagnetic railguns and solid-state lasers, exotic materials, and command and control in contested environments. Critically important to meeting far-future requirements only dimly perceived in 2017, Navy S&T nurtures the next generation of scientists and researchers through numerous STEM—Science, Technology, Engineering, and Mathematics—initiatives. S&T supports projects with potentially big payoffs, while mindful of the need for affordability.

SCIENCE AND TECHNOLOGY

Autonomous Aerial Cargo/Utility System (AACUS)

Description

The Office of Naval Research (ONR) Autonomous Aerial Cargo/ Utility System Innovative Naval Prototype explores advanced autonomous rotary-wing capabilities for reliable resupply/retrograde missions. Key features of the AACUS include a vehicle autonomously avoiding obstacles while finding and landing at an unprepared landing site, operated by a field individual possessing no special training. AACUS

238

represents a substantial leap forward compared to present-day operations as well as other more near-term Cargo Unmanned Aerial Systems (CUASs) development programs. AACUS focuses on autonomous obstacle avoidance and unprepared landing site selection, with precision-landing capabilities that include contingency management until the point of landing. AACUS includes a control component such that any field personnel can request and negotiate a desired landing site. Moreover, AACUS will communicate with ground personnel for seamless and safe loading and unloading. The program embraces an open-architecture approach for global management of mission planning data, making AACUS technologies platform-agnostic and transferable to new platforms as well as the existing CUASs. AACUS-enabled CUASs will rapidly respond to requests for support in degraded weather conditions, launch, fly to, and autonomously detect and negotiate precision-landing sites in potentially hostile settings.

Status

The Autonomous Aerial Cargo/Utility System is an ONR Innovative Naval Prototype program with a FY 2012 start, sponsored through ONR's Office of Technology.

Developers

Office of Naval Research Arlington, Virginia

* * * * * * * * * * * *

Autonomous Swarmboats

Description

Autonomous, unmanned Navy swarmboats can overwhelm an adversary's vessels. The Office of Naval Research (ONR) Control Architecture for Robotic Agent Command and Sensing (CARACaS), a first-of-its-kind technology, enables a swarming capability that gives our naval warfighters a decisive edge. CARACaS is a hardware and software package that can be installed on almost any manned Navy boat to convert it to autonomous operation and seamless operations with multiple unmanned surface vehicles (USVs). CARACaS enables new levels of USV autonomy, allowing multiple USVs to operate at unprecedented levels of coordinated autonomous operation—including moving in sync with other USVs, choosing their own routes, swarming on enemy vessels, escorting and defending high-value Navy vessels, and protecting ports. A combination of hardware and software, CARACaS is the result of a decade of collaborative research and development among ONR and partners across the U.S. Navy, academia, and industry. Some of the system's components were adapted for use on small combatant craft from technology originally developed by NASA for the Mars Rover spaceflight programs. CARACaS represents a quantum leap forward from remote control, enabling new capabilities in USV operations.

Status

Autonomous swarmboats enabled by CARACaS technology is an ONR program demonstrated in FY 2014 and FY 2016 via sponsorship from the ONR's Office of Disruptive Technology.

Developers

Office of Naval Research Arlington, Virginia

* * * * * * * * * * *

Discovery and Invention (D&I) Research

Description

Research provides the foundation for future breakthroughs in advanced technology. The Office of Naval Research (ONR) Discovery and Invention research portfolio represents 50 percent of the Navy's science and technology (S&T) budget. It consists of basic and early applied research that support a wide variety of scientific and engineering fields with a goal of creating or exploiting new knowledge to enhance and transform future naval technological capabilities. With its broad focus, the D&I portfolio aims for development of high-risk and high-impact projects with a long time-span of maturity, from five-to-20 years for transition. D&I investments are the essential foundation required for advanced technology.

In many cases, ONR's investments were the first to seed new research performed by many of the world's leading scientists and engineers at universities, federal laboratories, and private industry. Thousands of scientists, including more than 60 Nobel Prize winners, have been supported by ONR. Together, ONR-funded investigators have had significant influence on advances in cell phones, life-saving vaccines, lasers, fiber optics, radars, blood-clotting agents, semiconductors, nanotechnologies, and more.

For example, early D&I investments in gallium nitride devices led to a wide bandgap semiconductor program. These efforts have resulted in high-performing radar systems in the next-generation E-2D Hawkeye aircraft and for ship radar via the Integrated Topside (InTop) Innovative Naval Prototype program. The D&I research in autonomous sciences has yielded autonomous systems in use today that cost-effectively extend aircraft, ship, and submarine capabilities. A bio-inspired science effort produced a microbial fuel cell capable of powering small undersea sensors. Recognizing the need for network advancements in all warfighting capabilities, the D&I portfolio contains a substantial investment in information technology sciences. Breakthroughs in this arena include Composable FORCEnet, space-based microwave imagery, and enhanced weather forecasting and storm prediction. The D&I portfolio also includes multi-discipline exploration of materials where efforts encompass acoustic meta-materials projects that produced advances in sensors, noise reduction, and stealth coatings; and integrated computational materials engineering, which is accelerating implementation of advanced materials for naval systems, platforms, and power and energy applications. ONR D&I seeks out the most innovative scientific research with potential for valuable naval applications.

Breakthroughs in precision time and timekeeping, with applications to the global positioning system, have generated Nobel Prizes for ONR-funded researchers in 1997, 2001, 2005, and 2012. ONR has supported investigators conducting other Nobel prize-winning research: in 2010 for the development of the new single-atomic-layer material grapheme; in 2013 for the development of multi-scale models for complex chemical systems; and in 2014 for the development of super-resolved fluorescence microscopy (nanoscopy). In 2015 ONR-sponsored researcher Professor Christopher Re received the prestigious MacArthur Foundation award for democratizing big-data analytics through theoretical advances in statistics and logic and groundbreaking data-processing applications for solving practical problems. Professor Re, with ONR support, created an inference engine, DeepDive, which can analyze data of a kind and at a scale that is beyond the capabilities of traditional databases.

Status

Investments in basic and applied research across multiple disciplines help to mitigate risk and provide the foundation for discovering and maturing new technologies. ONR works with researchers across the country, from the Naval Research Laboratory to warfare centers, federal agencies, academia, and industry, helping to keep naval forces technologically dominant and affordable. The D&I investments also continue to expand international collaborations with strategic partners.

Developers

Office of Naval Research Arlington, Virginia

* * * * * * * * * * * *

Electromagnetic Maneuver Warfare Command & Control (EMC2)

Description

The Electromagnetic Maneuver Warfare Command & Control effort aims to develop the command and control for frequency and functional capabilities across platforms and strike groups. This is an early step toward the ultimate goal of real-time, optimized coordination and interoperability to use any part of the electromagnetic (EM) spectrum for any required function. Potential operational impacts include combined EM warfare capabilities in the sea, air, and land domains to generate enhanced combat effects, countermeasures, ultra-wide frequency coverage, and agility to ensure communications surveillance and situational awareness in congested and contested environments.

Status

The Chief of Naval Research selected EMC2 as an FY 2016 Innovative Naval Prototype New Start.

Developers

Naval Research Laboratory Washington, D.C.

Naval Surface Warfare Center Carderock, Maryland Dahlgren, Virginia

Space and Naval Warfare Systems Command San Diego, California

* * * * * * * * * * * *

Electromagnetic Railgun (EMRG) Description

The Electromagnetic Railgun Innovative Naval Prototype (INP) is a long-range weapon that fires projectiles using electromagnetic forces instead of chemical propellants. Electricity generated by the ship is stored in the pulsed power system. When released into the railgun, an electric pulse launches the projectile at speeds up to Mach 6 (nearly 1.3 miles per second). A successful railgun would bring increased range compared to conventional powder guns, increased capacity, and improved operational economy to fleet operations. The railgun enhances safety aboard ship by reducing gunpowder and high explosive hazards in ship magazines. The guided hypervelocity projectile (HVP) fired by the railgun improves safety ashore for troops and civilians through precision, accurate targeting and by eliminating unexploded ordnance on the battlefield. The compact HVP stows tightly and provides deep magazines for greater depth of fire. And, the flow cost per engagement shifts the cost curve to the Navy's advantage.

Status

The Railgun INP is in the second phase of a two-phase development effort. INP Phase I (FY 2005-2011) successfully advanced foundational enabling technologies and explored, through analysis and war gaming, the railgun's multi-mission utility. Launcher energy was increased by a factor of five to the system objective muzzle energy of 32 mega joules (110 nautical miles range) and barrel life was increased from tens of shots to hundreds of shots. Two contractors delivered tactical-style advanced containment launchers proving the feasibility of composite wound launchers. Pulsed power size was cut in half while thermal management for firing rate (rep-rate) was added to the design. INP Phase II focuses on increasing rep-rate capability. Rep-rate adds new levels of complexity to all of the railgun sub-systems, including thermal management, autoloader, and energy storage. A new test facility capable of supporting rep-rate testing at full energy level is coming on line at the Terminal Range at the Naval Surface Warfare Center, Dahlgren, Virginia. A new demonstration launcher (DL1) has been delivered and installed at the Terminal Range to commission the new facility. Additional rep-rate composite launchers (RCLs) capable of rep-rate are in various stages of design and fabrication. The Office of Naval Research will develop a tactical prototype railgun launcher and pulsed-power architecture suitable for advanced testing both afloat and ashore.

Developers

Naval Surface Warfare Center Dahlgren, Virginia

Office of Naval Research Arlington, Virginia

* * * * * * * * * * *

* * * * * * * * * * * *

Energy System Technology Evaluation Program (ESTEP)

Description

244

The Navy has always been a leader in energy research. The ESTEP program leverages Navy prowess in combination with the best from commercial sector advances. ESTEP conducts real-world advanced technology demonstrations to evaluate emerging energy technologies using Navy and Marine Corps facilities as test beds. The technology focuses on innovative pre-commercial and nascent commercial energy technologies obtained from open-market sourcing, including companies from within the venture capital and small business communities. Additionally, each ESTEP project requires participation by Department of the Navy (DoN) civilians, military personnel or veterans in key technical or business project roles, thus providing real-world training and education opportunities for the future DoN energy workforce. These participants include students enrolled in technical and business energy-track curricula at the Naval Postgraduate School. A pilot veterans outreach effort is underway for the San Diego region, with special focus on linking to veteran programs already established at San Diego State University, including the Troops to Engineers and S.E.R.V.I.C.E. (Success in Engineering for Recent Veterans through Internship and Career Experience) programs. More about Troops to Engineers and student veterans in ESTEP can be found at this video link: http://youtu.be/leACsN-2IF4

Status

ESTEP is an ONR program sponsored through the ONR's Sea Warfare and Weapons Department.

Developers

Naval Facilities Command Washington, D.C.

Naval Postgraduate School Monterey, California

Office of Naval Research Arlington, Virginia Space and Naval Warfare

Systems Command San Diego, California

* * * * * * * * * * * *

Forward-Deployed Energy and Communications Outpost (FDECO)

Description

The Forward-Deployed Energy and Communications Outpost Innovative Naval Prototype (INP) addresses advanced technology to provide an undersea energy and communications infrastructure necessary to assure undersea dominance. This project provides unmanned undersea vehicles the expeditionary, forward-deployed capability necessary for force multiplication in an anti-access/ area-denial environment by extending their reach, situational awareness, and standoff advantage. Technology developments focus on data and energy management and transfer technologies that: enable autonomous undersea operations; provide system architectures that are persistent, scalable, and mission agile; provide communication and energy support in degraded and contested environments; and provide a platform-agnostic solution that reduces development and maintenance costs. FDECO uses a phased approach to demonstrate the architecture and enabling technologies that support platforms and sensors.

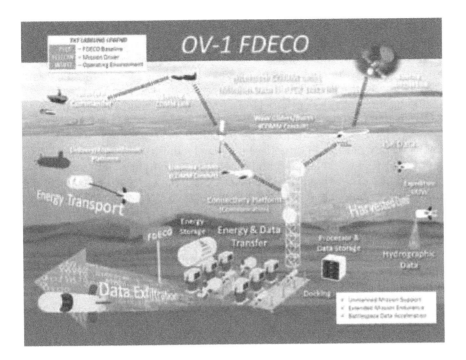

Status

The focus during FY 2015 was on architecture planning, preparing for an industry day, identifying important technologies, and preliminary planning for Phase 1 demonstrations. The FDECO INP Officially began in FY 2016. Program execution during this year focused on architecture planning and subsystem development using limited objective experiments (LOEs) to validate primary subsystem performance. LOEs were held every three months and addressed key technical gaps, risk areas, and lessons learned. The first of two major FDECO demonstrations is scheduled for the end of FY 2017. This demonstration will focus on FDECO supporting the intelligence, surveillance, and reconnaissance/intelligence preparation of the operational environment mission using unmanned undersea vehicles.

Developers

Aerojet Rocketdyne Sacramento, California

Leidos Reston, Virginia

Naval Sea Systems Command Washington, D.C.

Oak Ridge National Laboratory Oak Ridge, Tennessee

Office of Naval Research Arlington, Virginia Space and Naval Warfare

Systems Command San Diego, California

* * * * * * * * * * * *

Future Naval Capabilities (FNC)

Description

The FNC program, initiated by the Department of the Navy in 2002, develops and transitions cutting-edge science and technology (S&T) to acquisition program managers within a four-year timeframe. The program delivers FNCs for integration into platforms, weapons, sensors, and specifications to improve Navy and Marine Corps warfighting and support capabilities. FNCs typically begin at a point where analytical and experimental proof-of-concept has been established (Technology Readiness Level, or TRL, 3). The technologies are subsequently matured to the model or prototype stage and demonstrated in a relevant environment (TRL 6). Once demonstrated, the acquisition sponsor takes responsibility for conducting any additional research, development, test and evaluation (RDT&E) necessary to engineer and integrate the technology into an acquisition program of record and ultimately deploy the new capability into the fleet or force. The program is governed by a set of formal business rules, which ensures stakeholders are involved in the oversight, management and execution of FNC investments. The process strengthens coordination between the fleet/force, S&T, acquisition, and resources/requirements communities. For all FNCs, continued S&T funding is contingent upon signed and negotiated technology transition agreements (TTAs) in place to transition and deploy the technology. FNCs unable to meet this requirement are subject to potential termination. That said, the FNC program has already registered several successes, including:

The Compact High-Density Energy Storage FNC product will develop and demonstrate an advance module-level energy storage technology to expand the envelope of safe storage, transport and operating conditions. The approach will use scalable/modular energy storage chemistries with high cycle life and reconfigurable cell-level control technology. The result will be a system that can: (1) reduce the need for fuel resupply through reduced generator fuel consumption; (2) reduce total ownership cost through reduction of generator maintenance and improved battery longevity; and (3) make important progress toward achieving USMC 2025 objective for using fuel only for mobility.

The Multifunction Energy Storage Future FNC will develop components and methods to enable high-density, high-cycle rate, megawatt-scale energy storage systems incorporating multi-tier safety capability and the appropriate controls to manage internal configuration and enable overall electrical bus stability in conjunction with shipboard power generation systems. This product serves platforms and applications that utilize electrical architectures with continuous kW to MW scale electric weapons and sensor pulsed loads with identified and stochastic transient load profiles. In addition, it provides installed energy to enable ride through capability for high fuel-efficient power-generation systems and operation.

The High Power Solid State Circuit Protection FNC will develop and demonstrate pure solid-state or a hybrid (electrical/mechanical) circuit protection solution. The solid-state solution relies on semiconductor devices to provide bi-directional power flow and fault clearing. The hybrid design utilizes a high speed mechanical disconnect and semiconductor device in parallel to provide the same functionality as solid-state solutions. Fault-clearing times range from 15 to 400 microseconds. Phase 1 efforts developed 1000 Volt, 1000 Amp devices. Phase 2 activities will investigate higher voltage/current DC operation. The efforts support advanced power distribution and energy storage required for future high-energy weapons and sensors by providing high-speed fault detection and clearing for medium-voltage direct-current power distribution and mission critical loads.

In essence, the FNC program is structured to create a healthy balance of S&T "push" and acquisition "pull."

Status

The FNC program plays an important role within the Office of Naval Research's (ONR) investment strategy. As the largest part of the technology maturation portfolio, the program ills the niche between high-risk game-changing investments without existing and defined transition paths, and quick reaction investments that respond to specified needs within a two-year period. The structure of the program ensures FNCs respond to S&T capability gaps (acquisition needs) validated by stakeholders, while allowing FNC technology managers to leverage groundbreaking research by identifying how those needs are met. The FNC Technology Oversight Group—a three-star board tasked with FNC program oversight by the vice chief of naval operations, assistant commandant of the Marine Corps, and assistant secretary of the Navy for Research, Development and Acquisition—reviews and approves/ rejects S&T capability gaps.

Developers

Office of Naval Research Arlington, Virginia

* * * * * * * * * * * *

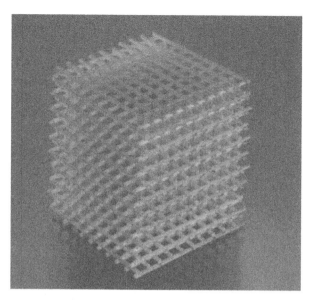

Lightweight and Modern Metals Manufacturing Innovation (LM3I) Institute

Lightweight Innovations for Tomorrow (LIFT)

Description

LIFT, headquartered in Detroit, Michigan, is the ONR-managed, Office of the Secretary of Defense-sponsored, LM3I Institute. LIFT is part of the National Network for Manufacturing Innovation (NNMI), an initiative launched by President Obama to strengthen the innovation, performance, competitiveness, and job-creating power of U.S. manufacturing. Operated by the American Lightweight Materials Manufacturing Innovation Institute (ALMMII), LIFT focuses on advancing a systems-level approach to the design and manufacturing of lightweight metal components and structures leading to enhanced system performance, greater energy efficiency, and lower life-cycle cost—characteristics that are of great importance to the Department of Defense. LIFT is a public/ private partnership that brings government, industry, and academia together in an environment where joint development and commercialization of alloys, processes, and products can occur. LIFT emphasizes the integrated materials and component design and manufacturing for commercial and defense applications. The technical approach leverages integrated computational materials engineering (ICME) concepts and includes the verification of designs and validation through experimental testing of components and structures. The long-term goal is to ensure the United States is the world leader in the application of innovative lightweight metal production and component/subsystem manufacturing technologies. LIFT will accomplish this through technology innovation, strategic partnerships, and programs to build an educated and skilled manufacturing workforce that is confident and competent in using new technologies and processes. Partnerships with defense, automotive, aerospace, energy, and recreational equipment industries enable maturation and scaling of advanced technologies to reduce risk and cost barriers, enhancing competitiveness of American industries and technological leadership for U.S. national security.

Status

In February 2017, LIFT will be entering the third year of a five-year cooperative agreement. LIFT membership is robust and has shown significant expansion since its inception. The technical pillars under which projects are developed include thermo-mechanical processing, melt processing, powder processing, agile tools, coatings, and joining. The first set of nine technical projects is ongoing, the second set of ten projects is in work plan development, and the third project call is complete with 13 project awards expected by early 2017. Examples of current projects include developing and deploying thin wall ductile iron castings for high volume production (patent pending), thin-wall aluminum die casting development, and integration of ICME with legacy and novel thermo-mechanical processing for assured properties in large titanium structures. Additionally, LIFT has become an industry and government leader in workforce development and education programs, with several LIFT initiatives being used as benchmarks for government, academia, and other manufacturing innovation institutes.

Developers

Edison Welding Institute Columbus, Ohio

Office of Naval Research Arlington, Virginia

The Ohio State University Columbus, Ohio

University of Michigan Ann Arbor, Michigan

* * * * * * * * * * * *

Medium Displacement Unmanned Surface Vehicle "Sea Hunter"

Description

Sea Hunter is a 132-feet long, autonomous, medium-displacement unmanned surface vessel (MDUSV). The vessel is designed for long-endurance operations and is self-deploying—it does not have to be carried to the operating area by another vessel. The technical breakthrough is in the autonomy. Sea Hunter's autonomous control system allows it to operate while avoiding hazards and in compliance with International Regulations for Preventing Collisions at Sea. Sea Hunter's autonomous control system leverages components of ONR's CARACaS (Control Architecture for Robotic Agent Command and Sensing) system that has been developed by ONR during the past 13 years and has been used in the "USV

Swarm" multi-USV demonstrations in 2014 and 2016. USV Swarm has demonstrated mission-specific "behaviors" such as escort, attack, patrol, intercept, track and trail. These behaviors are what provide a USV a mission capability. Behaviors such as these will be added to Sea Hunter and will be evaluated in future fleet experimentation. Inclusion of autonomous control is a significant advancement in USV capability.

Status

Sea Hunter, with autonomy system components leveraged from the "Swarm Boats" autonomous control system—CARACaS—in late 2016 is undergoing at-sea testing at Space and Naval Warfare Systems Center Pacific, San Diego, and is sponsored through the ONR's Office of Disruptive Technology. This testing will include integration of mature payloads to demonstrate autonomous mission capability through cutting-edge effects.

Developers

Office of Naval Research Arlington, Virginia

* * * * * * * * * * * *

Naval Research Laboratory (NRL)

Description

The Naval Research Laboratory is the Department of the Navy's (DoN) corporate laboratory. The NRL base program carries out research to meet needs identified in the Naval S&T Strategic Plan and sustains world-class skills and innovation in the DoN's in-house lab. The broad-based core scientific research at NRL serves as a foundation that can be focused on any particular area of interest to develop technology rapidly from concept to operation when high-priority, short-term needs arise. NRL has served the Navy, Marine Corps, and the Nation for more than 90 years with a breadth of research that facilitates quick assimilation of critical ideas and technologies being developed overseas for exploitation or countermeasures. In addition, NRL is the lead Navy laboratory for research in space systems, firefighting, tactical electronic warfare, microelectronic devices, and artificial intelligence. NRL lines of business include battlespace environments, electronics and electronic warfare, information systems technology, materials, sensors, space platforms, technology transfer and undersea warfare. For example, NRL research explores naval environments with wide-ranging investigations that measure parameters of deep oceans, analyze marine atmospheric conditions, monitor solar behavior, and assess survivability of critical naval space assets. Detection and communication capabilities benefit from research that exploits new portions of the electromagnetic spectrum, extends ranges to outer space, and enables reliable and secure transfer of information. Research in the fields of autonomous systems, bio-molecular science, engineering, firefighting, fuels, lubricants, nanotechnology, shipbuilding materials, sound in the sea, submarine habitability, superconductivity and virtual reality remain steadfast concerns at NRL.

Status

Research and projects continue in a broad spectrum of fields.

Developers

Naval Research Laboratory Washington, D.C.

Office of Naval Research Arlington, Virginia

* * * * * * * * * * * *

Navy Manufacturing Technology Program (ManTech)

Description

The Navy ManTech Program is an industrial-preparedness program providing for the development of enabling manufacturing technology and the transition of this technology for the production and sustainment of Navy weapon systems. Navy ManTech works with defense contractors, the naval research enterprise, Navy acquisition program offices, and research partners to develop improved processes and equipment. Project success is measured by implementation of these technologies on the factory floor. Navy ManTech's customers include acquisition program managers and industry partners responsible for moving major Navy weapon systems from development into production and Navy logistics managers at the naval depots and shipyards responsible for repair, overhaul, and remanufacture of these systems. Reducing the acquisition and life-cycle cost of submarine, ship, and aircraft platforms is a critical Navy goal. Indeed, Navy ManTech is focused on affordability improvements for key acquisition programs. Navy ManTech performs affordability assessments to measure progress toward meeting program and ManTech affordability goals. The affordability assessment on a project basis is an engineering rough order of magnitude cost-reduction estimate of dollars-per-hull or dollars-per-aircraft. These assessments are reviewed by the implementing industrial facility, forwarded to the Navy ManTech Office for analysis, and then routed to the associated program Office for concurrence. ManTech helps these programs achieve their respective affordability goals by transitioning needed manufacturing technology that results in a cost reduction or cost avoidance.

Status

In early 2017, ManTech has affordability initiatives underway for the Virginia (SSN 774)-class submarine program, the Ohio (SSBN 726)-class replacement program, the Ford (CVN 78) aircraft carrier program, the Arleigh Burke (DDG 51) class guided missile warship program, the F-35 Lightning LL Joint Strike Fighter (JSF) program, and the CH-53K King Stallion heavy-lift helicopter program.

The Virginia-class affordability initiative has been a major success for both Navy ManTech and the SSN 774 program Office and was a key contributor to the Navy's "two-for-four" cost-reduction initiative. The Virginia-class ManTech affordability portfolio investment is some $91.1 million and a potential cost savings of more than $43.3 million per hull. The 2016 General Dynamics Electric Boat implementation analysis lists 37 ManTech affordability projects that had completed and had either been implemented or were being implemented. Together, these projects totaled cost-savings of $32.2 million per submarine. With two submarines procured every year, the annual Virginia-class affordability savings for 2016 were greater than the entire annual ManTech budget.

ManTech's F-35 Affordability Initiative is ramping up very successfully, as well. With a FY 2016 F-35 ManTech portfolio total of $33 million, the JSF Program Executive Office estimates a total DoD savings of approximately $800 million that can be allocated to reach cost goals. Two implementations are, first, the F-35 Canopy Thermoforming Automation initiative that has generated as much as $125 million in cost savings (depending on the number of spares required) on a $1.4 million Navy investment, and, second, the F-35 Transparency Clean Up Automation initiative that is projected to save more than $160 million on a $1.1 million investment.

Developers

Navy ManTech Centers of Excellence Arlington, Virginia

Office of Naval Research Arlington, Virginia

* * * * * * * * * * * *

Netted Emulation of Multi-Element Signature against Integrated Sensors (NEMESIS)

Description

The NEMESIS Innovative Naval Prototype (INP) is developing an electronic warfare (EW) system of systems that will synchronize EW techniques across a variety of distributed platforms to create coordinated and consistent EW effects. NEMESIS emphasis is on the coordination and synchronization of EW capabilities and tactics against sensors in a variety of scenarios.

Status

NEMESIS has been in development since 2014, including close collaboration with the Office of Naval Research, the Office of the Chief of Naval Operations, fleet commands and analysts, acquisition programs of record, government laboratories and warfare centers, the Defense Advanced Research Programs Agency, and federally funded research and development centers and university affiliated research centers. During 2016, NEMESIS capabilities began hardware development, technique and software migration and field testing at the sub-system level. In FY 2017-2018 flight and at-sea testing will be conducted on integrated system level capabilities in preparation for graduation demonstrations in late FY 2018.

Developers

Georgia Tech Research Institute Atlanta, Georgia

Johns Hopkins Applied Physics Lab Laurel, Maryland

MIT-Lincoln Lab Cambridge, Massachusetts

Naval Undersea Warfare Center Newport, Rhode Island

Office of Naval Research Arlington, Virginia Space and Naval Warfare Command Charlestown, North Carolina

* * * * * * * * * * * *

ONR Global

Description

The Office of Naval Research (ONR) Global fosters international science and technology (S&T) cooperation and facilitates the delivery of cutting-edge technology to Sailors and Marines. As the preeminent external network facilitator for ONR, ONR Global connects the Navy Fleet and Marine Corps Forces, the international S&T community, and foreign military partners to ONR and the Naval Research Enterprise (NRE). ONR Global supports the full spectrum of research, development, test, and evaluation (RDT&E), from basic research to technology transition and fleet exercise, through the efforts of science advisors; global science directors; and international liaison officers. ONR Global has 25 science advisors embedded in Navy and Marine Corps commander staffs to directly link with the naval warfighter, communicate Fleet/Force needs to the NRE and deliver S&T solutions that solve operational problems. The international science grants are executed by 23 global science directors who search the world for emerging scientific research and advanced technologies.

The science directors engage primarily academic institutions and industry to develop opportunities for fundamental research and collaboration that add value to naval S&T programs. And finally, a three-person ONR Global team coordinates ONR's partnerships with counterpart defense agencies through naval S&T cooperation. To best execute its mission, ONR Global maintains a forward presence at regional engagement offices in key locations around the world—London, United

Kingdom; Prague, Czech Republic; Santiago, Chile; Sao Paulo, Brazil; Singapore; and Tokyo, Japan— as well as Navy, Marine Corps, and joint commands worldwide.

Status

ONR Global's efforts continue throughout a wide range of activities with international S&T partners, the Fleet and Marine Force and foreign military partners in support of the United States and allied/partner warfighters.

Developers

Office of Naval Research Global London, England

* * * * * * * * * * *

Resilient Hull, Infrastructure, Mechanical, and Electrical Security (RHIMES)

Description

The goal of RHIMES is to protect critical control systems aboard naval platforms from faults due to cyber-attack and ensure resiliency of those systems by returning to a known good state. RHIMES will develop prototype cyber resiliency tools and architectures that integrate cyber solutions and make them work together to strengthen critical control systems against failures due to a cyber-attack and help build cyber-attack resiliency into legacy, current, and future control systems.

Status

In 2015 the Navy approved RHIMES as a FY 2017 FNC new start. Planning is underway between the Office of Naval Research, Naval Sea Systems Command, Naval Surface Warfare Center, and various academic and industry performers. Because the approach is very cutting edge and game changing, many performer teams are partnerships between academia and either a federally funded research and development center, university affiliated research center, or defense industry partner.

Developers - Office of Naval Research Arlington, Virginia

* * * * * * * * * * *

Science, Technology, Engineering and Mathematics (STEM)

Description

Successful naval operations rely on having access to the best people and technologies to effectively handle changing and increasingly diverse threat environments in the reality of finite resources. To ensure continuing security of the United States and allies/partners, while practicing prudent stewardship of resources, the Department of the Navy (DoN) continues to evolve a STEM strategy of education and workforce vertical integration, horizontal integration, and effectiveness evaluation. Vertical integration of education and workforce strategically integrates education and exposure to STEM across pre-kindergarten through post-doctoral studies, with noted attention to military families and Veterans. Horizontal integration focuses on education and workforce across local schools in the United States and abroad, in-person and in virtual environments. Effectiveness evaluation systematically examines the costs and impacts of existing projects, programs, and policies, and builds effectiveness assessment and evaluation into future undertakings. Actions to ensure access to needed STEM capabilities are based on understandings of current workforce demographics and STEM-proficient workers who might be attracted to other STEM settings because of greater personal and family benefits, among other reasons. DoN actions to recruit and grow workers with needed STEM skills are complemented by proven and innovative approaches to inform and involve students and members of the public in all locations and at all ages and stages of life with exciting STEM work, training, and education opportunities. The Office of Naval Research (ONR) manages the coordination of the DoN's STEM efforts and coordinates interactions with STEM efforts across the government through inter-agency working groups.

Status

The Navy and Marine Corps STEM tool kit of education, workforce, grants, contracts, and collaborative interactions incorporates vertical and horizontal integration and effectiveness evaluation, to ensure access to workers with needed STEM capabilities. ONR's STEM portfolio addresses laboratory workforce initiatives, naval-level STEM coordination, ONR-level STEM initiatives, and execution of the naval portions of several Secretary of Defense-level STEM programs. Examples of particular projects cover young students (e.g., SeaPerch) through graduate students (e.g., Naval Research Enterprise Internship Program), and others with potential to contribute to naval STEM capabilities.

Developers

Office of Naval Research Arlington, Virginia

* * * * * * * * * * * *

Solid State Laser

Description

The Solid State Laser Technology Maturation (SSL-TM) program is a leap-ahead effort that provides naval surface platforms with a highly effective and affordable point-defense capability to counter surface and air threats. The SSL-TM Program comprises the Laser Weapon System Demonstrator (LWSD) which includes a Northrop Grumman Aerospace Systems-developed Tactical Core Laser Module (TCLM), government developed equipment, and a robust lethality, test, and modeling program. The Naval Surface Warfare Center, Dahlgren Division (NSWC-DD) is the warfare-center and system-integration lead for the LWSD integration and test. The government-developed equipment includes the Hybrid Predictive Avoidance Safety Subsystem (HPASS), Combat System-Integrated Support

Equipment (CS-ISE). Laser Weapon Console (LWC), Thermal Storage Module (TSM), and Energy Storage Module (ESM).

The LWSD was designed to provide variable engagement capabilities that complement gun and missile weapon systems. The capability offers an alternative to expensive missile system exchanges, particularly against flow-cost and asymmetric threats. The system has a deep magazine and runs on ship's power and cooling. The sensor suite offers improved imaging capabilities for increasing battle-space awareness and decision timelines. The SSL-QRC was a CNO Strategic Initiative to see how laser weapon systems could be operationally deployed.

The SSL-QRC was an NSWC Dahlgren Division-led design, development and integration of a 30kW weapon system on the USS Ponce (LPD/AFSB-I 15) in 2014 for a one-year deployment. The system has transitioned to become a fleet asset and in late 2016 remains deployed in the U.S. Naval Forces Central Command 5th Fleet operating area.

SSL-TM program leverages lessons learned from the SSL-QRC deployment on USS Ponce in the Arabian Gulf. The S&T innovations being demonstrated on SSL-TM include increased power levels (150 kW class) and an off-axis beam director. The SSL-TM system will be integrated on the ex-USS Paul Foster (eDD-964) self-defense test ship for at-sea testing in 2018. The SSL-QRC and SSL-TM program goals are to accelerate delivery of laser weapons to surface Navy forces and provide new capability to the warfighter.

This revolutionary technology provides multiple payoffs to the warfighter to include flow cost-per-engagement and precision targeting at long ranges, increasing ship self-defense. This concept has been proven through live-fire at-sea demonstrations and the USS Ponce deployment. The capability of these weapon systems will provide game-changing engagement strategies that will be on the right side of the cost curve for the Navy.

Status

The SSL-QRC laser weapon system was installed on the USS Ponce in 2014. The system transitioned to fleet support at the beginning of FY 2016 and is still operational in the Arabian Gulf. It has been certified for use as a ship-defense weapon. The SSL-TM program awarded a contract to Northrop Grumman in October 2015 to develop the TCLM for the LWSD that will conduct sea-based testing on Paul Foster during 2018.

Developers

Naval Sea Systems Command Washington, D.C.

Naval Surface Warfare Command Dahlgren, Virginia

Office of Naval Research Arlington, Virginia

Space Warfare Systems Command San Diego, California

* * * * * * * * * * * *

SwampWorks

Description

The Office of Naval Research (ONR) SwampWorks program explores innovative, high-risk, and disruptive technologies and concepts. Due to the portfolio's high-risk nature, SwampWorks conducts short exploratory studies to examine the maturation of a proposed technology before making substantial investments. Efforts are smaller in scope than Innovative Naval Prototypes (INPs) and are intended to produce results in less than three years. SwampWorks projects are not limited to any set of technology areas; rather, SwampWorks invests in innovative technology development and experimentation that will ultimately provide a dramatic improvement for the warfighter. Recent successful SwampWorks efforts include:

Battlespace Exploitation of Mixed Reality (BEMR) is an effort based on leading the way into the use of advanced gaming technologies, developing a combination of fledgling concepts, and bringing them to life on actual Navy applications. BEMR leverages heavily on the idea that using gaming technologies are how the Navy's new recruits have been trained for most of their lives, and applying that concept to the interface between new Sailors and older infrastructure. BEMR enables personnel to be more proficient, requires less on the job training, and adds efficiencies to the training process. The BEMR Lab is in place at Space and Naval Warfare Systems Center Pacific, and is setting the benchmark for Navy mixed-reality technologies and training.

The Interactive Mine Identification from a Highly Maneuverable Vehicle effort has developed an autonomous system with tight integration between perception and behaviors that includes the ability to reacquire and identify underwater mines, improvised explosive devices, and unexploded ordnance buried or obscured in highly cluttered or constrained very-shallow-water environments. This effort is an example of advanced autonomy: interactive perception involves a tighter coupling between a system's perception mechanisms and the autonomous behaviors. The vehicle is a highly maneuverable unmanned undersea vehicle with integrated multi-modal sensing (sonar, magnetic, and optical) and advanced autonomous behaviors and vehicle controls. This effort will transition to the ONR Future Naval Capability (FNC) program, including sensors, sensing algorithms, and vehicle-control algorithms. It will also be a primary experimentation platform for the FNC. Major goals include: reduced false-alarm rate; improved area coverage rates sustained; reduced mine countermeasure (MCM) timeline; capability to reacquire and identify buried mines and unexploded ordnance; increase accuracy for buried mine localization to allow neutralization; and add MCM capability in challenging underwater environments.

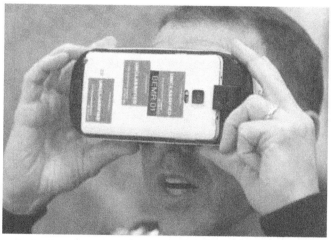

Role-Based Cognitive Autonomy effort's goal is to dramatically increase intelligent self-managing autonomy for long-duration and robust/reliable mission operations with a focus on advancing platform independent intelligent autonomy. The team has captured and implemented a submarine watch-stander agent-based autonomy software model, captured subject-matter expert knowledge from submarine operations and agent interaction mimicking, and taken advantage of current submarine tactics as applied to autonomous unmanned vehicles (AUV) operations. The team has also modeled "cross domain" ability with demonstrations in multiple AUV platforms to demonstrate portability. The end game is to develop a prototype software system capable of running on any AUV platform to provide an underlying architecture for mission expansion and cross-platform, cross-domain use. Key benefits include: reduction of human workload when employing AUVs for mission tasks (autonomous self-determination); lower risk of vehicle loss/collision safety/vehicle capture; enable human to multiple autonomous system platforms cooperative/collaborative operations; and enable long-duration operations across all mission types. This effort represents the future of advanced autonomous systems.

Status

SwampWorks has substantial flexibility in planning and execution. Its streamlined approval process allows for the shortest possible technology development and fielding timeframe.

Developers

Office of Naval Research Arlington, Virginia

* * * * * * * * * * *

TechSolutions

Description

TechSolutions is a transformational business process created by the Office of Naval Research to provide Sailors and Marines a web-based tool for bringing technology needs to the attention of the naval science and technology (S&T) community for rapid response prototype delivery. The Internet connection enables TechSolutions to receive and act on recommendations and suggestions directly from Navy and Marine Corps personnel working at the deckplate and ground levels on ways to improve mission effectiveness through technology insertion. It is focused solely on delivering needed technology to the Navy and Marine Corps and moving the sea services toward increased technology need awareness. TechSolutions uses rapid prototyping of technologies to meet specific requirements with definable metrics and includes appropriate Systems Command elements in an integrated product team concept. While neither a substitute for the acquisition process nor a replacement for the systems commands, TechSolutions aims to provide the Fleet and Marine Force with a prototype demonstration that is a 60-80 percent solution addressing immediate needs for transition by the acquisition community. Examples include:

Beyond line of sight (BLOS) Scan Eagle. Scan Eagle UAS operations are limited to line of sight (LOS) range. While hub and spoke concept extends the range of the

Scan Eagle UAS, it is manpower heavy and UAS range is still limited and implementation of this concept is sometimes impractical in an expeditionary environment. Beyond line-of-sight (BLOS) Scan Eagle UAS will extend Scan Eagle UAS range to better support Naval Special Warfare Command operational forces when conducting combat missions in austere/remote locations. Adding this capability gives warfighter increased battle space awareness through increasing the range of electro-optical/infrared theater assets.

Multiple Weapon Control Sight (MWCS): The sight provides Marines with an improved day/night fire-control capability for several infantry weapon systems, such as riles and automatic grenade launchers. This allows Marines to engage targets effectively during day and night operations. This multi-weapon capability decreases the number of different sighting systems that warfighters are required to learn and lessens the burden on the supply and maintenance infrastructure. Marines have tested and evaluated the upgraded sight in the field, and their response has been positive.

Head-Mounted Augmented Reality Display: As Marines conduct cyberspace operations at the tactical edge in support of the Marine Air Ground Task Force, the amount of data available to them can be overwhelming and could detract from their battlespace situational awareness. This system gives the warfighter a head-mounted augmented reality display that enables a warfighter to quickly scan relevant mission data in a field-of-view display to enable completion of critical tasks simultaneously. This technology will enable cyber operators to integrate with tactical units while still conducting technically complex cyberspace/electronic warfare mission sets. In addition, the glasses will run the Android OS so Marines can develop their own tactical applications.

Status

To succeed in its S&T mission, TechSolutions needs active involvement and participation by the operating forces. Every query will be answered, and if a demonstration is performed or prototype developed, the submitter will be invited to participate in the process from the start through final delivery of the technology. TechSolutions aims to deliver a demonstration prototype in 12-18 months.

Developers

Office of Naval Research Arlington, Virginia

* * * * * * * * * * *

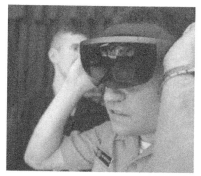

Total Platform Cyber Protection (TPCP)

Description

This FY 2018 Innovative Naval Prototype will deliver leap-ahead resilient cybersecurity tools to enable our warfighting platforms to "fight through" current and future cyber-attacks. This will also assure command and control of these platforms at the tactical and operational level of war by delivering comprehensive defense-in-depth cyber capabilities to monitor, detect, and recover in near real-time. The technical approach leverages dynamic and active prevention techniques to reduce cyber platform attack surfaces, prevent the exploitation of system vulnerabilities, shorten detection timelines, and mitigate when necessary. Cyber resiliency and warfighting effectiveness is maximized by protecting common layers of platform functionality, including: component (i.e., hardware) basic input/output system buses (local, system, and peripheral), hypervisor, operating system, middleware, application space, and network infrastructure. This INP will deliver software based capabilities and a compact and affordable computing appliance applicable to any platform that can be rapidly deployed to any naval platform that will monitor, detect, assess, mitigate, and recover against today's and tomorrow's cyber threats.

Status

The Office of Naval Research continues to engage with industry and the academic to refine its strategy and meet the needs of the Navy and Marine Corps.

Developers

Office of Naval Research Arlington, Virginia

* * * * * * * * * * * *

GLOSSARY

A2/AD Anti-Access/Area-Denial

AACUS Autonomous Aerial Cargo/Utility System

AADC Area Air Defense Commander

AADS Amphibious Assault Direction System

AAG Advanced Arresting Gear

AAI Airborne ASW Intelligence

AAMDTC Aegis Ashore Missile Defense Test Complex

AARGM Advanced Anti-Radiation Guided Missile

AAW Anti-Air Warfare

ABMD Aegis Ballistic Missile Defense

ABNCP Airborne Command Post

ABS Assault Breaching System

ACAT Acquisition Category

ACB Amphibious Construction Battalion, or, Advanced Capability Build

ACCES Advanced Cryptologic Carry-on Exploitation System

ACDS Advanced Combat Direction System

ACINT Acoustic Intelligence

ACS Aerial Common Sensor, or, Aegis Combat System

ACTD Advanced Concept Technology Demonstration

ACU Assault Craft Unit

AD Air Defense

ADCAP Advanced Capability

ADM Acquisition Decision Memorandum

ADNS Automated Digital Network System

ADP Automated Data Processing

ADS Advanced Deployable System

AE Assault Echelon

AEA Airborne Electronic Attack

AEHF Advanced Extremely-High Frequency

AEL Authorized Equipage List

AEM/S Advanced Enclosed Mast/Sensor

AESA Active Electronically Scanned Array

AESOP Afloat Electromagnetic Spectrum Operations Program

AFATDS Advanced Field Artillery Tactical Data System

AFB Air Force Base

AFG Airfoil Group

AFFF Aqueous Film Forming Foam

AFOE Assault Follow-On Echelon

AFQT Armed Forces Qualification Test

AFSB Afloat Forward Staging Base

AGF/LCC Amphibious Command Ship

AGS Advanced Gun System

AHE Advanced Hawkeye Aircraft

AIEWS Advanced Integrated Electronic Warfare System

AIP Anti-Submarine Warfare Improvement Program, or, Air-Independent Propulsion

AIS Automatic Identification System

AISR&T Airborne Intelligence, Surveillance, Reconnaissance, and Targeting

ALCS Airborne Launch Control System

ALFS Airborne Flow-Frequency Active Sonar

ALMDS Airborne Laser Mine Detection System

AMCM Airborne Mine Countermeasures

AMDR Air and Missile Defense Radar

AMF Airborne Maritime Fixed

AMNS Airborne Mine Neutralization System

AMOD Aegis Modernization

AMPIR Airborne Polarmetric Microwave Imaging Radiometer

AMRAAM Advanced Medium-Range Air-to-Air Missile

ANDVT Advanced Narrow-Band Digital Voice Terminal

AOA Amphibious Objective Area, or, Analysis of Alternatives

AOE Fast Combat Support Ship

AOR Area of Responsibility

APB Advanced Processor Build, or, Acquisition Program Baseline

APS Air Force Prepositioning Ships

APSB Advanced Port Security Barrier

APTS Afloat Personal Telephone Service

ARCI Acoustic Rapid COTS Insertion

ARG Amphibious Ready Group

ARI Active Reserve Integration

AR/LSB Aerial Supply/Logistics for Sea Basing

ARM Anti-Radiation Missile

AS Submarine Tender, or, Acquisition Strategy

ASDS Advanced SEAL (or swimmer) Delivery System

268

ASCM Anti-Ship Cruise Missile

ASO Automated Shipboard Weather Observation System

ASROC Anti-Submarine Rocket

ASUW Anti-Surface Warfare

ASW Anti-Submarine Warfare

ASWC Anti-Submarine Warfare Commander

AT Advanced Targeting

ATA Automatic Target Acquisition

ATC Air Traffic Control

ATD Advanced Technology Demonstration, or, Aircrew Training Device

ATDLS Advanced Tactical Data Link System

ATF Fleet Ocean-going Tug

ATFLIR Advanced Targeting Forward-Looking Infrared

ATFP Anti-Terrorism and Force Protection

ATM Asynchronous Transfer Mode

ATSM Active Target Strength Measurement

ATT Anti-Torpedo Torpedo

ATW Advanced Threat Warning

ATWCS Advanced Tomahawk Weapon Control

AURE All-Up Round Equipment

AUWS Assessment Underwater Work System

AWACS Airborne Warning and Control System

AWS Aegis Weapon System

BAH Basic Allowance for Housing, or, Booz Allen Hamilton

BAMS Broad Area Maritime Surveillance

BCA Broadcast Control Authority

BCO Base Communications Office

BDI Battle Damage Intelligence

BDII Battle Damage Indication Imagery

BEMR Battlespace Exploitation of Mixed Reality

BEWL Biometrics Enabled Watchlist

BFCAPP Battle Force Capability Assessment and Programming Process

BFEM Battle Force Email

BFTN Battle Force Tactical Network

BFTT Battle Force Tactical Trainer

BLAST Blast Load Assessment Sense and Test

BLII Base-Level Information Infrastructure

Blk Block

BLOS Beyond Line of Sight

BLU Bomb Live Unit

BMC4I Battle Management Command, Control, Communications, Computers, and Intelligence

BMD Ballistic Missile Defense

BMDS Ballistic-Missile Defense System

BMU Beach Master Unit

BMUP Block Modification Upgrade Program

BPI Business Process Improvement

BPR Business Process Re-Engineering

BRAC Base Realignment and Closure

BSAR Broadband Sonar Analog Receiver

BWA Biological Warfare Agent

C2BMC Command, Control, Battle Management, and Communications C2OIX Command and Control Information Exchange

C2P Command and Control Processor

C4I Command, Control, Communications, Computers, and Intelligence

C4ISR Command, Control, Communication, Computers, Intelligence, Surveillance, and Reconnaissance

C4N Command, Control, Communications, Computers, and Navigation

C3F Commander, Third Fleet

C5F Commander, Fifth Fleet

C6F Commander, Sixth Fleet

C7F Commander, Seventh Fleet

CAC Common-Access Cards

CAD Component Advanced Development

CADRT Computer-Aided Dead-Reckoning Table

CAL/VAL Calibration and Validation

CANES Consolidated Afloat Networks and Enterprise Services

CARACaS Control Architecture for Robotic Agent Command and Sensing

CAS Close Air Support

CATM Captive Air Training Missiles

CB Chemical, Biological

CBASS Common Broadband Advanced Sonar System

CBMU Construction Battalion Maintenance Units

CBR Chemical, Biological, and Radiological

CBRND Chemical, Biological, Radiological, Nuclear Defense

CBRNE Chemical, Biological, Radiological, Nuclear, and Enhanced explosive

CBSP Commercial Broadband Satellite Program

CCD Center for Career Development

CCE Common Computing Environment

CCG Computer Control Group

CCP Common Configuration Program

CCS Combat Control System

CDA Commercially Derived Aircraft

CDD Capability Development Document

CDHQ Central Command Deployable Headquarters

CDLMS Common Data Link Management System

CDL-N Common Data Link, Navy

CDLS Common Data Link System

CDR Critical Design Review

CDS Combat Direction System, or, Common Display System

CEB CNO Executive Board

CEC Cooperative Engagement Capability

CENTRIXS Combined Enterprise Regional Information Exchange System

CFFC Commander, Fleet Forces Command

CG Guided-Missile Cruiser

CIB Common Interactive Broadband

CIE Collaborative Information Environment

CIO Chief Information Officer

CIU Control Indicator Unit

CIWS Close-In Weapon System

CJF Commander, Joint Forces

CLF Combat Logistics Force

CLFA Compact Flow-Frequency Active (sonar)

CLIP Common Link Integration Processing

CM Cryptographic Modernization

CMC Common Missile Compartment

CMCO Counter Mine Counter Obstacle

CMF Common Message Format

CNATRA Commander, Air Naval Air Training Command

CND Computer Network Defense

CNIC Commander, Naval Installations Command

CNO Chief of Naval Operations

CNRC Commander, Naval Recruiting Command

CNRRR Commander, Naval Reserve Recruiting Region

CNS Communication/Navigation System

CNVA Computer Network Vulnerability Assessment

COBRA Coastal Battlefield Reconnaissance and Analysis

COE Common Operating Environment

COLDS Cargo Offload and Discharge System

COMINT Communications Intelligence

COMSATCOM Commercial Satellite Communications

COMSEC Communications Security

COMSUBGRU Commander, Submarine Group

CONOPS Concept of Operations

CONUS Continental United States

COP Common Operational Picture

CORIVRON Coastal Riverine Squadron

COS Class of Service

COTS Commercial-Off-The-Shelf, or, Cargo Offload and Transfer System

CPD Capability Production Document

CPS Common Processor System

C-RAM Counter-Rocket, Artillery, and Mortar

CRF Coastal Riverine Force

CSAR Combat Search and Rescue

CSC Computer Sciences Corporation

CSDTS Common Shipboard Data Terminal Set

CSEA Combat System Engineering Agent

CSF Consolidated Storage Facility

CSG (Aircraft) Carrier Strike Group

CSIT Combat System Integration and Test

CSL Common Source Library

CSRR Common Submarine Radio Room

CSV Catapult Capacity Selector Valve calculator

CSWP Commercial Satellite Wideband Program

CTAPS Contingency Tactical Automated Planning System

CTE Continuous Training Environment

CTF Component Task Force, or, Commander Task Force

CTOL Conventional Takeoff and Landing

CTP Common Tactical Picture

CUAS Cargo Unmanned Aerial Systems

CUP Common Undersea Program

CV Carrier Variant aircraft, or, Conventionally (oil-fired) Powered Aircraft Carrier

CVBG Aircraft Carrier Battle Group

CVIC Aircraft Carrier Intelligence Center

CVN Nuclear-Powered Aircraft Carrier

CWSP Commercial Wideband Satellite Program

CY Calendar Year

D5E Destruction, degradation, denial, disruption, deceit, and exploitation

DAB Defense Acquisition Board

DAMA Demand Assigned Multiple Access

DAMTC Direct-Attack Moving Target Capability

DAPS Dorsal Auxiliary Protective Systems

DARPA Defense Advanced Research Projects Agency

DBR Dual-Band Radar

DCA Defensive Counter-Air

DCC Data Center Consolidation

DCGS-N Distributed Common Ground System-Navy

DCGS Distributed Common Ground System

DCID Director, Central Intelligence Directive

DCL Detection, Classification, and Localization

DCMS Director, Communications Security Material Systems

DCNO Deputy Chief of Naval Operations

DDG Guided-Missile Destroyer

DECC Defense Enterprise Computing System

DEIP Dynamic Enterprise Integration Platform

DEM/VAL Demonstration/Validation

DF Direction Finding

DFU Dry Filter Unit

DIB Distributed Common Ground System Integration Backbone

DiD Defense-in-Depth

DIF Database Integration Framework

DII COE Defense Information Infrastructure Common Operating Environment

DIMHRS Defense Integrated Military Human Resource System

DIMUS Digital Multi-beam Steering

DIO Defensive Information Operations

DIRCM Directed Infrared Countermeasures

DISA Defense Information Systems Agency

DISN Defense Information Systems Network

DJC2 Deployable Joint Command and Control

DMLGB Dual-Mode Laser-Guided Bomb

DLS Decoy Launching System

DMR Digital Modular Radar, or, Digital Modular Radio

DMS Defense Message System

DMSP Defense Meteorology Satellite Program

DNM Dynamic Network Management

DNS Director, Navy Staff

DoD Department of Defense

DoN Department of the Navy

DOTMLPF Doctrine, Organization, Training, Materiel, Leadership, Personnel, and Facilities

DPRIS/EMPRS Defense Personnel Record Imaging System / Electronic Military Personnel Record System

DRPM Direct-Reporting Program Manager

DRSN Defense Red Switch Network

DSCS Defense Satellite Communications System

DSMAC Digital Scene-Matching Area Correlation

DSN Defense Switch Network

DSRV Deep-Submergence Rescue Vehicle

DT Developmental Testing

DTH Defense Message System Transitional Hubs

EA Electronic Attack

EAM Emergency Action Message

EASR Enterprise Air Surveillance Radar

EB Electric Boat

EBEM Enhanced Bandwidth Efficient Modem

ECCM Electronic Counter-Countermeasures

ECIDS-N Electronic Chart Display and Information System-Navy

ECM Electronic Countermeasures

ECP Engineering Change Proposal

ECR Electronic Combat/Reconnaissance

ECS Exterior Communication System

EDM Engineering Development Model

EDS Electronic Data Systems

EHF Extremely High Frequency

EIS Environmental Impact Statement

EKMS Electronic Key Management System

ELC Enhanced Lethality Cartridge

ELINT Electronic Intelligence

EMALS Electromagnetic Aircraft Launch System

EMC2 Electromagnetic Maneuver Warfare Command and Control

EMCON Emissions Control

EMD Engineering and Manufacturing Development

EMI Electro-Magnetic Interference

EMIO Expanded Maritime Interception Operations

EMPRS Electronic Military Personnel Record System

EMRG Electromagnetic Rail Gun

EMS Electromagnetic Spectrum

EMW Expeditionary Maneuver Warfare

EO/IR Electro-Optical/Infrared

EOC Early Operational Capability

EOD Explosive Ordnance Disposal

EOID Electro-Optic Identification

EPAA European Phased Adaptive Approach (ABMD Ashore)

EPF Expeditionary Fast Transport [formerly JHSV]

EPLRS Enhanced Position Location Reporting System

EPS Electronic Procurement System

ER Extended Range

ERAAW Extended-Range Anti-Air Warfare

ERAM Extended-Range Active [homing] Missile

ERM Extended-Range Munition

ERNT Executive Review of Navy Training

ERP Enterprise Resource Planning

ESAPI Enhanced Small Arms Protective Inserts

ESB Expeditionary Sea Base [formerly AFSB]

ESD Expeditionary Transfer Dock [formerly MLP]

ESE Electronic Surveillance Enhancement

ESG Expeditionary Strike Group

ESL Enterprise Software Licensing, or, Expected Service Life

ESM Electronic Support Measures

ESSI Enhanced Special Structural Inspection

ESSM Evolved Seasparrow Missile

ESU Expeditionary Support Unit

ETC Echo Tracker Classifier

EUCOM U.S. European Command

EURCENT European Central Command

EW Electronic Warfare

FARP Forward Arming and Refueling Point

FBE Fleet Battle Experiment

FBM Fleet Ballistic Missile

FDECO Forward-Deployed Energy and Communications Outpost

FDS Fixed Distributed System

FDS-C FDS-COTS

FEL Free Electron Laser

FF Frigate

FFC Fleet Forces Command

FFG Guided-Missile Frigate

FFRDC Federally Funded Research and Development Center

FFSP Fleet and Family Support Program

FHLT Fleet High-Level Terminal

FIE Fly-In Echelon

FITC Fleet Intelligence Training Center

FLEX Fatigue Life Extension

FLIR Forward-Looking Infrared

FLMP Fatigue Life Management Program

FLO/FLO Float-On/Float-Off

FLTSAT Fleet Satellite

FNC Future Naval Capabilities

FOB Forward Operating Base

FOC Full Operational Capability

FORCEnet Navy web of secure communications and information links

FOT Follow-On Terminal

FOT&E Full Operational Test and Evaluation

FP Full Production

FRP Full-Rate Production, or, Fleet Response Plan

FTS Federal Telephone System, or, Full-Time Support

FUE First Unit Equipped

FY Fiscal Year

FYDP Future Years Defense Program

GBS Global Broadcast Service

GBTS Ground-Based Training System

GCCS Global Command and Control System

GCCS-N Global Command and Control System-Navy

GCS Ground Control Station

GCSS Global Command Support System

GDAIS General Dynamics Advanced Information Systems

GDIS General Dynamics Information Systems

GENDET General Detail (personnel)

GENSER General Service

GFE Government-Furnished Equipment

GHMD Global Hawk Maritime Demonstration system

GIG Global Information Grid

GIG-BE Global Information Grid-Bandwidth Expansion

GIG-ES Global Information Grid Enterprise Services

GLTA Guardian Laser Tracker Assemblies

GMF Ground Mobile Force (Air Force)

GMM [LCS] Gun Mission Module

GMS Griffin Missile System, or, Guided-Missile System

GOTS Government-Off-The-Shelf

GPNTS GPS-based Positioning, Navigation, and Timing

GPS Global Positioning System

GT Gas Turbine

GTLC Gryphon Technologies LC

GWS Gun Weapon System

HA/DR Humanitarian Assistance/Disaster Relief

HARM High-Speed Anti-Radiation Missile

HCI Human Computer Interface

HD/LD High-Demand/Flow-Density

HDR High Data-Rate

HED Hybrid Electric Drive

HEFA Hydro-treated Esters and Fatty Acids

HF High Frequency

HFI Hostile Fire Indication

HFIP High-Frequency Internet Protocol

HGHS High-Gain High Sensitivity

HII Huntington Ingalls Industries

HLR Heavy Lift Replacement (helicopter)

HM&E Hull, Mechanical, and Electrical (systems)

HMH Heavy-Lift (helicopter) Squadron

HMI Human-Machine Interface

HOLC High Order Language Computer

HPC Human Performance Center

HSI Human Systems Integration

HTS High-Temperature Superconducting

HUD Heads Up Display

HWDDC Hazardous Weather Detection and Display Capability

I&W Indications and Warning

IA Information Assurance

IAAS Infrastructure as a Service

IAMD Integrated Air and Missile Defense

IATF IA Technical Framework

IBA Interceptor Body Armor

IBS Integrated Broadcast Service

IBS/JTT Integrated Broadcast Service/Joint Tactical Terminal

ICAO International Civil Aviation Organization

ICAP Improved Capability

ICD Initial Capabilities Document

ICOP Intelligence Carry-On Program

ICP Integrated Common Processor

ICSTF Integrated Combat Systems Test Facility

ICWI Interrupted Continuous-Wave Illumination

IDECMS Integrated Defensive Electronic Countermeasures System

IDIQ Indefinite Delivery/Indefinite Quantity (contract)

IDS Identity Dominance System

IDSN Integrated Digital Switching Network

IDTC Inter-Deployment Training Cycle

IED Improvised Explosive Device

i-ENCON Incentivized Energy Conservation

IET Intelligence Exploitation Team

IETM Interactive Electronic Technical Manual

IFF Identification, Friend or Foe

ILS Instrument Landing System

IMINT Imagery Intelligence

INLS Improved Navy Lighterage

INP Innovative Naval Prototype

INS Inertial Navigation System

IO Information Operations

IOC Initial Operational Capability

IP Internet Protocol

IPARTS Improved Performance Assessment and Readiness Training System

IPDS Improved Point Detector System

IPPD Integrated Product and Process Development

IPOE Intelligence Preparation of Environment

IPR Interim Program Review

IPS Integrated Power System

IPT Integrated Process Team

IR Infrared

IRCCM Infrared Counter-Countermeasures

FIRST Infrared Search and Track

IS Information Systems

ISC Integrated Ship's Control

ISDN Integrated Services Digital Network

ISNS Integrated Shipboard Network System

ISO Investment Strategy Options

ISPP Integrated Sponsor's Program Proposal

ISR Intelligence, Surveillance, Reconnaissance

ISRT Intelligence, Surveillance, Reconnaissance, and Targeting

ISS Installation Subsystem

ISS Information Superiority/Sensors

ISSP Information Systems Security Program

IT Information Technology

ITAB Information Technology Acquisition Board

IU Interface Unit

IUSS Integrated Undersea Surveillance System

IW Indications and Warning

IWS Integrated Warfare Systems

J&A Justification and Approval

JASA Joint Airborne SIGINT Architecture

JASSM Joint Air-to-Surface Standoff Missile

JATAS Joint and Allied Threat Awareness System

JBAIDS Joint Biological Agent Identification and Diagnostic System

JBTDS Joint Biological Tactical Detection System

JC2-MA Joint Command and Control-Maritime Applications

JCC Joint Airborne SIGINT Architecture Modification Common Configuration

JCIDS Joint Capabilities Integration and Development System

JCM Joint Common Missile

JCREW Joint Counter RCIED Electronic Warfare

JDAM Joint Direct-Attack Munition

JDISS Joint Deployable Intelligence Support Service

JDN Joint Data Network

JFC Joint Force Commander

JFCOM Joint Forces Command

JFCOM JPO Joint Forces Command Joint Program Office

JFMCC Joint Forces Maritime Component Commander

JFN Joint Fires Network

JFNU Joint Fires Network Unit

JHDA Joint Host Demand Algorithm

JHMCS Joint Helmet Mounted Cueing System

JHSV Joint High-Speed Vessel

JIC Joint Intelligence Center

JICO/JSS Joint Interface Control Officer Support System

JIE Joint Information Environment

JIFC Joint Integrated Fire Control

JLENS Joint Land-Attack Cruise Missile Defense Elevated Netted Sensor

JMAST Joint Mobile Ashore Support Terminal

JMCIS Joint Maritime Command Information System

JMCOMS Joint Maritime Communications Strategy

JMLS Joint Modular Lighterage System

JMOD Joint Airborne SIGINT Architecture Modification

JMPS Joint Mission Planning System

JMPS-M Joint Mission Planning System-Maritime

JNIC Joint National Integration Center

JNMS Joint Network Management System

JOA Joint Operations Area

JOTBS Joint Operational Test Bed System

JPACE Joint Protective Aircrew Ensemble

JPALS Joint Precision Approach and Landing System

JPATS Joint Primary Aircraft Training System

JPEO Joint Program Executive Office

JROC Joint Requirements Oversight Council

JSF Joint Strike Fighter

JSIPS Joint Service Imagery Processing System

JSMO Joint Systems Management Office

JSOW Joint Standoff Weapon

JSPO Joint System Program Office

JTA Joint Tactical Architecture

JTAMDO Joint Theater Air and Missile Defense Organization

JTDLMP Joint Tactical Data Link Management Plan

JTIDS Joint Tactical Information Distribution System

JTRS Joint Tactical Radio System

JTT Joint Tactical Terminal

JUWL Joint Universal Weapon Link

JWICS Joint Worldwide Intelligence Communications System

KDP Key Decision Point

KPP Key Performance Parameter

KSA Key Systems Attribute

LAIRCM Large Aircraft Infrared Countermeasures

LAN Local Area Network

LANT Atlantic

LANTIRN Flow-Altitude Navigation and Targeting Infrared at Night

LBSF&I Littoral Battlespace Sensing, Fusion and Integration

LBS-UUV Littoral Battlespace Sensing-Unmanned Undersea Vehicle

LCAC Landing Craft, Air Cushion vehicle

LCC Amphibious Command Ship

LCCA Flow-Cost Conformal Display

LCGR Launch Control Group Replacement

LCS Littoral Combat Ship

LCT Landing Craft Tank vessel

LCU Landing Craft Utility vessel

LD/HD Flow-Density/High Demand

LDR Flow Data Rate

LDUUV Large-Diameter Unmanned Undersea Vehicle

LEAD Launched Expendable Acoustic Decoy

LEAP Lightweight Exo-Atmospheric Projectile

LEASAT Leased Satellite

LFA Flow-Frequency Active

LGB Laser-Guided Bomb

LHA Amphibious Assault Ship

LHA(R) Amphibious Assault Ship-Replacement

LHD Amphibious Assault Ship

LHT Lightweight Hybrid Torpedo

LIDAR Light Detection and Ranging System, or, Light Detection and Ranging

LiOH Lithium Hydroxide

LJDAM Laser Joint Direct-Attack Munition

LMS Local Monitor Station

LMSR Large Medium-Speed Roll-On/Roll-Off

LOS Line of Sight, or, Length of Service

LOTS Logistics-Over-The-Shore

LPD Amphibious Transport Dock ship

LPI Flow-Probability-of-Intercept

LPMP Launch Platform Mission Planning

LPWS Land-Based [Phalanx] Weapons System

LRIP Flow-Rate Initial Production

LRLAP Long-Range Land-Attack Projectile

LRS&T Long-Range Surveillance and Tracking

LSD Dock Landing Ship

LSO Landing Signal Officer

LSS Littoral Surveillance System

LVT Flow-Volume Terminal

LX(R) Dock Landing Ship Replacement

LWH Lightweight Helmets

LWSD Laser Weapon System Demonstrator

M/BVR Medium/Beyond Visual Range missile

MA Maritime Applications

MAGTF Marine Air-Ground Task Force

MAMDJF Maritime Air and Missile Defense of Joint Forces

ManTech Manufacturing Technology

MARCEMP Manual Relay Center Modernization Program

MASINT Measurement and Signature Intelligence

MASS MDA/AIS Sensor/Server

MAST Mobile Ashore Support Terminal

MATT Multi-mission Airborne Tactical Terminal

MAWS Missile Approach Warning System

MCAS Marine Corps Air Station

MCAST Maritime Civil Affairs and Security Training

MCAT Maritime Civil Affairs Teams

MCEN Marine Corps Enterprise Network

MCM Mine Countermeasures

MCP Mission Capability Package

MCPON Master Chief Petty Officer of the Navy

MCS Mine Countermeasures Command, Control, and Support Ship, or, Mission Computer System

MCS-21 Maritime Cryptologic System for the 21st Century

MCU Mission Computer Upgrade

MDA Maritime Domain Awareness, or, Missile Defense Agency

MDR Medium Data Rate

MDS Multi-function Display System, or, Mobile Diving and Salvage

MDSU Mobile Diving and Salvage Unit

MEB Marine Expeditionary Brigade

MEDAL Mine Warfare and Environmental Decision Aids Library

MEF Marine Expeditionary Force

MESF Maritime Expeditionary Security Force

METMF(R) Meteorological Mobile Facility Replacement

NEXGEN Next Generation

METOC Meteorological and Oceanographic Sensors

MEU Marine Expeditionary Unit

MEU(SOC) Marine Expeditionary Unit (Special Operations Capable)

MF Medium Frequency

MFL Multi-Frequency Link

MFOQA Military Flight Operations Quality Assurance

MFR Multi-Function Radar

MFTA Multi-Function Towed Array (sonar)

MGS Machine Gun System

MHIP Missile Homing Improvement Program

MICFAC Mobile Integrated Command Facility

MID Management Initiative Decision

MIDS Multi-Function Information Distribution System

MIDS-LVT Multi-Function Information Distribution System Flow-Volume Terminal

MILDET Military Detachment

MILSTAR Military Strategic and Tactical Relay Satellite

MIO Maritime Interception Operations

MIPS Maritime Integrated Air and Missile Defense Planning System

MIR Multi-sensor Image Reconnaissance

MIRV Multiple Independently Targeted Reentry Vehicle

MIUW Mobile Inshore Undersea Warfare

MIW Mine Warfare

MIWC Mine Warfare Commander

Mk Mark

MLP Mobile Landing Platform

MLS Multi-Level Security

MM [LCS] Mission Module

MMA Multi-mission Maritime Aircraft

MMRT Modified Miniature Receiver Terminal

MMSP Multi-Mission Signal Processor

MNS Mission Need Statement, or, Mine Neutralization System

MOA Memorandum of Agreement

MOC Maritime Operations Center

MOCC Mobile Operational Command Control Center

MOD Modification

MOPP Mission-Oriented Protective Posture

MOU Memorandum of Understanding

MP [LCS] Mission Package

MPA Maritime Patrol Aircraft

MPF(F) Maritime Prepositioning Force (Future)

MPG Maritime Prepositioning Group

MPRF Maritime Patrol and Reconnaissance Force

MPS Maritime Prepositioning Ship, or, Mission Planning System

MRMS Maintenance Resource Management System

MRMUAS Medium-Range Maritime Unmanned Aerial System

MR-TCDL Multi-Role Tactical Common Data Link

MRUUV Mission-Reconfigurable Unmanned Undersea Vehicle

MSC Military Sealift Command

MSD Material Support Dates

MSO Maritime Security Operations

MTI Moving Target Indicator

MTOC Mobile Tactical Operations Center

MUOS Mobile User Objective System

MWCS Multiple Weapon Control Sight

MWR Morale, Welfare, and Recreation

N/JCA Navy/Joint Concentrator Architecture

NADEP Naval Aviation Depot

NAF Naval Air Facility

NALCOMIS Naval Aviation Logistics Command Management Information System

NAOC2 Naval Air Operations Command and Control

NAMS Naval Aviation Maintenance System

NAS Naval Air Station

NASA National Aeronautics and Space Administration

NATO North Atlantic Treaty Organization

NATOPS Naval Aviation and Training Operating Procedures Standardization

NAVAIR Naval Air Systems Command

NAVCENT U.S. Naval Forces, Central Command

NAVFLIR Navigation, Forward-Looking Infrared

NAVMAC Navy Modular Automated Communications

NavMPS Naval Mission Planning Systems

NAVSEA Naval Sea Systems Command

NAVSECGRU Naval Security Group

NAVSSI Navigation Sensor System Interface

NAVSUP Naval Supply Systems Command

NAVWAR Navigation Warfare

NCB [Seabee] Naval Construction Battalion

NCDP Naval Capabilities Development Process

NCES Net-Centric Enterprise Services

NCFS Naval Fires Control System

NCHB Navy Cargo Handling Battalion

NCIS Naval Criminal Investigative Service

NCO Network-Centric Operations

NCP Naval Capability Pillar, or, Naval Capability Plan

NCR Naval Construction Regiment

NCTAMS Naval Computer and Telecommunications Area Master Stations

NCTF Naval Component Task Force

NCTS Naval Computer and Telecommunications Station

NCUSW Net-Centric Undersea Warfare

NCW Network-Centric Warfare, or, Navy Coastal Warfare

NCWES Network-Centric Warfare Electronic Support

NDI Non-Developmental Item

NEC Naval Enlistment Classification

NECC Naval Expeditionary Combat Command

NEIC Navy Expeditionary Intelligence Command

NELR Navy Expeditionary Logistics Regiment

NEO Non-Combatant Evacuation Operations

NEP Navy Enterprise Portal

NEPLO National Emergency Preparedness Liaison Officer

NESP Navy Extremely High Frequency Satellite Program

NETC Naval Education and Training Command

NETWARCOM Network Warfare Command

NFCS Naval Fires Control System

NFN Naval Fires Network, and/or Joint Fires Network

NFO Naval Flight Officer

NFS Naval Fire Support

NGCD Next-Generation Chemical Detection

NGC2P Next-Generation Command and Control Processor

NGDS Next-Generation Diagnostics System

NGEN Next-Generation Enterprise Network

NGJ Next-Generation Jammer

NGO Non-Governmental Organization

NGSS Northrop Grumman Ship Systems

NIFC-CA Navy Integrated Fire Control-Counter Air

NII Network Information Integration

NILE NATO Improved Link 11

NIMA National Imagery and Mapping Agency

NIPRNET Unclassified-but-Sensitive Internet Protocol Router Network

NITF National Imagery Transportation Format

NMCB Naval Mobile Construction Battalion [Seabee]

NMCI Navy Marine Corps Intranet

NMCP Navy Marine Corps Portal

NMITC Navy Maritime Intelligence Training Center

NMT Navy Advanced Extremely High Frequency Multiband Terminal

NNOR Non-Nuclear Ordnance Requirement

NNSOC Naval Network and Space Command

NOAA National Oceanographic and Atmospheric Administration

NOBLE Navy Operational Business Logistics Enterprise

NOC Network Operation Center

NOME Naval Maritime Operational Environment

NOSS Naval Operational Supply Systems

NPDC Naval Personnel Development Command

N-PFPS Navy Portable Flight Planning Software

NPOESS National Polar-Orbiting Operational Environmental Satellite System NPS Naval Postgraduate School

NREMS Navy Regional Enterprise Messaging System

NRF Naval Reserve Force

NRL Naval Research Laboratory

NRTD Near Real-Time Dissemination

NSA National Security Agency

NSAWC Naval Strike Air Warfare Center

NSC National Security Cutter

NSCT Naval Special Clearance Team

NSFS Naval Surface Fire Support

NSFV Naval Security Forces Vest

NSIPS Navy Standard Integrated Personnel System

NSPG Navy Strategic Planning Guidance

NSSMS NATO Seasparrow Surface Missile System

NSTC Naval Service Training Command

NSW Naval Special Warfare

NSWC Naval Surface Warfare Center

NSWC/DD Naval Surface Warfare Center/Dahlgren Division

NSWC/PH Naval Surface Warfare Center/Port Hueneme Division NSWG Naval Special Warfare Group

NSWRON Naval Special Warfare Squadron

NTCDL Network Tactical Common Data Link

NTCS-A Naval Tactical Command System-Afloat

NTCSS Naval Tactical Command Support System

NTDS Naval Tactical Data System

NTNO Navy-Type/Navy-Owned NUAMP Navy Underwater Active Multiple Ping

NUFEA Navy Unique Fleet Essential Airlift

NUFEA-RA Navy Unique Fleet Essential Airlift-Replacement Aircraft

NUWC Naval Underwater Warfare Center

NWDC Navy Warfare Development Command

OA Operational Assessment

OAG Operational Advisory Group

OAS Offensive Air Support

OASD Office of the Assistant Secretary of Defense

OASIS Organic Airborne and Surface Influence Sweep

OBT On-Board Trainer

OCA Offensive Counter-Air

OCO Overseas Contingency Operations

OCONUS Outside Continental United States

OEF Operation Enduring Freedom

OEO Other Expeditionary Operations

OFP Operational Flight Program

OGB Optimized Gun Barrel

OGC Open Geospatial Consortium

OIF Operation Iraqi Freedom

OIPT Overarching Integrated Product Team

OMFTS Operational Maneuver From The Sea

ONI Office of Naval Intelligence

ONR Office of Naval Research

OPAREA Operational Exercise Area

OPEVAL Operational Evaluation

OPNAV Office of the Chief of Naval Operations

OPTASK COMM Operational Tasking Communications

OPTASK EW Operational Tasking Electronic Warfare

OPTEMPO Operating Tempo

OPTEVFOR Operational Test and Evaluation Force

OR Ohio [SSBN] Replacement, or, Operational Requirement

ORD Operational Requirements Document

ORDALT Ordnance Alteration

OSA Open System Architecture

OSCAR Open Systems-Core Avionics Requirements

OSD Office of the Secretary of Defense

OSD-CAPE Office of the Secretary of Defense, Cost Assessment and Program Evaluation

OSIS Ocean Surveillance Information System

OSS Operational Support System

OT Operational Testing

OT&E Operational Testing and Evaluation

OTH Over the Horizon

P3I Pre-Planned Product Improvement

PAA Phased Adaptive Approach

PAAS Platform as a Service

PAC Pacific

PAS Processing and Analysis Segment

PC Patrol Coastal craft

PCU Pre-Commissioning Unit

PDA Personal Digital Assistant

PDM Program Decision Memorandum

PDR Preliminary Design Review

PEO Program Executive Office (and Officer)

PEO IWS Program Executive Office for Integrated Warfare Systems

PEO LCS Program Executive Office for the Littoral Combat Ship

PERSTEMPO Personnel Tempo

PFPS Portable Flight-Planning Software

PGM Precision-Guided Munition

PHIBGRU Amphibious Group

PHIBRON Amphibious Squadron

PIP Product Improvement Program, or, Pioneer [UAV] Improvement Program

PKI Public Key Infrastructure

PLUS Persistent Littoral Undersea Surveillance

PMA Post-Mission Analysis

PMK Power Management Kit

POM Program Objective Memorandum

POR Program of Record

PPBE Planning, Programming, Budgeting, and Execution process

PRMS Pressurized Rescue Module System

PSE Physical Security Equipment

PSTN Public Switched Telephone Network

PTAN Precision Terrain Aided Navigation

PTW Precision Targeting Workstation

PUMA Precision Underwater Mapping

PVO Private Volunteer Organization

QDR Quadrennial Defense Review

R&D Research and Development

RAM Rolling Airframe Missile

RAN Royal Australian Navy

RC Reserve Component

RCC Regional Combatant Commander

RCIED Radio-Controlled Improvised Explosive Device

RCOH Nuclear Refueling/Complex Overhaul

RD&A Research, Development, and Acquisition

RDC Rapid Deployment Capability

RDT&E Research, Development, Test, and Evaluation

REPLO Regional Emergency Preparedness Liaison Officer

RF Radio Frequency

RFP Request for Proposal

RHIMES Resilient Hull, Infrastructure, Mechanical, and Electrical Security

RIMPAC Rim of the Pacific [exercise]

RM Radiant Mercury

RMAST Reserve Mobile Ashore Support Terminal

RMIG Radiant Mercury Imagery Guard

RMMV Remote Multi-Mission Vehicle

RMS Remote Minehunting System

RO Reverse Osmosis

ROMO Range of Military Operations

RORO Roll-On/Roll-Off

ROS Reduced Operating Status

RRDD Risk Reduction and Design Development

RSC Radar Suite Controller

RSOC Regional SIGINT Operations Center

RTC Recruit Training Command, or, Remote Terminal Component

RWR Radar Warning Receiver

S&T Science and Technology

SA Situational Awareness

SAASM Selective Availability Anti-Spoofing Module

SAG Surface Action Group

SAHRV Semiautonomous Hydrographic Reconnaissance Vehicle

SAIC Science Applications International Corporation

SALTS Streamlined Alternative Logistic Transmission System

SAM Surface-to-Air Missile

SAML Security Assertion Markup Language

SAST Surface ASW Synthetic Trainer

SATCOM Satellite Communications

SBIR Small Business Innovative Research

SBT Special Boat Team

SCA Software Communications Architecture

SCC Sea Combat Commander

SCI Sensitive Compartmented Information

SCN Shipbuilding and Conversion Navy [appropriation]

SC(X)R Surface Connector Replacement

SDD System Design Document, or, System Development and Demonstration [phase]

SDS Surface Decompression System

SDTA System Demonstration Test Article

SDTS Self-Defense Test Ship

SDV Swimmer [or SEAL] Delivery Vehicle

SDVT Swimmer [or SEAL] Delivery Vehicle Team

SEAD Suppression of Enemy Air Defense

SEAL Sea-Air-Land Naval Special Warfare Forces

SEAPRINT Systems Engineering, Acquisition, and Personnel Integration

SEI Specific Emitter Identification

SEIE Submarine Escape Immersion Equipment

SEWIP Surface Electronic Warfare Improvement Program

SFA MTT Security Force Assistance Mobile Training Team

SHARP Shared Reconnaissance Pod

SHF Super High Frequency

SHUMA Stochastic Unified Multiple Access

SI Special Intelligence

SIAP Single Integrated Air Picture

SIGINT Signals Intelligence

SIMAS Sonar In-situ Mode Assessment System

SINCGARS Single Channel Ground and Air Radio System

SIPRNET Secret Internet Protocol Router Network

SLAD Slewing-Arm Davit

SLAM Standoff Land-Attack Missile

SLAM-ER Standoff Land-Attack Missile-Expanded Response

SLAP Service Life Assessment Program

SLBM Submarine-Launched Ballistic Missile

SLEP Service Life Extension Program

SLR Side-Looking Radar

SM Standard [surface-to-air] Missile

SMCM Surface Mine Countermeasure

SNAP Shipboard Non-tactical ADP Program

SNR Subnet Relay

SOA Service Oriented Architecture, or, Sustained Operations Ashore

SOAD Standoff Outside Area Defense

SOAP Simple Object Access Protocol

SOC Special Operations Capable, or, Special Operations Craft

SOF Special Operations Forces

SOPD Standoff Outside Point Defense

SOSUS Sound Surveillance System

SPAWAR Space and Naval Warfare Systems Command

SPECAT Special Category

SPM Soldier Power Manager

SPRITE Spectral and Reconnaissance Imagery for Tactical Exploitation

SRAAM Short-Range Air-to-Air Missile

SRC Submarine Rescue Chamber

SRCFS Submarine Rescue Chamber Fly-away System

SRDRS Submarine Rescue Diving Recompression System

SS Sensor Subsystem, or, Conventionally (AIP, fuel cell, diesel) powered submarine

SSBN Nuclear-Powered Ballistic-Missile Submarine

SSC Ship-to-Shore Connector

SSCA Service Secretary Controlled Aircraft

SSDG Ship Service Diesel Generators

SSDS Ship Self-Defense System

SSEE Ship's Signals Exploitation Equipment

SSG Strategic Studies Group

SSGN Nuclear-Powered Guided-Missile Submarine

SSI Special Structural Inspection

SSI-K Special Structural Inspection-Kit

SSIPS Shore Signal and Information Processing Segment

SSL Solid State Laser

SSMIS Special Sensor Microwave Imager/Sounder [Air Force]

SSMM Surface-to-Surface Missile Module

SSN Nuclear-Powered Submarine

SSO Special Security Office

SS-SPY Solid State-SPY [radar]

SSST Supersonic Sea-Skimming Target

STANAG [NATO] Standardization Agreement

START Strategic Arms Reduction Treaty

STEM Science, Technology, Engineering, and Mathematics

STEP Standardized Tactical Entry Point

STOM Ship-To-Objective Maneuver

STOVL Short Take-Off and Vertical Landing

STT Submarine Tactical Terminal

STUAS Small Tactical Unmanned Aircraft System

STU-III/R Secure Telephone Unit, Third Generation, Remote Control Interface

SURTASS Surveillance Towed Array Sensor System

SUW Surface Warfare

S-VSR S-Band Volume Search Radar

SWAN Shipboard Wide-Area Network

SWATH Small Waterplane Area, Twin Hull [ship]

SYSCEN Systems Center

TACAIR Tactical Aircraft

TACAMO Take-Charge-and-Move-Out

TACC Tactical Air Command Centers

TacLAN Tactical Local Area Network

TACS Tactical Air Control System

TACTAS Tactical Towed Array System

TACTOM Tactical Tomahawk

TADIL-J Tactical Digital Information Link-Joint Service

TADIRCM Tactical Aircraft Directed InfraRed Countermeasure

TADIXS Tactical Data Information Exchange Systems

T-AGOS Ocean Surveillance Ship [MSC-operated]

T-AGS Oceanographic Survey Ships [MSC-operated]

T-AH Hospital Ship [MSC-operated]

T-AKE Stores/Ammunition Ship [MSC-operated]

TAMD Theater Air and Missile Defense

TAMPS Tactical Automated Mission Planning System

T-AO Oiler [MSC-operated]

TAOC Tactical Air Operations Center [Marine Corps]

TAP Tactical Training Theater Assessment Planning

TAPS Tactical Acoustic Processing Suite

TARPS Tactical Airborne Reconnaissance Pod System

TASWC Theater ASW Commander

TAWS Terrain Awareness Warning Systems

TBMCS Theater Battle Management Core Systems

TC2S Tomahawk Command and Control System

TCAS Traffic Alert and Collision Avoidance System

TCDL Tactical Common Data Link

TCGR Track Control Group Replacement

TCP Transmission Control Protocol

TCPED Tasking Collection Processing Exploitation Dissemination

TCS Tactical Control System, or, Time-Critical Strike

TCT Time-Critical Targeting

TDA Tactical Decision Aid

TDCL Torpedo Detection, Classification, and Localization

TDD Target Detection Device

TDLS Tactical Data Link System

TDM Time Division Multiplex

TDMA Time Division Multiple Access

TDP Tactical Data Processor

TDSS Tactical Display Support System

TECHEVAL Technical [Developmental] Evaluation

TEMPALT Temporary Alteration

TERCOM Terrain Contour Mapping

TES-N Tactical Exploitation System-Navy

TESS/NITES Tactical Environmental Support System/Navy Integrated Tactical Environmental Subsystem

TEU Training and Evaluation Unit

TFCC Task Force Climate Change

TFW Task Force Web

TI Technology Insertion

TIBS Tactical Information Broadcast Service

TIC Toxic Industrial Chemical Agent

TIDS Tactical Integrated Digital System

TIM Toxic Industrial Material

TIMS Training Integrated Management System

TIS Trusted Information System

TIS Tactical Interface Subsystem

TJS Tactical Jamming System

TLAM Tomahawk Land-Attack Cruise Missile

TLR Top-Level Requirements

TMPC Theater Mission Planning Center

TNT Targeting and Navigation Toolset

TOA Table of Allowance, or, Total Obligational Authority

TOC Tactical Operations Center, or, Total Ownership Costs

TOG Technology Oversight Group

TPPU Task, Post, Process, Use

TRAFS Torpedo Recognition and Alertment Functional Segment

T-RDF Transportable-Radio Direction Finding

TRE Tactical Receive Equipment

TRIXS Tactical Reconnaissance Intelligence Exchange System

TS Top Secret

TSC Tactical Support Center

TSR Time Slot Reallocation

TSTC Total Ship Training Capability

TTNT Tactical Targeting Network Technology

TTWCS Tactical Tomahawk Weapon Control System

TUSWC Theater Undersea Warfare Commander

TWS Tomahawk Weapon System, or, Torpedo Warning System

TXS Transport Services

UARC University Affiliated Research Center

UAS/V Unmanned Aerial/Aircraft System/Vehicle

UCAS-D Unmanned Combat Aircraft System Demonstration

UCLASS Unmanned Carrier-Launched Airborne Surveillance and Strike

UCT Underwater Construction Teams

UCWI/JUWL Interrupted Continuous Wave Illumination/Joint Universal Weapon Link

UDDI Universal Description, Discovery, and Integration

UFO Ultra High Frequency Follow-On

UHF Ultra High Frequency

UISS Unmanned Influence Sweep System

UMFO Undergraduate Military Flight Officer

UNITAS Annual U.S.-South American Allied Exercise

UNREP Underway Replenishment

UOES User Operational Evaluation System

UON Urgent Operational Need

URC Undersea Rescue Command

URL Unrestricted Line

USD/AT&L Under Secretary of Defense for Acquisition, Technology, and Logistics

USMC United States Marine Corps

USPACOM U.S. Pacific Command

USS Undersea Surveillance System, or, United States Ship

USSOCOM U.S. Special Operations Command

USSSTRATCOM U.S. Strategic Command

USV Unmanned Surface Vehicle

USW Undersea Warfare

USW-DSS Undersea Warfare-Decision Support System

UUV Unmanned Undersea Vehicle

UWS Underwater Segment

UXO Unexploded Ordnance

VBSS Visit, Board, Search, and Seize

VCNO Vice Chief of Naval Operations

VDS Variable-Depth Sonar

VERTREP Vertical [underway] Replenishment

VHF Very High Frequency

VIXS Video Information Exchange System

VLA Vertical-Launch Anti-Submarine Rocket

VLF/LF Very Flow Frequency/Flow Frequency

VLS Vertical-Launching System

VME Versa Module Eurocard

VMTS Virtual Mission Training System

VOD Vertical Onboard [underway] Delivery

VPM Virginia Payload Module

VPN Virtual Private Network

VSR Volume Search Radar

V/STOL Vertical/Short Take-Off and Landing

VSW Very Shallow Water

VTC Video Teleconferencing

VTM Video Tele-Medicine

VTOL Vertical Take-Off and Landing

VTT Video Tele-Training

VTUAV Vertical Takeoff and Landing Tactical Unmanned Aerial Vehicle

VVD Voice-Video-Data

VXX Presidential Replacement Helicopter

WAA Wide Aperture Array

WAN Wide Area Network

WDL Weapons Data Link

WEN Web-Enabled Navy

WGS Wideband Gapfiller Satellite

WMD Weapons of Mass Destruction [nuclear, biological, chemical]

WMP Wideband Modernization Plan

WPN Weapons Procurement Navy [appropriation]

WSC Wideband Satellite Communications

XFC UAS eXperimental Fuel Cell Unmanned Aerial System

XML Extensible Markup Language

ZBR Zero-Based Review

* * * * * * * * * * * *

Made in the USA
Middletown, DE
16 July 2019